The Gothic Imagination in the
Music of Franz Schubert

The Gothic Imagination in the Music of Franz Schubert

Joe Davies

THE BOYDELL PRESS

© Joe Davies 2024

All rights reserved. Except as permitted under current legislation
no part of this work may be photocopied, stored in a retrieval system,
published, performed in public, adapted, broadcast,
transmitted, recorded or reproduced in any form or by any means,
without the prior permission of the copyright owner

The right of Joe Davies to be identified as
the author of this work has been asserted in accordance with
sections 77 and 78 of the Copyright, Designs and Patents Act 1988

First published 2024
The Boydell Press, Woodbridge

ISBN 978 1 83765 162 7

The Boydell Press is an imprint of Boydell & Brewer Ltd
PO Box 9, Woodbridge, Suffolk IP12 3DF, UK
and of Boydell & Brewer Inc.
668 Mt Hope Avenue, Rochester, NY 14620–2731, USA
website: www.boydellandbrewer.com

A catalogue record for this book is available
from the British Library

The publisher has no responsibility for the continued existence or accuracy of URLs for
external or third-party internet websites referred to in this book, and does not guarantee
that any content on such websites is, or will remain, accurate or appropriate

In loving memory of my father
Peter Jonathan Davies (1961–2021)

Contents

List of Illustrations	ix
Foreword	xiii
NINA SCOLNIK	
Acknowledgements	xvii
Introduction: Schubert and the Gothic	1
1 Songs of the Grave	23
2 Doubles and Distortions	53
3 Songs of the Night	89
4 Grotesquerie	119
Epilogue	151
Select Bibliography	157
Index	171

Illustrations

Figures

0.1	Caspar David Friedrich, 'Abbey in an Oak Forest' (1809–10)	10
0.2	Carl Blechen, 'Gotische Kirchenruine' (1826)	11
4.1	Henry Fuseli, 'The Nightmare' (1781)	124

Music Examples

1.1	Schubert, 'Leichenfantasie', D 7, bars 1–22	28
1.2	Schubert, 'Leichenfantasie', D 7, bars 23–44	30
1.3	Mozart, Rondo in A minor, K 511, bars 1–8	31
1.4	Schubert, 'Leichenfantasie', D 7, bars 303–16	32
1.5	Schubert, 'Leichenfantasie', D 7, bars 431–53	35
1.6	Schubert, 'Schwestergruss', D 762, bars 1–6	39
1.7	Schubert, 'Schwestergruss', D 762, bars 6–20	40
1.8	Schubert, 'Schwestergruss', D 762, bars 41–48	41
1.9	Schubert, 'Thekla: Eine Geisterstimme', D 595, bars 7–10	43
1.10	Schubert, 'Thekla: Eine Geisterstimme', D 595, bars 15–18	43
1.11	Schubert, 'Grablied', D 218, bars 1–13	46
1.12	Schubert, 'Totengräbers Heimweh', D 842, bars 1–9	48
1.13	Schubert, 'Totengräbers Heimweh', D 842, bars 40–48	49
1.14	Schubert, 'Totengräbers Heimweh', D 842, bars 49–62	51
1.15	Schubert, 'Totengräbers Heimweh', D 842, bars 82–86	52
2.1	Schubert, Piano Trio in E flat major, D 929, IV, bars 273–86	54
2.2	Schubert, Piano Trio in E flat major, D 929, II, bars 1–21	55

x *Illustrations*

2.3	Schubert, *Grand Marche Funèbre* in C minor for four hands, D 859, bars 1–6	60
2.4	Schubert, *Grande Marche Funèbre* in C minor for four hands, D 859, bars 15–28	61
2.5	Schubert, Impromptu in C minor, D 899/1, bars 1–17	62
2.6	Schubert, Fantasy in G minor for four hands, D 9, bars 1–7	63
2.7	Schubert, Fantasy in C minor for four hands, D 48, bars 1–4	63
2.8	Schubert, Piano Sonata in A minor, D 784, II, bars 1–8	65
2.9	Schubert, Piano Sonata in A minor, D 784, I, bars 1–22	65
2.10	Schubert, Piano Sonata in A minor, D 845, I, bars 1–10	66
2.11	Schubert, Impromptu in C minor, D 899/1, bars 95–118	67
2.12	Schubert, String Quartet in D minor, D 810, II, bars 1–8	69
2.13	Schubert, String Quartet in D minor, D 810, II, bars 73–75	69
2.14	Schubert, String Quartet in D minor, D 810, II, bars 81–92	70
2.15	Schubert, Piano Trio in E flat major, D 929, II, bars 104–14	71
2.16	Schubert, Impromptu in C minor, D 899/1, bars 33–51	73
2.17	Schubert, Impromptu in C minor, D 899/1, bars 124–29	75
2.18	Schubert, Piano Trio in E flat major, D 929, II, bars 41–44	75
2.19	Schubert, Piano Trio in E flat major, D 929, II, bars 67–84	76
2.20	Schubert, Fantasy in F minor for four hands, D 940, I, bars 1–8	79
2.21	Schubert, Fantasy in F minor for four hands, D 940, II, bars 121–32	80
2.22	Schubert, Fantasy in F minor for four hands, D 940, IV, bars 474–81	82
2.23	Schubert, Impromptu in C minor, D 899/1, bars 193–204	83
2.24	Schubert, Piano Trio in E flat major, D 929, II, bars 196–212	84
2.25	Schubert, Fantasy in F minor for four hands, D 940, IV, bars 556–70	85
3.1	Schubert, 'Nachtstück', D 672, bars 1–10	99
3.2	Schubert, 'Nachtstück', D 672, bars 17–29	100
3.3	Schubert, 'Bertas Lied in der Nacht', D 653, bars 1–8	105
3.4	Schubert, 'Bertas Lied in der Nacht', D 653, bars 8–15	106
3.5	Schubert, 'Der Unglückliche', D 713, bars 1–30	110

3.6	Schubert, 'Der Unglückliche', D 713, bars 31–47	112
3.7	Schubert, 'Der Zwerg', D 771, bars 37–50	113
3.8	Schubert, 'Der Unglückliche', D 713, bars 47–55	114
3.9	Schubert, 'Der Unglückliche', D 713, bars 114–23	115
3.10	Schubert, 'Nacht und Träume', D 827, bars 1–6	117
3.11	Schubert, 'Nacht und Träume', D 827, bars 14–21	118
4.1	Schubert, 'Wanderer' Fantasy in C major, D 760, II, bars 227–35	120
4.2	Schubert, 'Wanderer' Fantasy in C major, D 760, II, bars 206–13	129
4.3	Schubert, *Klavierstück* in E flat minor, D 946/1, bars 1–8	131
4.4	Schubert, *Klavierstück* in E flat minor, D 946/1, bars 118–24	131
4.5	Schubert, *Klavierstück* in E flat minor, D 946/1, bars 129–37	132
4.6	Schubert, *Klavierstück* in E flat major, D 946/2, bars 1–9	134
4.7	Schubert, *Klavierstück* in E flat major, D 946/2, bars 30–45	134
4.8	Schubert, *Klavierstück* in E flat major, D 946/2, bars 46–59	135
4.9	Schubert, String Quintet in C major, D 956, II, bars 28–31	137
4.10	Schubert, String Quintet in C major, D 956, II, bars 1–4	138
4.11	Schubert, String Quintet in C major, D 956, II, bars 64–67	140
4.12	Schubert, Piano Sonata in A major, D 959, II, bars 1–8	143
4.13	Schubert, Piano Sonata in A major, D 959, II, bars 69–122	144
5.1	Schubert, Piano Sonata in B flat major, D 960, I, bars 1–9	155
5.2	Schubert, Piano Sonata in B flat major, D 960, IV, bars 537–40	155

Full credit details are provided in the captions to the images in the text. The author and publisher are grateful to all the institutions and individuals for permission to reproduce the materials in which they hold copyright. Every effort has been made to trace the copyright holders; apologies are offered for any omission, and the publisher will be pleased to add any necessary acknowledgement in subsequent editions.

Foreword

Nina Scolnik

I first encountered Franz Schubert when I was five. An easy, bare-bones piano solo transcription of the song 'Ständchen' rested against the music desk of our old Köhler upright piano in the living room. My mother, intent on teaching it to me by rote, played it slowly and only a few notes at a time. I stopped her after many bars of this process and asked why the music was so sad. She paused and answered cryptically: 'Schubert died of a broken heart.' Whether she knew the truth of Schubert's tragic end or not, her words hung in the air merged with the sounds that issued forth from that old, out-of-tune upright, and unknowingly she cemented a notion that the music's sadness was connected to something beyond the notes.

My mother's response, even if only poetically true, aligns well with hermeneutic readings that link Schubert's awareness of his own mortality to depictions of death in his music. Not surprisingly, I gravitated towards these narratives as a performer and as a teacher, finding in them satisfying entry points for engaging with Schubert's music.

Joe Davies's seminal book, *The Gothic Imagination in the Music of Franz Schubert*, turns away from biographical considerations to a cross-disciplinary, multisensory exploration of death and the gothic at the intersection of music, literature, and the visual arts. Davies's breadth of erudition and depth of insight is striking for its balance of analytical/critical commentary that is grounded in musical engagement while still being accessible to a wide audience. In a book for scholars, performers, and readers outside the discipline of music, Davies guides us on a revelatory journey through a lesser-known village in Schubert country and opens new vistas for Schubert analysis, interpretation, and performance.

Public fascination with the gothic in the eighteenth and nineteenth centuries sets the stage for Schubert's preoccupation with death, the macabre, and the strange. Davies observes that these gothic tropes, appearing as early as Schubert's 1810 *Schauerballaden*, extend throughout his oeuvre to the later instrumental and piano works of his final years. Through case studies, Davies identifies a non-linear 'constellation of ideas' that intermingle, fragment, loop, and metamorphose in sonic estuaries of gothic Romanticism, the sublime, and the grotesque. As he traces elements from eeriness to the sublime and violent disjuncture, the reader is forced to ask what is the sound, the sight, and the feel of the gothic? Do words alter its effect? Schubert's gothic also reciprocally enlarges how we perceive its many permutations in the visual arts and literature while offering a deeper understanding of the relationship of these aesthetic categories to each other.

Gothic themes of blurred boundaries, eerie sounds, 'presences without explicit sources', and that of finding meaning in the 'in-between spaces' provide a focal point for grappling with the unexpected, the paradoxical, the strange, the perplexing, the irrational, and even the violence in Schubert's music. These ideas come to the fore in the discussion of the C minor Impromptu, D 899/1, in chapter 2. Davies's reading provokes new ways to hear and perform the forceful double octaves with fermatas and their dissipation at the beginning of the piece. From where do the octaves originate? What happens in the moments before their shocking presence? What must be conjured in the gap between the octaves' initial sounding and the theme's funereal entry in the right hand? How will the theme emerge from the sound of the octaves as they decay? At what moment should the pedal be changed? Does the theme emerge out of the violence of the octaves, or is it something unto itself, whispering from a world beyond?

Where the opening octave figure invites consideration of where material originates, the coda of the Impromptu foregrounds gothic themes of presence and absence. Davies writes: 'As the major takes hold, there is a glimpse of a theme never fully realized – a suggestion of "fragility", through the pared-down texture and gradual dissipation of the funereal rhythms, that was "evident at the (hesitant) start of the piece"' (p. 83). This description stimulates further thoughts. While the funereal rhythms dissipate with major and minor 'entwining', the eerie octaves heard in the beginning of the piece are now split off from each other in haunting off-beat minims, first in the left hand, then in the right hand. Syncopated this time and even more ominous, the octaves carry a memory of their previous iterations from their first appearance to their distortive impact when they are heard in triplets. When the octaves finally relinquish their grip, their presence continues to be felt past their last evocation. Davies concludes: 'The piece closes in a space between presence and absence, its echoing chain of cadences commingling with the eeriness heard at the outset' (p. 83). Davies's poetic analysis, as with all the examples in the book, offers a springboard for interpreting manifestations of the gothic in Schubert's music in imaginative and generative ways.

I met Joe Davies in the spring of 2021 when he joined our faculty at the University of California, Irvine, as a Marie Skłodowska-Curie Global Fellow in a joint affiliation with Maynooth University, Ireland. From our first meeting, which coincided with a guest lecture he gave at UCI, 'Rethinking Strangeness: Franz Schubert and the Gothic', I sensed my relationship to 'all things Schubert' was about to change. But even more than that, a relationship born of our shared love for the music of Franz Schubert blossomed into a professional and personal friendship that has offered the deepest kind of nourishment.

Joe's residency brimmed with a passion for collaboration. His rich engagement with faculty, students, and the community propelled interdisciplinary dialogues

Foreword

that continue to resonate in mentorships, collaborative projects, and friendships. So ethos-changing was his presence at UCI that we are left to re-evaluate old habits of separateness and contemplate the enriching consequences of scholarship and collaboration combined with a generosity of spirit. This book, too, shines through with a generosity of spirit in the manner in which Davies engages with extant scholarship. Such an inclusive mode of discourse will no doubt generate further crucial interdisciplinary dialogue on the gothic and Schubert's expressive world.

Acknowledgements

This book has roots in three countries: the United Kingdom, where its seeds were sown, Ireland, and most recently the United States. In each I have been blessed with friends and colleagues whose inspiration has enriched its content and life more generally.

My abiding thanks go to Susan Wollenberg – friend, mentor, collaborator, and constant presence since my days as a graduate student at the University of Oxford. Susan has sharpened my thinking in myriad ways: from reading the manuscript with an unparalleled eye for detail, to highlighting through her own example the power of scholarship imbued with kindness. For this, and for Susan's wisdom, I shall be forever grateful.

In Ireland, I am fortunate to be part of a community of scholars whose intellectual creativity is matched only by their generosity of spirit. I thank colleagues in the Music Department at Maynooth University, as well as friends through the Society for Musicology in Ireland, especially Harry White, for their warm embrace. To Lorraine Byrne Bodley, I owe gratitude not only for her encouragement to write this book, but also for her friendship and engagement with the material in the years since. Our conversations about Schubert or all else besides provided light at the end of a day of writing, a reminder of the joys of immersing oneself in music and words.

The Music Department at the University of California, Irvine, where the finishing touches were made, has offered a space in which to think at the intersection of scholarship and performance. Heartfelt thanks are extended to Nicole Grimes, who has gone above and beyond to make my move across the Atlantic so life-affirming. Nicole's inspiration – from our working together on Clara Schumann, to musing on life over walks at Crystal Cove – resonates throughout these pages and beyond. That she read large portions of the manuscript, with an ear for musical detail and an eye for critical thought, is a privilege for which I owe further gratitude. To Nina Scolnik, I extend thanks for a friendship that knows no bounds, for making Irvine feel like home, and for her generous sharing of ideas about the intricacies of Schubert's piano music. Nina's approach, as both pianist and scholar, provided a boost of creativity in those moments where it is cherished most. I extend thanks also to colleagues across the UCI Music Department and the Claire Trevor School of the Arts, especially Amy Bauer, David Brodbeck, Lorna Griffitt, Tifanny Ana López, and Colleen Reardon; and to Peter Chang for his brilliance with administrative matters.

The inspiration of friends around the world has never been far from reach. Among them are Matthew Head, whose mentorship during my time at King's College

London provided the foundations for everything that has followed since; and Laura Tunbridge, whose guidance from the earliest stages of the project leaves an imprint on my approach to Schubert and musicology more broadly. Gascia Ouzounian's friendship has always been close to hand. Working together at Lady Margaret Hall, Oxford, a time I recall with fondness, opened up ways of engaging with music that live on in all aspects of my life.

Susan Youens, an inspiration to us all, has enhanced my thinking on occasions too numerable to list here. It is one of life's privileges to be on the receiving end of Susan's friendship, personally and professionally, and to learn from her treasure trove of knowledge. Natasha Loges, to whom I offer further thanks, read drafts of the manuscript with the breadth of vision that characterizes her own work. Our collaborations, whether on Schubert or on the global history of women pianists, have deepened the interweaving of music and ideas throughout the pages that follow.

I am grateful also to James Sobaskie for the many stimulating exchanges since our co-editing of *Drama in the Music of Franz Schubert*; and to Roe-Min Kok for the joy of co-editing *Clara and Robert Schumann in Context* together. These projects, infused with collegiality and an openness to learning from one another, have been front of mind while working on this monograph.

It was an honour to complete this book while holding a Postdoctoral Fellowship from the Irish Research Council (Project ID: GOIPD/2019/296) and to present material at international conferences or lectures at, among other institutions, Bristol University, the University of Huddersfield, the Hochschule für Musik, Freiburg, Maynooth University, the Catholic University of America, the University of Tübingen, and the University of California, Irvine. I am grateful for the engagement of attendees at those events, as well as to numerous colleagues for their insights over the course of the book's development: Kofi Agawu, Scott Burnham, Matthew Gardner, Christopher Gibbs, Martyn Harry, Anne Hyland, David Kasunic, Christine Martin, Clive McClelland, Stephen Rodgers, Alexander Stefaniak, and Katharina Uhde. I thank also the doctoral students whom I have had the pleasure of advising, among them Louis De Nil, Ruth Minton, and Deirdre Toh, together with generations of Oxford students for their creative engagement with ideas explored throughout this book.

Friends from various phases of life – Fernanda Carneiro, Mary Jean Chan, Gerard Gormley, Louis Jack, Yvonne Liao, Alex Lopes Rocha Lima, Pamela Michaelidou, Hannah Millington, Wei Tan, Beverley Vong, Linde Wester, Bryan Whitelaw – have been an inspiring presence throughout, always willing to share their creativity, supportive to the last.

Special thanks are reserved for Michael Middeke, Editorial Director for Music and Modern History at Boydell & Brewer, who has guided the project with empathy for the realities of bringing a book to life. Michael's endorsement, constant since our earlier work together, has been central to the journey from proposal to publication, his patience unwavering throughout. I extend thanks also to Crispin Peet

Acknowledgements xix

and colleagues in the Production Department for their work in the latter stages of the process; and to the anonymous readers whose feedback has enriched the arguments. Further gratitude goes to Robin Hagues for producing the music examples; Wendy Baskett for preparing the Index; and Ingalo Thomson for copy-editing the text with a flair for the subtleties of language. I am grateful for permission to develop material for chapters 2 and 4 from my contributions to *Drama in the Music of Franz Schubert* (Boydell & Brewer) and *Schubert's Piano* (Cambridge University Press). All translations of Schubert's songs are taken with kind permission of the translator, Richard Wigmore, from Graham Johnson, *Franz Schubert: The Complete Songs* (Yale University Press).

My partner Min Sern Teh has lived through this project as if it were his own. Your inspiration, Min Sern, as someone who thinks and listens with depth of spirit, has shaped everything that follows. Thank you for the life we share together, whether in the UK, the US, or Malaysia, and for all that you do to enrich those around you.

My final thanks are for my family, especially my parents and grandparents, whose steadfast belief in my work has propelled me to the finishing line; and my extended family in Malaysia for their support and kindness. Mum, none of this would be possible without you – thank you for always being there, for offering encouragement when it is needed most. The immediacies of the subject matter – of love and pain entwined, as Schubert expressed in 'My Dream' (1822) – were brought home to me by the sudden death of my father during the late stages of writing. Dad, this book is for you, with gratitude for everything.

Introduction: Schubert and the Gothic

Evening light. Dreamer (A). His dreamt self (B). Dreamt hands R (right) and L (left). Last 7 bars of Schubert's Lied, 'Nacht und Träume'.[1]

A dreamer sits in darkness, head bowed, hands resting in front of him. All is hushed, no words, little movement. A male voice hums the last seven bars of Schubert's 'Nacht und Träume', D 827 – 'sweet dreams, come back!' ('Holde Träume, kehret wieder!'). Haunting in its fragmentation, the music is repeated, this time with words, the man's head sinking deeper into his hands. At the words 'Holde Träume', the light reveals the man's own reflection, his dreamt self, gazing down on him from a podium suspended in mid-air: a mirror image of his waking self.

This scene from Samuel Beckett's last television play, 'Nacht und Träume', broadcast on 19 May 1983, provides a springboard for thinking about the prominence of death (whether real or imagined) in Schubert's music.[2] Central to the discussion is the relationship between biography and art – or, more specifically, the relationship between depictions of death and Schubert's confrontation with his own mortality, as intimated in his oft-quoted letter to Leopold Kupelwieser:[3]

---

[1] Samuel Beckett, 'Nacht und Träume', in *Collected Shorter Plays* (New York: Grove, 1984), 303–6. See Paul Lawley, '"The Grim Journey": Beckett Listens to Schubert', *Samuel Beckett Today* 11 (2001), 255–66; Noel Witts, 'Beckett and Schubert', *Performance Research* 12/1 (2007), 138–44; and Graley Herren, 'Splitting Images: Samuel Beckett's Nacht und Träume', *Modern Drama* 43/2 (2000), 182–91. I thank Nicole Grimes for bringing to mind the Schubert–Beckett association.

[2] See https://www.youtube.com/watch?v=Uj-CZw8PMFY.

[3] On the issues surrounding Schubert and death, see Lorraine Byrne Bodley, 'Introduction: Schubert's Late Style and Current Musical Scholarship', in *Schubert's Late Music: History, Theory, Style*, ed. Byrne Bodley and Julian Horton (Cambridge: Cambridge University Press, 2016), 1–16; Byrne Bodley, 'A Place at the Edge: Reflections on Schubert's Late Style', *Oxford German Studies* 44/1 (2015), 18–29; Byrne Bodley, 'Music of the Orphaned Self? Schubert and Concepts of Late Style', in *Schubert's Late Music*, 331–56; and Lauri Suurpää, *Death in Winterreise: Music-Poetic Associations in Schubert's Song Cycle* (Bloomington: Indiana University Press, 2014). On Schubert's illness, see (among others) Elizabeth Norman McKay, *Franz Schubert: A Biography* (New York: Oxford University Press, 1996), chapter 7; and Eric Sams, 'Schubert's Illness Re-examined', *Musical Times* 121 (1980), 15–22; John O'Shea, *Music and Medicine: Medical Profiles of Great Composers* (London: J.M. Dent, 1990), 109–17; Peter Gilroy Bevan, 'Adversity: Schubert's Illnesses and their Background', in *Schubert Studies*, ed. Brian Newbould (Farnham: Ashgate, 1998), 244–66; Anton Neumayr, *Musik und Medizin: am Beispiel der Wiener Klassik* (Vienna: Edition Wien, 1987), 189–226; Deborah Hayden, *Pox: Genius, Madness, and the Mysteries of Syphilis* (New York: Basic Books, 2003), chapter 9, 'Franz Schubert, 1797–1828'; and Joseph N. Straus, *Extraordinary*

I feel myself to be the most unhappy and wretched creature in the world. Imagine a man whose health will never be right again, and who in sheer despair over this ever makes things worse and worse, instead of better; imagine a man, I say, whose most brilliant hopes have perished, for whom the felicity of love and friendship have nothing to offer but at best pain, whose enthusiasm (at least of the stimulating kind) for all things beautiful threatens to forsake him, and I ask you, is he not a miserable, unhappy being? My peace is gone, my heart is sore, I shall find it never and nevermore [*'Meine Ruh' ist hin, Mein Herz ist schwer, Ich finde sie nimmer und nimmermehr'*], I may well sing every day now, for each night, on retiring to bed, I hope I may not wake again, and each morning but recalls yesterday's grief. Thus, joyless and friendless, I should pass my days, did not Schwind visit me now and again and turn on me a ray of those sweet days of the past.[4]

Much ink has been spilled over the extent to which these words capture Schubert's psychological and creative mindset in the last years of his life. In some cases, the connection between life and music is rendered explicit, as in Benjamin Korstvedt's observation of the last three Piano Sonatas, D 958–960 (1828), that 'these works feel, often uncannily so, as if they were written under the star of looming mortality'.[5] Eric Wen, in his analysis of the slow movement of the B flat Sonata, D 960, is similarly drawn to the music's biographical resonances, his concluding remark striking a poignant tone: 'at the end of this sorrowful *Wiegenlied* – this final lullaby before death – Schubert has at last found peace.'[6] For James Sobaskie, this movement represents an expression of 'self-elegy' – a 'mourning of one's own anticipated death' – rooted in while also allowing for 'realities' beyond Schubert's own circumstances.[7]

Yet death does not always reach such existential heights in Schubert's music. As Lorraine Byrne Bodley writes, 'an awareness of his own mortality unquestionably

---

Measures: Disability in Music (New York: Oxford University Press, 2011), chapter 3, 'Musical Narratives of Disability Accommodated: Schubert'.

4 Letter to Leopold Kupelwieser, 31 March 1824, in Otto Erich Deutsch (ed.), *The Schubert Reader: A Life of Franz Schubert in Letters and Documents*, trans. Eric Blom (New York: W.W. Norton & Co., 1949), 339. The quotation of *'Meine Ruh' ist hin, Mein Herz ist schwer, Ich finde sie nimmer und nimmermehr'*, borrowed from the opening lines of Schubert's setting of Goethe's 'Gretchen am Spinnrade', D 118, evokes the blurring of life and death that is central to what follows. While the opening of this letter conveys Schubert's immersion in the harsh realities of his situation, the closing passage presents a more optimistic perspective. Here, moving from the personal to the professional realm, Schubert outlines his ambitions to 'pave his way towards a grand symphony'. For further discussion of this letter – a rare, uncensored entrée into Schubert's psychological world – see (among others) John Gingerich, *Schubert's Beethoven Project*, 41 ff.; and Lorraine Byrne Bodley, *Schubert: A Musical Wayfarer* (New Haven: Yale University Press, 2023), 371.

5 Benjamin K. Korstvedt, '"The Prerogative of Schubert's Late Style": Thoughts on the Expressive World of Schubert's Late Works', in *Schubert's Late Music*, 412–13.

6 Eric Wen, 'Schubert's *Wiegenlied*: The Andante sostenuto from the Piano Sonata in B♭, D. 960', in *Schubert's Late Music*, 148. Further on Wen's argument, see my review of *Schubert's Late Music*, in *Nineteenth-Century Music Review* 16/1 (2019), 97–104, at 99–100.

7 James William Sobaskie, 'Schubert's Self-Elegies', *Nineteenth-Century Music Review* 5/2 (2008), 71–105, at 105.

Introduction: Schubert and the Gothic

deepened Schubert's preoccupation with death, but did not instigate it.'[8] Those initial seeds can be traced back to his *Schauerballaden* of the 1810s, where gothic subject matter takes centre stage:[9] from the graveyard imagery of 'Leichenfantasie', D 7, to the portrayal of patricide in 'Der Vatermörder', D 10, and the ghostliness of his three 'Der Geistertanz' settings, D 15, D 15A, and D 116, discussed below.

The Gothic Imagination in the Music of Franz Schubert, taking its cue from these early ballads, disentangles death from biographical considerations and contextualizes strangeness in relation to a phenomenon that captivated the late eighteenth- and early nineteenth-century imagination.[10] Just as Beckett became 'almost obsessed' with the 'Death and the Maiden' Quartet, D 810, so this book invites readers to locate meanings in the intersections of death and the gothic that run through Schubert's oeuvre – sometimes explicitly, other times implicitly. The interpretations, grounded in close reading of musical and poetic material, move beyond the ghostly or macabre towards a framework in which ideas of death, the sublime, and the grotesque intersect across generic boundaries. In doing so, they offer new perspectives for contextualizing Schubert's creative approach and for understanding the gothic imagination more generally.[11]

Defining the Gothic

The gothic resists neat categorization. It has been defined as an 'indeterminate genre',[12] a 'literature of terror',[13] a 'discourse of the supernatural', a 'psychology', 'a particular form, or set of forms, of the imagination'.[14] Not a fixed mode, the gothic

---

[8] Byrne Bodley, 'Introduction: Schubert's Late Style and Current Musical Scholarship', 8.

[9] Clive McClelland, 'Death and the Composer: The Context of Schubert's Supernatural Lieder', in *Schubert the Progressive: History, Performance Practice, Analysis*, ed. Brian Newbould (Aldershot: Ashgate, 2003), 21–35.

[10] On strangeness, a long-standing trope in Schubert criticism, see Hugh Macdonald, 'Schubert's Volcanic Temper', *Musical Times* 119 (1978), 949–52; and Susan Wollenberg, *Schubert's Fingerprints: Studies in the Instrumental Works* (Farnham: Ashgate, 2011), 161–90.

[11] On the growing body of literature addressing the gothic in music, to which this study contributes, see Marjorie Hirsch, 'Schubert's Reconciliation of Gothic and Classical Influences', in *Schubert's Late Music*, 149–70; Matthew Head, 'Mozart's Gothic: Feelings for History in the Rondo in A minor, K. 511', *Keyboard Perspectives* 4 (2012), 69–114; Laura Protano-Biggs, 'Bellini's Gothic Voices: Bellini, "Un grido io sento" (Alaide), *La straniera*, Act I', *Cambridge Opera Journal* 28 (2016), 149–54; Melina Esse, 'Donizetti's Gothic Resurrections', *19th-Century Music* 33 (2009), 81–109; Anatole Leikin, 'Chopin and the Gothic', in *Chopin and his World*, ed. Jonathan D. Bellman and Halina Goldberg (Princeton, NJ: Princeton University Press, 2017), 85–102; and Jessie Fillerup, 'Lucia's Ghosts: Sonic, Gothic and Postmodern', *Cambridge Opera Journal* 28/3 (2016), 313–45.

[12] Jacqueline Howard, 'Theories of the Gothic', in *Reading Gothic Fiction: A Bakhtinian Approach* (Oxford: Oxford Academic Books, 1994), 12–52.

[13] David Punter, 'Introductory: Dimensions of Gothic', in *The Literature of Terror: A History of Gothic Fiction from 1765 to the Present Day* (New York: Longman Group, 1980), 1–21.

[14] On the last three descriptions, see David Punter, 'Introduction', in *The Edinburgh Companion to Gothic and the Arts*, ed. Punter (Edinburgh: Edinburgh University Press, 2019), 1–12, esp. 1–2.

is, in Michael Gamer's words, 'something more organic and protean', a 'shifting aesthetic' that fuses the literary, the visual, and the sonic.[15] At its core is an emphasis on 'the responses it provokes (fear, terror, horror)', and on 'the places from which it originates (dream, fantasy)'.[16] It resides as much in material sounds as in the gaps, those in-between moments where the distinction between fantasy and reality is 'no longer secure'.[17] These elements point, as Isabella van Elferen observes, to a phenomenon defined above all by the 'crossing of boundaries, the exploration of limits'; it is located in a 'perpetual and self-perpetuating in-between'.[18]

Methodologically, the 'in-between' space of the gothic can be problematic, for it requires interpreters to look beyond established categories of knowledge, and to work at the boundaries of what is stated and that which is implied. As Elizabeth Napier notes, the gothic 'seems to demand an activity of consolidating on the part of its readership that its own design subverts. The result is fundamentally unstable, both in theory and in practice.'[19] Yet, its precariousness notwithstanding, such territory allows for cross-disciplinary innovation as larger enquiries unfold regarding the role of the gothic across the arts. What role do words play in conjuring the gothic? What does the gothic look like? And how does it sound? These questions, central to what follows, form the basis of an approach positioned between seeing, reading, hearing, and sensing – one that captures the fluidity of the gothic imagination as it moves across music, literature, and the visual arts.[20]

This book situates these multisensory strands within 'gothic necropoetics', a framework comprised of 'death-focused symbols and tropes' such as spectrality and the concept of *memento mori*.[21] It grapples not only with the sonic dimension of death – where it resides, its stylistic properties – but also with the gothic as a space in which to 'indulge death-related fantasies and fears';[22] or to encounter, in the words

[15] Michael Gamer, *Romanticism and the Gothic: Genre, Reception, and Canon Formation* (Cambridge: Cambridge University Press, 2000), 4.

[16] See Chris Baldick and Robert Mighall, 'Gothic Criticism', in *A New Companion to the Gothic*, ed. David Punter (West Sussex: Blackwell Publishing, 2012), 274.

[17] Fred Botting, *Gothic* (London and New York: Routledge, 1996), 11.

[18] Isabella van Elferen, *Gothic Music: The Sounds of the Uncanny* (Cardiff: University of Wales Press, 2012), 18.

[19] Elizabeth R. Napier, *The Failure of Gothic: Problems of Disjunction in an Eighteenth-Century Literary Form* (New York: Oxford University Press, 1987), 44.

[20] Multisensory studies of this kind intersect with the category of fantasy, as explored in Francesca Brittan, *Music and Fantasy in the Age of Berlioz* (Cambridge: Cambridge University Press, 2017); see my review in *Nineteenth-Century Music Review* 17/2 (2020), 287–91, for further discussion of this approach.

[21] See Carol Margaret Davison, 'Introduction – The Corpse in the Closet: The Gothic, Death, and Modernity', in *The Gothic and Death*, ed. Davison (Manchester: Manchester University Press, 2017), 1–17, at 2. See also Davison, 'Trafficking in Death and (Un)dead Bodies: Necro-Politics and Poetics in the Works of Ann Radcliffe', *Irish Journal of Gothic and Horror Studies* 14 (2015), 37–47.

[22] Davison, 'The Corpse in the Closet', 7

of Elisabeth Bronfen, 'death by proxy', an 'attractive and even desirable experience because "apparently unreal".[23]

Framing the gothic in terms of death allows for a rethinking of its chronological and geographical boundaries, as Andrew Smith shows in his literary history of gothic death, 1740–1914.[24] The approach he takes charts the evolution of the gothic from its origins, commonly located in Horace Walpole's *The Castle of Otranto* (1764), through the 1790s, the heyday of the gothic novel,[25] into the Romantic gothic of the early 1800s. This last emerges not as an exclusively English phenomenon, as is well established, but also with roots in German literature, from Friedrich Schiller to E.T.A. Hoffmann, and in the artwork of Caspar David Friedrich and Carl Blechen (discussed below).[26] Such thinking disrupts linear or teleological trajectories, by placing emphasis on how Romanticism looks back to and transforms tropes from earlier phases of gothic discourse, the two intersecting in ways difficult to disentangle.

Ideas of German Romanticism – rooted in subjectivity, the creative imagination, death as a release or communion with the universe – may seem worlds apart from the ghostliness and supernaturalism associated with the gothic.[27] Yet, as explored in the chapters that follow, the boundaries between the two coalesce around the

---

[23] Quoted in Davison, 'The Corpse in the Closet', 7; see also Elisabeth Bronfen, 'Death', in *The Handbook of Gothic Literature*, ed. Marie Mulvey-Roberts (Basingstoke: Palgrave Macmillan, 2009), 113–14.

[24] Andrew Smith, *Gothic Death 1740–1914: A Literary History* (Manchester: Manchester University Press, 2016). Further on the history of the gothic, see Jonathan Dent, 'Introduction: History and the Gothic in the Eighteenth Century', in *Sinister Histories: Gothic Novels and Representations of the Past, from Horace Walpole to Mary Wollstonecraft* (Manchester: Manchester University Press, 2016), 1–28; Punter, 'Introductory: Dimensions of Gothic'; Fred Botting, 'Introduction: Negative Aesthetics', in *Gothic* (New York: Routledge, 2014), 1–19; Jerrold E. Hogle, 'Introduction: The Gothic in Western Culture', in *The Cambridge Companion to Gothic Fiction*, ed. Hogle (Cambridge: Cambridge University Press, 2002), 1–20; and Gamer, 'Gothic and its Contexts', in *Romanticism and the Gothic*, 48–89.

[25] See Terry Castle, 'The Gothic Novel', in *The Cambridge History of English Literature, 1660–1780*, ed. John Richetti (Cambridge: Cambridge University Press, 2005), 673–706.

[26] On the gothic in German culture, see Curtis Maughan and Jeffrey High (eds), *German Gothic Literature: Origins, Adaptions, Transformations* (London, New York, Melbourne, Delhi: Anthem Press, forthcoming); Andrew Cusack and Barry Murnane (eds), *Popular Revenants: The German Gothic and its International Reception, 1800–2000* (Rochester, NY: Camden House, 2012); Heide Crawford and Linda Kraus Worley, 'The German Gothic: Introduction', in 'The German Gothic', special issue, *Colloquia Germanica* 42/1 (2009), 1–3; Andrew Philip Seeger, 'Crosscurrents between the English Gothic Novel and the German Schauerroman' (PhD dissertation, University of Nebraska, Lincoln, 2004).

[27] For a recent reappraisal, see Benedict Taylor (ed.), *The Cambridge Companion to Music and Romanticism* (Cambridge: Cambridge University Press, 2021); see further Nicholas Saul (ed.), *The Cambridge Companion to German Romanticism* (Cambridge: Cambridge University Press, 2013); John Daverio, *Nineteenth-Century Music and the German Romantic Ideology* (New York: Schirmer, 1993); Lisa Feurzeig, *Schubert's Lieder and the Philosophy of Early German Romanticism* (Farnham: Ashgate, 2014); and Denis Mahoney (ed.), *The Literature of German Romanticism* (Woodbridge: Boydell & Brewer, 2004).

'central paradox' of the Romantic gothic: the issue, as Smith defines it, of 'how to write the gothic [becoming] subsumed by the problem of how to write about death'.[28] At times, death is bound up with a distorted past; in other moments it becomes entwined with ideas of doubling and the Doppelgänger phenomenon, or with nocturnal imagery at once gothic and Romantic.[29]

Conjuring Death

Spectrality is one such trope that cuts across the development of the gothic.[30] For Walpole and early exponents, ghostly presences offered the possibility of encountering the supernatural – as in *The Castle of Otranto*, where Isabella is haunted by sighs as she wanders through a 'subterraneous passage' in the vaults of an ancient castle:

> Every murmur struck her with new terror. [...] She trod as softly as impatience would give her leave, – yet frequently stopped and listened to hear if she was followed. In one of those moments, she thought she heard a sigh. She shuddered, and recoiled a few paces. In a moment she thought she heard the step of some person.[31]

Evocations of this kind gradually gave way over the eighteenth century to Ann Radcliffe's notion of the 'explained supernatural' – an approach whereby supernatural occurrences, initially creating suspense, turn out to be the 'product of natural causes'.[32] There became, in other words, an increasing distance between the real and the imagined. One example is Radcliffe's *The Mysteries of Udolpho* (1794), where protagonist Emily believes her chamber is haunted only later to find out the rational explanation for the ghostly sounds emanating from unknown places:[33]

---

[28] Smith, *Gothic Death*, 9.

[29] See Carol Margaret Davison, 'Death and Gothic Romanticism: Dilating in/upon the Graveyard, Meditating among the Tombs', in *The Routledge Companion to Death and Literature*, ed. W. Michelle Wang, Daniel Jernigan, and Neil Murphy (New York: Routledge, 2020), 276–87.

[30] On spectrality, see Andrew Smith, 'Hauntings', in *The Routledge Companion to Gothic*, ed. Catherine Spooner and Emma McEvoy (New York: Routledge, 2007), 147–54; Yael Shapira, *Inventing the Gothic Corpse: The Thrill of Human Remains in the Eighteenth-Century Novel* (Cham, Switzerland: Palgrave Macmillan, 2018); and Terry Castle, 'The Spectralization of the Other in *The Mysteries of Udolpho*', in *The Female Thermometer: Eighteenth-Century Culture and the Invention of the Uncanny* (New York: Oxford University Press, 1995), 120–39.

[31] Horace Walpole, *The Castle of Otranto*, ed. N. Groom, 3rd edn (Oxford: Oxford University Press, 1982), 27–28 [1st edn, London: T. Lownds, 1765].

[32] See Dale Townshend and Angela Wright (eds), *Ann Radcliffe, Romanticism and the Gothic* (Cambridge: Cambridge University Press, 2014).

[33] See Noelle Chao, 'Musical Listening in *The Mysteries of Udolpho*', in *Words and Notes in the Long Nineteenth Century*, ed. Phyllis Weliver and Katharine Ellis (Woodbridge: Boydell & Brewer, 2013), 85–102.

Introduction: Schubert and the Gothic

Are there two instruments, or is it an echo I hear? […] That guitar is often heard at night, when all is still, but nobody knows who touches it; and it is sometimes accompanied by a voice so sweet, and so sad, that one would almost think the woods were haunted. […] I have sometimes got up to the window to look if I could see anybody; but […] all was hushed, and nobody to be seen; and I have listened, and listened, till I have been so timorous that even the trembling of the leaves in the breeze has made me start. They say it often comes to warn people of their death.[34]

Depictions of the supernatural as all too real yet unreal find a parallel in Friedrich Schiller's *Der Geisterseher* (*The Ghost-Seer*), first published in instalments in the journal *Thalia*, 1787–89, then subsequently printed as a three-volume book.[35] Here elements of Walpole's style – strange settings, unearthly noises – meet with apparitions that are displaced as soon as they are invoked:[36]

All of a sudden, we all felt … a stroke as of a flash of lightning, so powerful that our hands flew apart; a terrible thunder shook the house, the locks jarred; the doors fell shut; the cover of the silver box fell down and extinguished the light, and on the opposite wall, above the chimney piece, appeared a human figure in a bloody shirt, with the paleness of death on its countenance.

– – –

The house again trembled; a dreadful thunder rolled; a flash of lightning illuminated the room; the doors flew open, and another bodily form, bloody and pale as the first, but even more terrifying, appeared on the threshold. […] The first apparition was seen no more.[37]

---

34 Ann W. Radcliffe, *The Mysteries of Udolpho: And a Sicilian Romance* (London: J. Limbird, 1826), 308.

35 See Friedrich Schiller, 'Der Geisterseher, aus den Papieren des Grafen von O', *Thalia* 4 (1787), 68–94; Schiller, *Der Geisterseher: Eine Geschichte aus den Memoires des Grafen von O*** (Leipzig: bei Georg Joachim Göschen, 1789); Schiller, *The Ghost Seer; or, Apparitionist: An Interesting Fragment, Found among the Papers of Count O***, trans. Daniel Boileau (London: Vernor and Hood, 1795). See also Schiller, 'Der Geisterseher, aus den Papieren des Grafen von O', in *Historische Schriften und Erzählungen II*, 588–725; *The Ghost Seer; or, Apparitionist*, ed. Jeffrey L. Sammons, trans. H. Bohn (Columbia, SC: Camden House, 1992).

36 Further on Schiller and the gothic, see Stefan Andriopoulos, *Ghostly Apparitions: German Idealism, the Gothic Novel, and Optical Media* (Princeton, NJ: Zone Books, 2013); Roger Lüdeke, 'Gothic Truth and Mimetic Practice: On the Realism of Schiller's *Geisterseher*', *European Romantic Review* 28/1 (2017), 37–50; Jeffrey L. High, 'Schiller, Coleridge, and the Reception of the "German (Gothic) Tale"', Themenheft, 'The German Gothic', *Colloquia Germanica* 42/1, (2009), 49–66; Edward K. Maier, 'Gothic Horror, the Windowless Monad, and the Self: The Limits of Enlightenment in Schiller's "Der Geisterseher"', *Colloquia Germanica* 3/4 (2006), 243–55.

37 'Auf einmal empfanden wir alle zugleich einen Streich wie vom Blitze, daß unsre Hände auseinander flogen, ein plötzlicher Donnerschlag erschütterte das Haus, alle Schlösser klangen, alle Türen schlugen zusammen, der Deckel an der Kapsel fiel zu, das Licht löschte aus und an der entgegengesetzten Wand, über dem Kamine zeigte sich eine menschliche Figur, in blutigem Hemde, bleich und mit sterbendem Gesicht.' 'Hier

8 *The Gothic Imagination in the Music of Franz Schubert*

These examples speak to the widening gulf between death and the supernatural as gothic discourse evolved. By the late eighteenth century, rather than being synonymous with the gothic, the supernatural was problematized or treated as a context in which to probe the boundaries between the dead and the undead. Such questioning led to varied ways of understanding the aesthetics of death – as a source of horror, something to be feared, or an occasion to confront what lies beyond the realm of the living – that continued to evolve in the early decades of the nineteenth century.

One such context is that of the sublime, particularly as defined by Edmund Burke in his influential treatise of 1757.[38] Burke's notion of sublime terror, with its 'apprehension of pain or death', is stirred up through the examples discussed thus far.[39] Each places emphasis on a dark or terrifying experience, and collectively they speak to the dialectical representation of pain and pleasure at the heart of Burke's thinking. 'When danger or pain press too nearly', Burke observed, 'they are incapable of giving any delight, and are simply terrible but at certain distances, and with certain modifications, they are delightful.'[40] Whether conjuring death at a distance, or revealing the limits of the supernatural, the quoted passages from Walpole to Schiller can be seen as part of this larger movement towards thoughts and feelings redolent of the sublime.

Notions of the gothic as bound up with the sublime find further application in the writings of Johann Wolfgang von Goethe and Friedrich Schlegel. On encountering the (rather bewildering) design of Strasbourg cathedral, Goethe envisioned the gothic as 'undefined, disorganized, unnatural, patched-together, tacked-on': 'Quite smothered with ornament!' 'And I shuddered as I went', Goethe continued, '[at] the prospect of some misshapen, curly-bristled monster':

> How surprised I was when I was confronted by it! The impression which filled my soul was whole and large, and of a sort that (since it was composed of a thousand harmonizing details) I could relish and enjoy, but by no means identify and explain.[41]

---

erzitterte das Haus von neuem. Die Türe sprang freiwillig unter einem heftigen Donner auf, ein Blitz erleuchtete das Zimmer und eine andre körperliche Gestalt, blutig und blaß wie die erste aber schrecklicher, erschien an der Schwelle. [...] Die erste Figur war nicht mehr.' Translation adapted from Stefan Andriopoulos, 'Occult Conspiracies: Spirits and Secret Societies in Schiller's "Ghost Seer"', in 'Dark Powers: Conspiracies and Conspiracy Theory in History and Literature', *New German Critique* 103 (2008), 65–81, at 68.

[38] See Vijay Mishra, *The Gothic Sublime* (Albany, NY: State University of New York Press, 1994); Andrew Smith, 'The Gothic and the Sublime', in *Gothic Radicalism: Literature, Philosophy, and Psychoanalysis in the Nineteenth Century* (London: Palgrave Macmillan, 2020), 11–37; and David B. Morris, 'Gothic Sublimity', in 'The Sublime and the Beautiful: Reconsiderations', *New Literary History* 16/2 (1985), 299–319.

[39] Edmund Burke, *A Philosophical Enquiry into the Origin of our Ideas of the Sublime and Beautiful* (London: R. and J. Dodsley, 1757, repr. 1767), 96.

[40] Burke, *Ideas of the Sublime and Beautiful*, 60.

[41] Johann Wolfgang von Goethe, 'On German Architecture', in *Goethe on Art*, ed. and trans. John Gage (London: Scholar Press, 1980), 106–7.

Introduction: Schubert and the Gothic

Schlegel, too, was drawn to a view of the gothic as 'unit[ing] an extreme delicacy and inconceivable skill in mechanical execution, with the grand, the boundless, and infinite'. It is, in his words, 'a rare and truly beautiful combination of contrasting elements'.[42]

The idea of the gothic as intermingling the 'minutest details' with the 'lofty grandeur of the design', as Schlegel put it, comes to the fore in Caspar David Friedrich's 'Abbey in an Oak Forest' (1809–10) and Carl Blechen's 'Gotische Kirchenruine' (1826), featured on the cover (Figures 0.1 and 0.2 respectively).[43] Friedrich's painting suggests dialogues between Romantic themes that permeate his wider corpus, namely the figure of the Wanderer, isolated amid vast landscapes, seeking death or release from the realities of life, and gothic graveyard imagery that flourished in the mid- to late eighteenth century. The image is frozen in time while being also about change, reflected in the movement towards the grave and in the transition from day to night as the sun sets over the wintry landscape. Darkness paradoxically illuminates the presence of death, with the mixture of awe and terror that lies at the heart of the sublime. The crumbling abbey, with its broken window, refracts the fading light without offering a clear pathway to what lies beyond the graveyard. Traces of human presence blend with the skeletal trees, barely alive, and the silence that accompanies the procession to the inner realms of the abbey. Blechen's 'Gotische Kirchenruine' offers a close-up depiction, at once haunted and haunting, of Goethe's description of the gothic: 'quite smothered with ornament!'[44] Themes of growth and decay, palpable in Friedrich's painting, resurface here in the juxtaposition of trees that tower above the abbey and those that are drained of life, and through the dissolution of a monument that simultaneously stands the test of time. Death as something to be feared, suggested through the imposing stature of the ruins, intersects with the portrayal of the pilgrim, who is engulfed by the surroundings, seemingly poised between life and death. The fusion of eeriness and terror in Friedrich's painting is rendered even more enigmatic here as sleep slips between the temporary and the eternal.

Just as the gothic revolves around death and the sublime, so it also draws ideas of the grotesque into its web of references, especially as it developed in tandem with Romanticism.[45] Features of the grotesque – stylistic disjuncture, incongru-

---

[42] Friedrich Schlegel, 'Principles of Gothic Architecture (1804–5)', in *The Aesthetic and Miscellaneous Works of Frederick Von Schlegel*, trans. E.J. Millington (London: Henry G. Bohn, 1860), 156.

[43] On Caspar David Friedrich (1774–1840), a leading figure in the realm of landscape painting, see Joseph Leo Koerner, *Caspar David Friedrich and the Subject of Landscape* (2nd edn, Chicago: Chicago University Press, 2009); on Carl Blechen (1798–1840), landscape painter and professor at the Academy of Arts, Berlin, see John Sarn and Hertha Heller, 'Angst in der Natur: Die frühen Landschaften von Carl Blechen', *Zeitschrift für Kunstgeschichte* 43/2 (1980), 181–95; Annik Pietsch, '"Gottes Natur empfunden und erkannt" – Carl Blechens "Naturgemälde"', *Jahrbuch der Berliner Museen* 48 (2006), 89–116.

[44] Goethe, 'On German Architecture', 106–7.

[45] See Fragments 305, 389, and 424 in Friedrich Schlegel, *Philosophical Fragments*, trans. Peter Firchow (Minnesota: University of Minnesota Press, 1991), 60, 79, and 86. For

Figure 0.1. Caspar David Friedrich, 'Abbey in an Oak Forest' (1809–10). bpk Bildagentur / Nationalgalerie/Staatliche Museen/Berlin/Germany / Art Resource, NY.

ous configurations – are particularly pronounced in Mary Shelley's *Frankenstein* (1816) and E.T.A. Hoffmann's *Der Sandmann* (1816), wherein 'death and the creative imagination [are] given new affiliation', as Smith writes of the former.[46] Their approaches highlight the 'self-consciousness of the Romantic gothic', through the juxtaposition of physical formations with strange, 'mentally constructed' realities.[47] In Frankenstein, a hybrid creature – composed of dead human and animal body parts – is scientifically brought to life;[48] in *Der Sandmann*, the world of automata is

---

broader discussion of Schlegel's ideas, see Frederick Burwick, 'The Grotesque in the Romantic Movement', in *European Romanticism: Literary Cross-Currents, Modes, and Models*, ed. Gerhart Hoffmeister (Detroit: Wayne State University Press, 1989), 45–46.

[46] Smith, *Gothic Death*, 2–3.

[47] Smith, *Gothic Death*, 3.

[48] Mary Shelley located the inspiration for *Frankenstein*, a novel that would 'speak to the mysterious fears of our nature, and awaken thrilling horror', in the realm of dreams: 'When I placed my head on my pillow, I did not sleep, nor could I be said to think. My imagination, unbidden, possessed and guided me, gifting the successive images that arose in my mind with a vividness far beyond the usual bounds of reverie. I saw – with shut eyes, but acute mental vision – I saw the pale student of unhallowed arts kneeling beside the thing he had put together. I saw the hideous phantasm of a man stretched out, and then, on the working of some powerful engine, show signs of life, and stir with an uneasy, half vital motion. [...] He sleeps; but he is awakened; he opens his eyes; behold the horrid thing stands at his bedside, opening his curtains, and looking on him with yellow, watery, but speculative eyes.' Mary Shelley, *Frankenstein* (New York: Dover Publications, 1994),

Figure 0.2. Carl Blechen, 'Gotische Kirchenruine' (1826). bpk / Staatliche Kunstsammlungen Dresden / Elke Estel / Hans-Peter Klut.

represented by Olympia: 'Nathanael stood transfixed; he had only too clearly seen that in the deathly pale waxen face of Olympia there were no eyes, but merely black holes. She was a lifeless doll.'[49] The grotesque extends from physical descriptions – the mixture of beauty and deathliness in the case of Olympia, or the 'yellow skin scarcely cover[ing] the work of arteries and muscles' beneath Frankenstein's creature[50] – to the hybridity that defines their curious ontologies.

The examples given here – Walpole to Schiller, Shelley to Hoffmann – reflect the breadth of gothic necropoetics: from ideas of spectrality, strange sounds, or presences without explicit sources, to terror associated with the sublime and distortions characteristic of the grotesque. Death is evoked through direct references, or implied through blurred temporal boundaries, fissures between past and present, and narratives that are 'resistant to linearity, constantly looping, circling, reinventing' their content.[51] In the end, these elements represent entry points, rather than endpoints, for they spark ways of thinking about – and listening to – the gothic imagination in the eighteenth and nineteenth centuries.

Hearing the Gothic

One way of hearing gothic necropoetics in Schubert's music is to examine his numerous songs that feature graveyards, ghostliness, and parricide, or death and the supernatural more generally. Song, with its fusion of words and music, offers crucial insights into the semantics of the gothic, its poetic frames of reference, as well as opening out onto the literary contexts to which Schubert was drawn time and again. His contributions to this genre reveal a fascination with gothic discourse that developed over the course of his creative output.

Early signs of the gothic include Schubert's three settings of Friedrich von Matthisson's 'Der Geistertanz', two fragments in C minor (D 15, *c.*1812) and F minor (D 15A, *c.*1812), followed by a complete setting in C minor two years later (D 116). Matthisson's poem, bearing the subtitle '*Pulvis et umbra sumus – we are dust and shadows*' (Horace, Book IV, ode vii), stands out as strangely cheery.[52] Airy spirits strike up a dance around graves and rotting bones. Dogs whine, while ravens soar above the graveyard gates, flitting up and down like will-o'-the-wisps. Grief, buried deep in the gloomy chamber, is stamped with a cheerful farewell ('Dir fröhlich Ade!') at odds with the frames of reference throughout. The distance between the deathly and the

---

viii–ix. See Jonathan Crimmins, 'Mediation's Sleight of Hand: The Two Vectors of the Gothic in Mary Shelley's "Frankenstein"', *Studies in Romanticism* 52/4 (2013), 561–83.

49 Leonard J. Kent and Elizabeth C. Knight (eds), *Tales of E.T.A. Hoffmann* (Chicago: University of Chicago Press, 1972), 120.

50 Shelley, *Frankenstein*, 35.

51 Punter, 'Introduction', 1.

52 Graham Johnson, *Franz Schubert: The Complete Songs*, 3 vols (New Haven and London: Yale University Press, 2014), Vol. 1, 673.

Introduction: Schubert and the Gothic

jovial, this ending implies, is a matter of semantics, the two intertwining around the dance of the night spirits.

The multiple versions of 'Der Geistertanz', while highlighting the fluidity of ghostliness across Schubert's songs, share textural and rhythmic features.[53] Hushed octave unisons in D 15, outlining a tonic to dominant trajectory, resurface in D 15A as *fortissimo* iterations of the tonic, above which the inscription 'Mitternacht' mirrors the striking of midnight ('Wenn zwölfmal den Hammer / Die Mitternacht hebt'). D 116, underscored 'etwas geschwind', conveys restlessness through its distorted dactylic pattern (in compound duple metre) and through the doubling of the vocal line in the piano part. Hints of the supernatural materialize in the swirling diminished figurations (marked 'geschwinder'), from which the ravens take flight in stanza 4. The airy spirits dance throughout, their contours rising and falling, finding little time to rest. Common to all three settings is the way in which Schubert, while maintaining the musical signifiers of his graveyard songs, plays up the jovial side of Matthisson's text in a dance both merry and ghostly.

Elsewhere, as in Schubert's setting of Gottlieb Pfeffel's 'Der Vatermörder', D 10 (1811), associations between death and the gothic are captured in visceral terms:

Ein Vater starb von des Sohnes Hand.	A father died by his son's hand.
Kein Wolf, kein Tiger, nein!	No wolf, no tiger,
Der Mensch allein, der Tiere Fürst, erfand	but man alone, the prince of beasts,
Den Vatermord allein.	He alone invented parricide.[54]

The son, after killing his father, flees to the woods, where he is interrogated by a hunter:

Der Täter floh, um dem Gericht	To cheat the law of its victim,
Sein Opfer zu entziehn,	the murderer fled
In einen Wald, doch konnt er nicht	Into a wood, yet he could not
Den innern Richter fliehn.	Escape the inner judge.
Verzehrt und hager, stumm und bleich,	Consumed and haggard, silent and pale,
Mit Lumpen angetan,	Dressed in rags,
Dem Dämon der Verzweiflung gleich,	Like the demon of despair
Traf ihn ein Häscher an.	He was found by a henchman.[55]

---

[53] Its imagery points ahead to that of 'Die Nacht', D 534, discussed below, as well as the supernatural presences in *Winterreise*, D 911. Whining dogs find a parallel in those that bark in 'Im Dorfe', D 911/17; fluttering ravens cross paths with that which stalks – or guides? – the wanderer in 'Die Krähe', D 911/15; and the will-o'-the-wisps pre-empt that which entices the protagonist into the 'deepest rocky chasms' ('die tiefsten Felsengründe') in 'Irrlicht', D 911/9. Johnson, *The Complete Songs*, Vol. 3, 663.

[54] Johnson, *The Complete Songs*, Vol. 3, 462.

[55] Johnson, *The Complete Songs*, Vol. 3, 462–63.

Schubert wrought from Pfeffel's text, its content encompassing the human and the bestial, music that juxtaposes physical intensity with eeriness of the kind found in his settings of 'Der Geistertanz'. These contrasts are captured in the pianistic depiction of the woods through an abrupt shift from a full texture, marked *forte* and foreshadowing that of 'Erlkönig', D 328, to split tremolo-like octaves, marked *pianissimo*, in E flat minor. The tremolo, central to the soundworlds explored throughout this book, becomes increasingly disruptive in the piano interlude (bars 25–30) as it rises to *fortissimo* in the right hand and entwines with jagged, descending octaves in the left hand. The music associated with the hunter similarly draws on *schauerlicher* devices germane to gothic expression. Chromatic intervals, notably the augmented fourth for the words 'halt ein!' ('stop!'), diminished chords, further tremolos, and sudden dynamic contrasts mirror the portrayal of death in Pfeffel's text as both physical and imaginary.

Further signs of the gothic can be heard in Schubert's Ossian settings, from 'Kolmas Klage', D 217, to 'Die Nacht', D 534, through the coalescence of the night, death, and ghostliness.[56] The text of 'Kolmas Klage', penned by James Macpherson (Ossian), moves from the nocturnal landscape of the first stanza, to the contemplation of death in the penultimate stanza:

Stanza 1

Rund um mich Nacht,	Around me is night.
Ich irr' allein,	I wander alone,
Verloren am stürmischen Hügel;	Lost on the stormy hill;
Der Sturm braust vom Gebirg,	The storm roars from the mountains,
Der Strom die Felsen hinab,	The torrent pours down the rocks;
Mich schützt kein Dach vor Regen,	No roof shelters me from the rain.
Verloren am stürmischen Hügel,	Lost on the stormy hill,
Irr' ich allein.	I wander alone.

---

[56] On Schubert's Ossian settings, see James Porter, *Beyond Fingal's Cave: Ossian in the Musical Imagination* (Rochester, NY: University of Rochester Press, 2019), esp. 123–45; Walther Dürr, 'Schuberts Ossian-Gesänge. Vom Lied zur Szene', in *Schubert: Interpretationen*, ed. Ivana Rentsch and Klaus Pietschmann (Stuttgart: Franz Steiner, 2014), 11–26. For wider context on Ossian and the gothic, see Dale Townshend, 'Shakespeare, Ossian and the Problem of "Scottish Gothic"', in *Gothic Renaissance: A Reassessment*, ed. Elisabeth Bronfen and Beate Neumeier (Manchester: Manchester University Press, 2014), 218–40; Catherine Spooner, 'The Gothic in Nineteenth-Century Scotland', in *The Cambridge History of Gothic*, Vol. 2: *The Gothic in the Nineteenth Century*, ed. Dale Townshend and Angela Wright (Cambridge: Cambridge University Press, 2020), 328–58; and David Punter, 'Scottish Gothic', in *The Cambridge Companion to Scottish Literature*, ed. Gerard Carruthers and Liam McIlvanney (Cambridge: Cambridge University Press, 2013), 132–44.

Stanza 6

Geister meiner Toten,	Ghosts of my dead,
Sprecht vom Felsenhügel,	Speak from the rocky hillside,
Von des Berges Gipfel,	From the mountain top;
Nimmer schreckt ihr mich!	You will never frighten me!
Wo gingt ihr zur Ruhe,	Where are you gone to rest?
Ach, in welcher Höhle	Ah, in what cave
Soll ich euch nun finden?	Shall I find you now?
Doch es tönt kein Hauch.	But there is no sound.[57]

Schubert's setting mirrors the trajectory of Ossian's text through the dissipation of the restless opening accompaniment – its tremolo texture, couched in repeated triplet chords, recalling the depiction of night in 'Erlkönig' – into stylistic vocabulary associated with graveyard imagery. Ghostly tones of the dead pass between the elaborated turn figure in the vocal line and the main contours of the piano accompaniment, before receding into the *pianissimo* arpeggiated texture for the words 'kein Hauch' ('no sound'), this last-mentioned effect being a feature that recurs throughout the music discussed here.

These associations between the night and graveyard imagery are even more explicit in Schubert's setting of 'Die Nacht', the last of his Ossian settings. In his introduction (two sections of which Schubert set), Macpherson describes the scene as follows: 'Five bards, passing the night in the house of a chieftain, who was a poet himself, went severally to make their observations on, and returned with a description of, night.'[58] The opening section, devoted to the First Bard, summons a 'dull and dark' landscape, obscured by the clouds resting on the moors:

Erster Barde:

Die Nacht ist dumpfig und finster. An den Hügeln ruhn die Wolken. Kein Stern mit grünzitterndem Strahl; kein Mond schaut durch die Luft. Im Walde hör' ich den Hauch; aber ich hör' ihn weit in der Ferne. Der Strom des Tals erbraust; aber sein Brausen ist stürmisch und trüb.

First bard:

Night is dull and dark. The clouds rest on the hills. No star with green trembling beam; no moon looks from the sky. I hear the blast in the wood; but I hear it distant far. The stream of the valley murmurs; but its murmur is sullen and sad.

---

[57] Johnson, *The Complete Songs*, Vol. 2, 87–88.
[58] Johnson, *The Complete Songs*, Vol. 2, 417–18.

Vom Baum beim Grabe der Toten, hört man lang die krächzende Eul. An der Ebne erblick ich eine dämmernde Bildung! es ist ein Geist! Er schwindet, er flieht. Durch diesen Weg wird eine Leiche getragen: ihren Pfad bezeichnet das Luftbild.	From the tree at the grave of the dead the long-howling owl is heard. I see a dim form on the plain! It is a ghost! it fades, it flies. Some funeral shall pass this way: the meteor marks the path.
Der fernere Dogge heult von der Hütte des Hügels. Der Hirsch liegt im Moose des Bergs: neben ihm ruht die Hindin. In seinem astigten Geweihe hört sie den Wind; fährt auf, und legt sich zur Ruhe wieder nieder.	The distant dog is howling from the hut on the hill. The stag lies on the mountain moss: the hind is at his side. She hears the wind in his branchy horns. She starts, but lies again.[59]

Schubert's setting captures the dread of night – its blasts, distant sounds, and murmurs – through music combining the lyrical and the chant-like. Recitative, another recurring feature of the soundworlds explored here, is central to these slippages, as in the depiction of the night as 'dull and dark' in bars 5–6, its sounds emerging in the distance, audible but not fully tangible. Swirling figurations in bars 14–15 similarly echo the murmurs in the text, their sources unknown, while the funereal style of bars 30–34 brings the evocation of death into the foreground.

Later examples of the gothic range from Schubert's setting of Friedrich Schiller's 'Gruppe aus dem Tartarus', D 583 (1816), where it is bound up with the underworld, to his setting of Matthäus von Collin's 'Der Zwerg', D 771 (early 1820s), a 'subtle apotheosis of the horror genre'.[60] The text of Schiller's 'Gruppe aus dem Tartarus' turns away from the eeriness discussed thus far to the pain of entering Hades, the mythological realm of the dead. 'Utmost pattern, rigid architecture, combines with utmost instability in Dante-esque fashion', writes Susan Youens, central to which is the *ombra* topos: chromaticism within chromaticism, a rising up of tremolos from the depths of the accompaniment, doubling of pitches, and 'phrase compression and distortion' all make palpable the torment of encountering Hell.[61] 'Der Zwerg', by contrast, exhibits the materiality of the dead body, sonically and textually, as the dwarf declares to the queen: 'now you must grow pale for an early grave'; 'then the dwarf kisses her pale cheeks, whereupon her senses fade' ('Doch müsst zum frühen Grab du nun erblassen'; 'da küsst der Zwerg die bleichen Wangen, / Drauf alsobald

---

[59] (Ossian – Macpherson – Harold). The translation is James Macpherson's original text (rather than an exact translation of Edmund Baron von Harold's German), in Johnson, *The Complete Songs*, Vol. 2, 415–16. For wider commentary on the setting, including the authorial issues surrounding Macpherson and Ossian, see 415–19.

[60] Johnson, *The Complete Songs*, Vol. 3, 772.

[61] Susan Youens, 'Reentering Mozart's Hell: Schubert's "Gruppe aus dem Tartarus", D. 538', in *Drama in the Music of Franz Schubert*, ed. Joe Davies and James William Sobaskie (Woodbridge: Boydell & Brewer, 2019), 184.

Introduction: Schubert and the Gothic 17

vergehen ihr die Sinnen').[62] Schubert's setting harnesses the depiction of death as perverse yet enticing. Bare octaves, diminished chords, and repeated tremolos 'fill the air with incessant sound, a constant vibratory thrumming of dread', as the dwarf ties a cord of red silk around the queen's neck.[63] Such writing comes full circle from the soundworlds of his 'Der Geistertanz' to the exploration of sublime terror and grotesquerie in the chapters that follow.

Another way of hearing the gothic, beyond the realm of song, is to explore its manifestations in Schubert's first opera, *Des Teufels Lustschloss*, D 84 (1813/14), a three-act Singspiel with libretto by August von Kotzebue (1761–1819).[64] One example occurs in the scene of the haunted castle, Act I, where ghostliness fluctuates between the subject of mockery – 'Hexen Gespenster ha, ha, ha!' – and a physical presence that suddenly seizes Robert and breaks all his bones ('es kam plötzlich, wo ich stand, aus der Tiefe eine weisse Hand'; 'und dass mir alle Knochen krachten'). Schubert captures these tensions through the *ombra* style, notably sustained chordal entries in the winds and trombones, 'music of the dark shadows where demons, furies, and malevolent deities lurk', juxtaposed with rushing scalar passages and tremolo figurations in the strings and timpani.[65] Tremolando figures are linked directly with Robert's encounter with ghostliness – jabs of sound, interspersed with silence, that unsettle through their sonic oscillations and skeletal texture. Another example, in a twist of events characteristic of gothic narratives, occurs in the Finale of Act I, set in an ancient temple with monuments and tombstones. Oswald, after dismissing the existence of ghostly presences, comes face to face here with four statues who suddenly rise from the dead with swords drawn ('Die vier Statuen am Grabmal springen plötzlich auf und ziehen ihre Schwerter'). This encounter with the undead draws again on the fusion of tremolos and sustained sonorities, here couched in soft, eerie tones. These devices, tied to contrasting representations of the spirit world, feature also in Luitgarde's aria, 'Ihr

---

[62] Johnson, *The Complete Songs*, Vol. 3, 771.

[63] Susan Youens, 'Of Dwarves, Perversion, and Patriotism: Schubert's "Der Zwerg", D. 771', *19th-Century Music* 21/2 (1997), 177–207, at 202. See also Youens, *Schubert's Late Lieder: Beyond the Song-Cycles* (Cambridge: Cambridge University Press, 2002), 1–92.

[64] For an overview of Schubert's operas, see Lorraine Byrne Bodley, 'Opera that Vanished: Goethe, Schubert, and Claudine von Villa Bella', in *Drama in the Music of Franz Schubert*, 11–34; Christine Martin, 'Pioneering German Musical Drama: Sung and Spoken Word in Schubert's *Fierabras*', in *Drama in the Music of Franz Schubert*, 35–50; Thomas A. Denny, 'Schubert's Operas: "The Judgement of History?"', in *The Cambridge Companion to Schubert*, ed. Christoper H. Gibbs (Cambridge: Cambridge University Press, 1997), 224–38; and Richard Douglas Bruce, 'Schubert's Mature Operas: An Analytical Study' (PhD dissertation, University of Durham, 2003).

[65] Youens, 'Reentering Mozart's Hell', 180. On *ombra* music, see Birgitte Moyer, 'Ombra and Fantasia in Late Eighteenth-Century Theory and Practice', in *Convention in Eighteenth- and Nineteenth-Century Music: Essays in Honor of Leonard G. Ratner*, ed. Wye J. Allanbrook, Janet M. Levy, and William P. Mahrt (Stuyvesant, NY: Pendragon Press, 1992), 283–306; and Clive McClelland, 'Ombra after Mozart', in *Ombra: Supernatural Music in the Eighteenth Century* (Lanham, MD: Lexington Books, 2013), 215–25.

unsichtbaren Geister, erbarmt auch meiner Qual', Act III, wherein she pleads for the invisible spirits to have mercy on her torment. This example repurposes stylistic figurations associated with supernatural presences – tremolos, chordal interjections, rising chromatic bass lines (an inversion of the descending tetrachord) – in a depiction of death as both despairing and consolatory. Its sound is connected to the examples from Act I while reflecting the malleability of such writing across the gothic imagination.

A third, complementary way of hearing the gothic in Schubert's music is to examine the presence of stylistic figurations derived from song or opera in the context of instrumental genres. This approach, in the absence of textual cues, requires analytical thinking to be combined with inference and rumination[66] – not to impose a specific narrative on instrumental pieces, but rather to explore a shared vocabulary that traverses generic boundaries. Such thinking underpins John Gingerich's characterization of the Andante of Schubert's Octet in F major, D 803, as a 'full-fledged operatic *ombra* scene, of an eerie, gothic cast, replete with continuous tremolo in the strings'; and Marjorie Hirsch's reading of the Andantino of Schubert's A major Piano Sonata, D 959, as recalling the outbursts in 'Der Vatermörder', and 'Gruppe aus dem Tartarus', while displaying signs of the 'long-dormant anguish' manifested in 'Der Doppelgänger', D 957/13.[67] These examples spark further study of the gothic in Schubert's instrumental music, whether in terms of implicit dialogues with specific songs, or through a stylistic vocabulary of 'swirling figuration, trills and tremolos, scales and hammering chords' common to both genres.[68]

Mention of Heinrich Heine's 'Der Doppelgänger' brings to the fore a further thread throughout this book: the relationship between the gothic and Romantic aspects of Schubert's music.[69] Heine, less a gothic writer than a critical, disillusioned

---

[66] Cf. the wider emphasis on the figurative dimension of Schubert's instrumental music, as explored in the articles on memory and nostalgia by Walter Frisch, John Daverio, John Gingerich, Charles Fisk, and Scott Burnham in 'Music and Culture', special issue, *Musical Quarterly* 84/4 (2000); Benedict Taylor, 'Schubert and the Construction of Memory: The String Quartet in A Minor, D. 804 ("Rosamunde")', *Journal of the Royal Musical Association* 139/1 (2014), 41–88; Xavier Hascher, 'Music as Poetry: An Analysis of the First Movement of Schubert's Piano Sonata in A Major, D. 959', in *Drama in the Music of Franz Schubert*, 257–82.

[67] John Gingerich, 'The *Ombra* Scene and its Return', in *Schubert's Beethoven Project* (Cambridge: Cambridge University Press, 2014), 165; Hirsch, 'Gothic and Classical Influences', 159, 165. See for wider references to the gothic Sio Pan Leong, 'Recurring Hauntings and Trauma in Schubert's "Unfinished" Symphony', *Nineteenth-Century Music Review*, FirstView (2023), 1–27.

[68] Hirsch, 'Gothic and Classical Influences', 156.

[69] On the numerous interpretations of 'Der Doppelgänger', see Benjamin Binder, 'Disability, Self-Critique, and Failure in Schubert's "Der Doppelgänger"', in *Rethinking Schubert*, ed. Lorraine Byrne Bodley and Julian Horton (New York: Oxford University Press, 2016), 418–36; David Ferris, 'Dissociation and Declamation in Schubert's Heine Songs', in *Rethinking Schubert*, 383–403; Richard Kurth, 'Music and Poetry, A Wilderness of Doubles: Heine–Nietzsche–Schubert–Derrida', *19th-Century Music* 21/1 (1997), 3–37; David Code, 'Listening for Schubert's "Doppelgängers"', *Music Theory Online* 1/4 (1995),

Introduction: Schubert and the Gothic   19

Romantic, might seem out of place in this discussion. Yet the combination of eeriness and doubles in 'Der Doppelgänger' offers productive territory for contemplating how ideas of the gothic intersect with Romantic tropes. Two strands are salient here: eeriness as a feature of the gothic, often in relation to the supernatural, and eeriness as a by-product of the double, the splitting of the self, in the context of Romanticism. Schubert's setting of 'Der Doppelgänger', with its evocation of Baroque passacaglia through the repeated accompaniment, brings these dimensions into close contact.[70] The blurring of temporal boundaries, together with the outburst as the protagonist envisions his double, can be seen in the spirit of 'double vision', as distorted allusions to the soundworlds of Schubert's early ballads.[71] At the same time, the separation from those earlier manifestations allows for the critical distance that is central to the Romantic gothic under consideration here.

❧ ❧ ❧

These themes – distinctions between the gothic and Romantic, the relationship between song and instrumental music – form the starting points for the chapters that follow. Chapters 1 and 3, focusing on song, examine signs of the gothic, its poetic and semantic features, through the fusion of words and music.[72] Examples range from the associations between the gothic and graveyard imagery in 'Leichenfantasie', D 7, and 'Totengräbers Heimweh', D 842, explored in chapter 1, to connections between nocturnal imagery and the sublime in 'Bertas Lied in der Nacht', D 653, and 'Der Unglückliche', D 713, discussed in chapter 3. Both these chapters demonstrate dialogues across chronological boundaries as Schubert's songs open out onto the wider intersections between the gothic and Romanticism within his creative world. Chapters 2 and 4 broaden the constellation of gothic tropes and their intertex-

---

218–28; Susan Youens, 'Echoes of the Wounded Self: Schubert's "Ihr Bild"', in *Goethe and Schubert: Across the Divide*, ed. Lorraine Byrne and Dan Farrelly (Dublin: Carysfort Press, 2003), 1–18; Youens, *Heinrich Heine and the Lied* (Cambridge: Cambridge University Press, 2007), 22–34; David Bretherton, 'In Search of Schubert's Doppelgänger', *Musical Times* 144 (2003), 45–50; and Robert Samuels, 'The Double Articulation of Schubert: Reflections on *Der Doppelgänger*', *Musical Quarterly* 93/1 (2010), 192–233.

[70] On the sound of the past in Schubert's setting, see Christopher H. Gibbs, *The Life of Schubert* (Cambridge: Cambridge University Press, 2000), 165, who detects echoes of the fugal subject of the C sharp minor Fugue from Book I of J.S. Bach's *Well-Tempered Clavier* in the piano part.

[71] Andrew J. Webber, *The Doppelgänger: Double Visions in German Literature* (Oxford: Oxford University Press, 1996).

[72] Further on musical signs in Schubert's music, see Robert S. Hatten, *Interpreting Musical Gestures, Topics, and Tropes: Mozart, Beethoven, and Schubert* (Bloomington: Indiana University Press, 2004); and Hatten, 'Schubert's Alchemy: Transformative Surfaces, Transfiguring Depths', in *Schubert's Late Music*, 91–111.

tual references through consideration of instrumental genres.[73] Focal points extend from doubles and distortion, as chapter 2 explores in Schubert's *Grande Marche Funèbre*, D 859, and his C minor Impromptu, D 889/1,[74] to ideas of grotesquerie in the Adagio of the String Quintet in C major, D 956, and the Andantino of his A major Piano Sonata, D 959, discussed in chapter 4.[75] These readings similarly reflect the ways in which gothic and Romantic ideas, especially that of double vision, become entwined in the sonic lexicon mapped out across the case studies.

As the book traces the gothic across Schubert's music, it not only recontextualizes death, how it manifests textually and sonically, but also problematizes the delineation of 'lateness', a prominent trope in recent scholarship.[76] Markers of late style, such as irreconcilable contrasts,[77] dissolve within the soundworlds of the gothic,

[73] My approach to intertextuality takes inspiration from Richard Kramer's account of the 'shared lexicon of tropes and figures' between the first movement of Schubert's G major Piano Sonata, D 894, and his setting of Franz Bruchmann's 'Schwestergruss', D 762. These resonances extend beyond the 'literal and tactile' towards the metaphorical, demonstrated through the affinities Kramer hears between the tolling F sharp octaves in bars 10–16 of D 894 and the ghostly tones, the 'Geisterhauch', that suffuse the opening of 'Schwestergruss'. See Richard Kramer, 'Against the Grain: The Sonata in G (D. 894) and a Hermeneutics of Late Style', in *Schubert's Late Music*, 116–21. For wider discussion of intertextuality in Schubert's music, see Scott Messing, *Self-Quotation in Schubert: 'Ave Maria', the Second Piano Trio, and Other Works* (Rochester, NY: University of Rochester Press, 2020); and Charles Fisk, *Returning Cycles: Contexts for the Interpretation of Schubert's Impromptus and Last Sonatas* (Berkeley: University of California Press, 2001). On intertextuality more generally, see Christopher A. Reynolds, *Motives for Allusion: Context and Content in Nineteenth-Century Music* (Cambridge, MA: Harvard University Press, 2003); and Michael L. Klein, *Intertextuality in Western Art Music* (Bloomington: Indiana University Press, 2004).

[74] Chapter 2 expands on material in Joe Davies, 'Franz Schubert, Death, and the Gothic', in *Schubert's Piano*, ed. Matthew Gardner and Christine Martin (Cambridge: Cambridge University Press, forthcoming).

[75] Ideas in chapter 4 are developed from Joe Davies, 'Stylistic Disjuncture as a Source of Drama in Schubert's Late Instrumental Works', in *Drama in the Music of Franz Schubert*, 303–30, at 321–23.

[76] On the contrasting approaches to Schubert and lateness, see Joe Davies, 'Introduction: Schubert and Lateness', in 'Interpreting the Expressive Worlds of Schubert's Late Instrumental Works' (DPhil dissertation, University of Oxford, 2018), 4–30; together with Byrne Bodley, 'Introduction: Schubert's Late Style and Current Musical Scholarship', 1–16; Hans-Joachim Hinrichsen, 'Is There a Late Style in Schubert's Oeuvre?', in *Rethinking Schubert*, 17–28; Walther Dürr, 'Compositional Strategies in Schubert's Late Music', in *Rethinking Schubert*, 29–40; and William Kinderman, 'Franz Schubert's "New Style" and the Legacy of Beethoven', in *Rethinking Schubert*, 41–60. For earlier discussion of these issues, see Werner Aderhold, Walther Dürr, and Walburga Litschauer (eds), *Franz Schubert: Jahre der Krise 1818–1823, Arnold Feil zum 60. Geburtstag* (Kassel and Basel: Bärenreiter, 1985), 57–71; and Peter Gülke, 'Zum Bilde des späten Schubert: Vorwiegend analytische Betrachtungen zum Streichquintett, Op. 163', *Musik-Konzepte. Franz Schubert*, ed. Heinz-Klaus Metzger and Rainer Riehn (Munich: Edition Text+Kritik, 1979), 107–66.

[77] See Edward Said, *On Late Style: Literature and Music against the Grain* (London: Bloomsbury, 2006), 148, where he refers to the 'prerogative of late style' as 'the power to render disenchantment and pleasure without resolving the contradiction between them';

Introduction: Schubert and the Gothic

such that the strangeness of music from Schubert's final years sits alongside that of songs composed in his early years. These dialogues reveal a continuity of gothic tropes with varying associations across time and genre. If his early songs showcase the macabre and the supernatural, later music, from solo piano music to duets and chamber music, displays the critical and psychological complexity of the Romantic gothic. Yet, within this trajectory, the case studies resist a linear or unified development, for past and present continually intersect through stylistic allusions and shared vocabulary.

Collectively, the chapters assembled here grapple with the challenge of how to contextualize gothic tropes that fluctuate between the audible and the ungraspable. Their features – rooted in 'the peculiar, often ingenious, but rather strange procedures of [Schubert's] creations', as the publisher Artaria put it in 1826[78] – are suggested through stylistic vocabulary, but their tangibility slips out of reach when words come into the picture. The interpretations that follow offer ways of confronting this paradox, while embracing the slippages between presence and absence, sound and silence.[79] The gothic is thus conjured, problematized, reimagined, yet in the end left to percolate within and beyond the nineteenth-century artistic imagination.[80]

---

for wider contextualization, see Gordon McMullan and Sam Smiles, 'Introduction: Late Style and its Discontents', in *Late Style and its Discontents: Essays in Art, Literature, and Music*, ed. McMullan and Smiles (New York: Oxford University Press, 2016), 1–12.

[78] Quoted in Marjorie W. Hirsch, *Schubert's Dramatic Lieder* (Cambridge: Cambridge University Press, 1993), 1.

[79] In keeping with this approach, the score excerpts are unannotated throughout, to allow readers to imagine the music directly, rather than via analytical interventions, and to (re)hear and (re)see the gothic with repeated reading. The commentary, while drawing on technical language where needed, is geared towards a wide readership.

[80] This perspective aligns with the vision of Lorraine Byrne Bodley and James William Sobaskie in 'Introduction', in 'Schubert Familiar and Unfamiliar: Continuing Conversations', special issue, *Nineteenth-Century Music Review* 13/1 (2016), 9: 'a definitive version of Schubert must remain a phantom possibility; there always will be new readings, new ways of listening to that definitive sound ringing in the ear.'

1

Songs of the Grave

Strange things, the neighbours say, have happen'd here:
Wild shrieks have issued from the hollow tombs;
Dead men have come again, and walk'd about;
And the great bell has toll'd, unrung, untouch'd!

—Robert Blair, 'The Grave' (1743)[1]

The grave is at once silent and sonorous in Schubert's songs. Early manifestations extend back to the dance of the spirits in his settings of Friedrich von Matthisson's 'Der Geistertanz', discussed in the Introduction: 'Quickly we airy spirits / Strike up a whirling dance / Around graves / And rotting bones' ('Rasch tanzen um Gräber / Und morsches Gebein / Wir luftigen Schweber / Den sausenden Reih'n').[2] Here, the grave gives rise to supernatural presences, not yet fully formed, whirling around in the spirit of *danse macabre* (a theme taken up in chapter 4). Death, seemingly unburdened by morbid thoughts, is tinged with a cheerful 'farewell': 'You have buried our grief / Deep in the gloomy Chamber; / Happy we, who whisper you / A cheerful farewell!' ('Tief bargst du im düstern / Gemach unser Weh; / Wir Glücklichen flüstern / Dir fröhlich Ade!').[3] The ghostliness of the night spirit is juxtaposed with critical distancing from the grave as a site of the supernatural through imagery all too real (rotten bones, whimpering dogs). Such tensions play out in varied ways across Schubert's graveyard settings – sometimes affirming supernatural presences, while other times questioning or shifting away from such phenomena entirely.

Later songs revolving around graveyard diggers, such as his setting of his friend Franz von Schober's 'Schatzgräbers Begehr', D 761 (1822), weigh down the airiness

---

[1] Robert Blair, 'The Grave', in *Roach's Beauties of the Poets of Great Britain* (London: J. Roach, 1794), 25–53, at 51–53. On graveyards and the gothic, see Samantha Matthews, *Poetical Remains: Poets' Graves, Bodies, and Books in the Nineteenth Century* (Oxford: Oxford University Press, 2004); Andrew Smith, 'Touched by the Dead: Eighteenth-Century Gothic Poetics', in *Gothic Death 1740–1914: A Literary History* (Manchester: Manchester University Press, 2016), 11–14; and Serena Trowbridge, 'Past, Present, and Future in the Gothic Graveyard', in *The Gothic and Death*, ed. Carol M. Davison (Manchester: Manchester University Press, 2017), 21–33.

[2] Graham Johnson, *Franz Schubert: The Complete Songs*, 3 vols (New Haven and London: Yale University Press, 2014), Vol. 1, 672.

[3] Johnson, *The Complete Songs*, Vol. 1, 673.

of the night spirits with the weariness of lived experience: 'So leave me in peace with my endeavour. / Surely a grave is gladly given to every man; / Will you then not grant me one, friends?' ('Drum lasset Ruhe mir in meinem Streben! / Ein Grab mag man wohl jedem gerne geben, / Wollt ihr es denn nicht mir, ihr Lieben, gönnen?').[4] Here the grave offers a desirable escape from life, as apostrophized in the penultimate stanza: 'If I am digging my own grave with this hope, / Yet I will gladly climb down, / for then my longing will be stilled' ('Sollt' ich mein Grab mit dieser Hoffnung graben: / Ich steige gern hinab, / gestillt ist dann mein Sehnen').[5]

These examples speak to the shifting associations between graveyard imagery and gothic necropoetics across Schubert's creative endeavour. His settings of Matthisson's 'Der Geistertanz' display a kinship with graveyard poetry of the mid-eighteenth century, especially Robert Blair's 'The Grave' (1743), quoted in the epigraph above. The 'psychological effects' of the graveyard are captured through Blair's description of 'wild shrieks' as dead men return from the hollow tombs and through Matthisson's depiction of the night spirit as fluttering and teasing.[6] Schubert's 'Schatzgräbers Begehr' turns from ideas of the supernatural, or the grave as a 'rational, because understandable, fear', towards a tormented soul seeking, in the spirit of *Sehnsucht* (Romantic longing), release beyond life.[7] The grave serves less as an endpoint in this case than an invitation to imagine alternate realities offered by the prospect of death.

The songs discussed in what follows span the range of creative possibilities within the pillars of death as bound up with the supernatural, and death as a release from the oppressions of life. In some instances, such as 'Leichenfantasie', D 7 (1811), death is governed by the finality of the grave's closing bolts, while other examples, notably 'Schwestergruss', D 762, fluctuate between the eeriness of the grave and the spirits that arise from it. In the final case study, 'Totengräbers Heimweh', D 842 (1825), the graveyard offers a site for pondering finite existence, as in 'Schatzgräbers Begehr', and entering a realm beyond death. The readings offered here chart a pathway from the immediacies of the grave in 'Leichenfantasie' to a fusion of the physical (represented through constant motion) and the figurative (a space for reimagining the boundaries between life and death) in 'Totengräbers Heimweh'. These shifts between the world of eighteenth-century graveyard poetics and conceptions of the Romantic gothic take place within a shared vocabulary of funereal elements, textural sparsity, octave doubling, and tremolo-saturated textures. The recurrence of these devices demonstrates the fluidity of graveyard poetics, with past and present entwining, as the sound of death turns from the supernatural to the metaphysical.

---

[4] Johnson, *The Complete Songs*, Vol. 2, 731.

[5] Johnson, *The Complete Songs*, Vol. 2, 731.

[6] Smith, *Gothic Death*, 22.

[7] Smith, *Gothic Death*, 22–23.

Funereal Fantasies

It would be easy to dismiss Schubert's setting of Friedrich Schiller's 'Leichenfantasie', D 7, one of his earliest and lengthiest graveyard settings, as the product of an adolescent fascination with all things macabre;[8] or to hear in it the criticism levelled at his early ballads – too long, too lacking in unity.[9] In the words of a contemporaneous critic:

> Herr Fr[anz] S[chubert] does not write actual songs and has no desire to do so [...] but rather free vocal works, many so free, that one might perhaps call them caprices or fantasies. [He] tries to compensate for the lack of inner unity, order and regularity by eccentricities, barely or not at all motivated, and by often rather wild goings-on. With only these qualities [i.e. unity, order, and regularity], no artist's work can become a beautiful work of art. Without them, however, certainly only bizarre, grotesque things will result.[10]

'Leichenfantasie', shot through with ghostly subject matter and eccentric stylistic vocabulary, is susceptible to all these charges. Yet to write it off as early experimentation would be to overlook a burgeoning symbolism for the grave that runs through the songs discussed here and across the corpus of music explored throughout this book.

The text of 'Leichenfantasie' (1797) sits between the style of popular ghost tales, such as Schiller's own *Der Geisterseher* (1787–89),[11] and that of Blair's 'The Grave' (1743):

Mit erstorb'nem Scheinen	With dim light
Steht der Mond auf totenstillen Hainen;	the moon shines over the death-still groves;
Seufzend streicht der Nachtgeist durch die Luft –	Sighing, the night spirit skims through the air –
Nebelwolken trauern,	Mist-clouds lament,
Sterne trauern	Pale stars shine down mournfully
Bleich herab, wie Lampen in der Gruft.	Like lamps in a vault.
Gleich Gespenstern, stumm und hohl und hager,	Like ghosts silent, hollow, gaunt
Zieht in schwarzem Totenpompe dort	In black funeral pomp

---

[8] For general context on 'Leichenfantasie', see Clive McClelland, 'Death and the Composer: The Context of Schubert's Supernatural Lieder', in *Schubert the Progressive: History, Performance Practice, Analysis*, ed. Brian Newbould (Aldershot: Ashgate, 2003), 21–35; and Marjorie W. Hirsch, *Schubert's Dramatic Lieder* (Cambridge: Cambridge University Press, 1993), 82–88.

[9] On the reception of Schubert's early ballads, see Susan Wollenberg, 'Schubert's Dramatic Lieder: Rehabilitating "Adelwold und Emma", D. 211', in *Drama in the Music of Franz Schubert*, 85–106, at 85–88; and Hirsch, *Schubert's Dramatic Lieder*.

[10] Quoted in Hirsch, *Schubert's Dramatic Lieder*, 1.

[11] See notes 35–37 in the Introduction for literature on Schiller's *Der Geisterseher* and his approach to the gothic.

Ein Gewimmel nach dem Leichenlager	A procession moves towards the graveyard
Unterm Schauerflor der Grabnacht fort.	Beneath the dread veil of the burial night.
Zitternd an der Krücke,	Who is he who trembling on crutches
Wer mit düstern, rückgesunknem Blicke	With sombre, sunken gaze,
Ausgegossen in ein heulend Ach,	Pouring out his misery in a cry of pain,
Schwer geneckt vom eisernen Geschicke,	And harshly tormented by an iron fate
Schwankt dem stummgetragnen Sarge nach?	Totters behind the silently borne coffin?
Floss es 'Vater' von des Jünglings Lippe?	Did the boy's lips say 'Father'?
Nasse Schauer schauern fürchterlich	Damp, fearful shudders run through
Durch sein gramgeschmolzenes Gerippe,	His frame, racked with grief;
Seine Silberhaare bäumen sich –	His silver hair stands on end.
Aufgerissen seine Feuerwunde!	His burning soul is torn open
Durch die Seele Höllenschmerz!	Throughout his soul, hellish pain!
'Vater' floss es von des Jünglings Munde,	'Father' uttered the boy's lips.
'Sohn' gelispelt hat das Vaterherz.	'Son' spoke the father's heart in a whisper.
Eiskalt, eiskalt liegt er hier im Tuche,	Ice-cold, he lies here in his shroud,
Und dein Traum, so golden einst, so süss!	And your dream, once so golden, so sweet,
Süss und golden, Vater, dir zum Fluche!	Sweet and golden, now a curse on you, father!
Eiskalt, eiskalt liegt er hier im Tuche!	Ice-cold he lies here in his shroud,
Deine Wonne und dein Paradies. –	Your joy and your paradise![12]

These opening stanzas map out a constellation of tropes associated with the grave-yard and the gothic imagination. The nocturnal setting, with its 'dim light', illumi-nates the night spirit as the procession moves towards the graveyard: 'like ghosts silent, hollow, gaunt'. Evocation of and resistance to ghostliness work in tandem here, particularly when the father, racked with grief, hears the voice of his deceased son – 'did the boy's lips say "Father"? / "Father" uttered the boy's lips. / "Son" spoke the father's heart in a whisper.' These exchanges – pre-empting the father's questioning of the supernatural in 'Erlkönig', D 328 – bring the displacement of a dream 'once so golden, so sweet' into dialogue with the psychological realities of the grave.[13]

---

[12] Johnson, *The Complete Songs*, Vol. 2, 146.

[13] Further parallels between 'Leichenfantasie' and 'Erlkönig' are suggested through their relationship to the supernatural – the former song fluctuating between the real and the unreal, in the latter problematized throughout. As the Erlking lures the boy to his death – 'Sweet child, come with me! / I'll play wonderful games with you' ('Du liebes Kind, komm, geh mit mir! / Gar schöne Spiele spiel ich mit dir') – the father seeks to rationalize his presence by recourse to natural phenomena – a wisp of fog, sighing winds, shimmering willows. It is only in the final stanza, after the boy shrieks 'The Erlking has hurt me!', that he realizes his son is dead: 'The father shudders, he rides swiftly, / He holds the moaning child in his arms; / With one last effort he reaches home; / The child lay dead in his arms'

Songs of the Grave 27

The juxtaposition of a Schillerian father 'mourning his glorious dead son' and Schubert as a living 'son of (dead) Mozart', to quote Susan Youens,[14] suffuses the soundscape of 'Leichenfantasie'. The introduction, bars 1–10, looks back to eighteenth-century keyboard culture through the scalar runs depicting the 'Nachtgeist' (Example 1.1), and through an allusion to the expressive world of Mozart's Fantasia in D minor, K 397. Echoes of Mozart's music, specifically the theme of his Rondo in A minor, K 511, resurface in the portrayal of ghostliness in stanza 1, bars 27–30.[15] Its turn-like contours, E, D sharp, E, A, together with the split chordal accompaniment, find a distant return, doubled at the octave in the right hand of the piano part, at the words 'pale stars shine down mournfully / like lamps in a vault. / Like ghosts silent, hollow, gaunt' ('Sterne trauern / Bleich herab, wie Lampen in der Gruft. / Gleich Gespenstern, stumm und hohl und hager') (Examples 1.2 and 1.3).[16] Transparency of texture and hushed dynamics (barely rising above *pianissimo*) intensify the impression of music that, like the 'Nachtgeist', is seemingly of the present while tied to the (returning) past.

The eeriness of the opening material – its octave doubling and scalar runs being hallmarks of the music studied here – is thrown into sharp relief by the visceral outburst in bar 30 at the mention of 'black funeral pomp' ('schwarzem Totenpompe') (Example 1.2). This textural inversion of bar 23, with the chordal pattern now rising forcefully in the right hand, underpinned by jagged octave bass lines, unleashes what has been latent all along. Those earlier allusions to Mozart's music are further displaced in bar 33 by the rearing up of a tremolo figuration as the grave draws nearer. Outbursts of this kind dissipate as quickly as they materialize, notably in bars 43–44, where the texture is stripped to three repeated chords, each punctuated by silence, akin to the death knell that remains 'unrung' and 'untouch'd' in Blair's 'The Grave'.

('Erlkönig hat mir ein Leids getan! – / Dem Vater grauset's, er reitet geschwind, / Er hält in Armen das ächzende Kind, / Erreicht den Hof mit Müh' und Not: / In seinen Armen das Kind war tot'). Johnson, *The Complete Songs*, Vol. 1, 518. On the supernatural in 'Erlkönig', see Christopher H. Gibbs, '"Komm geh mit mir": Schubert's Uncanny "Erlkönig"', *19th-Century Music* 19/2 (1995), 115–35.

[14] I thank Susan Youens for framing the juxtaposition of Schillerian and Schubertian poetics in these evocative terms and for her inspiration more generally (personal correspondence).

[15] On Mozart's K 511, see Matthew Head, 'Mozart's Gothic: Feelings for History in the Rondo in A minor, K. 511', *Keyboard Perspectives* 4 (2012), 69–114.

[16] On Schubert's engagement with Mozart's music, see Susan Wollenberg, 'Schubert and Mozart', *Schubert's Fingerprints: Studies in the Instrumental Works* (Farnham: Ashgate, 2011), 133–59; and Susan Youens, 'Reentering Mozart's Hell: Schubert's "Gruppe aus dem Tartarus", D. 538', in *Drama in the Music of Franz Schubert*, 171–204.

Example 1.1. Schubert, 'Leichenfantasie', D 7, bars 1–22.
Franz Schubert. *Lieder*, volume 5, high voice (BA 9105), editor: Walther Dürr.
© 2011 Bärenreiter-Verlag Karl Vötterle GmbH & Co KG, Kassel.

—(continued)

Example 1.1—concluded

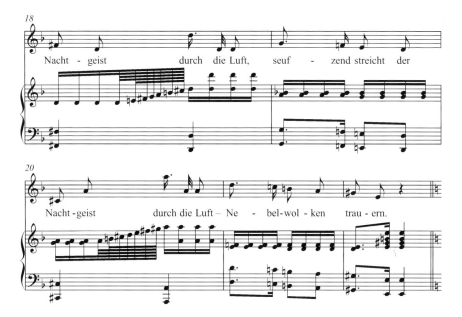

Example 1.2. Schubert, 'Leichenfantasie', D 7, bars 23–44.
Franz Schubert. *Lieder*, volume 5, high voice (BA 9105), editor: Walther Dürr.
© 2011 Bärenreiter-Verlag Karl Vötterle GmbH & Co KG, Kassel.

Example 1.3. Mozart, Rondo in A minor, K 511, bars 1–8.
Neue Mozart Ausgabe IX/27/2: Piano Pieces, volume 2, Individual Pieces.
Internationale Stifung Mozarteum, Online Publications (2006).

Sound, whether muted or physically intense, is central to the gothic worlds of 'Leichenfantasie', musically and textually. The churchyard gate rattles, iron hinges creak open, in stanza 7, as the father peers into the grave:[17]

Nein doch, Vater – Horch! die Kirchhoftüre brauset,	But no, father hark! The churchyard gate is rattling,
Und die ehr'nen Angel klirren auf –	And the iron hinges are creaking open
Wie's hinein ins Grabgewölbe grauset!	How terrifying it is to peer into the grave!
Nein doch lass den Tränen ihren Lauf! –	But no let the tears flow!
Geh, du Holder, geh im Pfade der Sonne	Go, gracious youth, in the sun's path,
Freudig weiter der Vollendung zu,	Joyfully onwards to perfection,
Lösche nun den edlen Durst nach Wonne,	Quench your noble thirst for joy,
Gramentbundner, in Walhallas Ruh!	Released from pain, in the peace of Valhalla![18]

Schubert's setting, similarly driven by harsh sonority, juxtaposes diminished harmonies in tremolo figuration, a welling up of sound in octaves and chordal combinations that mirrors the rattling and creaking of the gates, with the starkness of the vocal line (Example 1.4).[19] Signs of the textural and dynamic contrasts found

---

[17] See Noelle Chao, 'Musical Listening in *The Mysteries of Udolpho*', in *Words and Notes in the Long Nineteenth Century*, ed. Phyllis Weliver and Katharine Ellis (Woodbridge: Boydell & Brewer, 2013), 85–102.

[18] Johnson, *The Complete Songs*, Vol. 2, 146.

[19] The repeated chordal texture recalls the icy shivers in stanza 3, 'Eiskalt, eiskalt', depicted by split octaves (a tremolo pattern in miniature) and diminished seventh chords. These

Example 1.4. Schubert, 'Leichenfantasie', D 7, bars 303–16.
Franz Schubert. *Lieder*, volume 5, high voice (BA 9105), editor: Walther Dürr.
© 2011 Bärenreiter-Verlag Karl Vötterle GmbH & Co KG, Kassel.

Songs of the Grave 33

in stanza 1 resurface in the sudden reduction to *pianissimo* in bar 313, its eeriness enhanced through the *con sordini* marking: 'How terrifying it is to peer into the grave. / But no, let the tears flow' ('Wie's hinein ins Grabgewölbe grauset! / Nein doch lass den Tränen ihren Lauf!'). The unaccompanied vocal line, as the piano part suddenly falls silent, conveys the sound of terror by paring down the music to its skeletal features. Here, in contrast to the outburst of bar 30, silence renders Schiller's text all the more disturbing.

Ideas of gothic necropoetics as blurring the boundaries among death, the supernatural, and visions beyond the grave come together in the penultimate stanza of 'Leichenfantasie':

Wiedersehn – himmlischer Gedanke! –	To see him again – heavenly thought!
Wiedersehn dort an Edens Tor!	To see him again at the gates of Eden!
Horch der Sarg versinkt mit dumpfigem Geschwanke,	Hear the dull sound of the swaying coffin as it goes down,
Wimmernd schnurrt das Totenseil empor!	The ropes whirr upwards with a whine!
Da wir trunken um einander rollten,	As we staggered about each other
Lippen schwiegen, und das Auge sprach	Our lips were silent, but our eyes spoke:
'Haltet! Haltet!' da wir boshaft grollten –	'Stop! Stop!' as we grew angry –
Aber Tränen stürzten wärmer nach.	But afterwards tears fell more warmly.[20]

Schubert's setting of this stanza – as the father dreams of his son returning from the dead – evokes an alternate reality that is simultaneously close to its surroundings.[21] The modulation to A flat major, ushering in the 'heavenly thought' ('himmlischer Gedanke') of the son's return, is one such sign of what lurks in the shadows; its tritonal relationship to D minor (the song's home

---

earlier disturbances are rooted in the perishing of dreams, things that were once 'so golden, so sweet' becoming a curse on the protagonist's inner consciousness.

[20] Johnson, *The Complete Songs*, Vol. 2, 147–48.

[21] The language of dreams is foreshadowed in stanza 4, where the sound of the past is paradisial, rather than eerie, 'stroked by Elysian breezes' ('wie umweht von Elysiumslüften'). The rhythmic poise in recalling minuet style, underscored by the change in tempo marking (Allegretto) and time signature (3/4), the balance between melody and accompaniment, its *dolce* marking, all suggest a further throwback to late eighteenth-century keyboard culture – a flashback to a bygone era. The telescoping to a minuet framing (with allusions to a music-box topic) points to a fingerprint in Schubert's music, with later examples found in the Trio sections of the third movements of the String Quartet in G major, D 887, and the Piano Sonata in G major, D 894, both composed in 1826. See Walter Frisch, '"You Must Remember This": Memory and Structure in Schubert's String Quartet in G Major, D. 887', *Musical Quarterly* 84/4 (2000), 582–603 at 593 (apropos of D 894): 'this pastoral mode and the childlike, music-box tone create a temporal distance; the trio seems to evoke a more carefree and innocent past.'

key) represents in Youens's words 'the tonal abyss between life and death'.[22] The boundaries between the two coalesce around the sight and sound of the swaying coffin, as death intrudes more explicitly on the father's thoughts. The three-note figures in the piano part (bars 363 ff.), rising to a diminished seventh in the right hand, falling by step in the left hand, bring the dull thud of the coffin into the foreground while forcing the evocation of dreams to the background.

The final stanza of 'Leichenfantasie', in contrast to those earlier visions, affirms the idea of the grave as a place for confronting ghostliness and the inevitability of death:

Mit erstorbnem Scheinen	With dimmed light
Steht der Mond auf totenstillen Hainen,	The moon shines over the death-still groves;
Seufzend streicht der Nachtgeist durch die Luft –	Sighing, the night spirit skims through the air –
Nebelwolken trauern,	Mist-clouds are mourning,
Sterne trauern	Pale stars shine down mournfully,
Bleich herab, wie Lampen in der Gruft.	Like lamps in a vault.
Dumpfig schollerts überm Sarg zum Hügel	The clods pile over the coffin with a dull thud.
O um Erdballs Schätze nur noch einen Blick!	Oh, for just *one* more glimpse of the earth's treasure!
Starr und ewig schliesst des Grabes Riegel,	The grave's bolts close, rigid and eternal;
Dumpfer – dumpfer schollerts über'm Sarg Zum Hügel,	The thud of the clods grows duller as they pile over the coffin
Nimmer gibt das Grab züruck.	The grave will never yield up![23]

The music journeys full circle, signalled by the return of the piano introduction in bar 384, while appearing frozen in time; the sounds of the 'Nachtgeist' assume a strangely permanent presence. Yet the closing stanza is not altogether the same, for it now confirms what has been intimated throughout – perished dreams giving way to the finality of death – as the grave's bolts close. The grave is once more the sound of eerie ephemerality, poised between *pianissimo* and triple *piano* quivering chordal interjections, lingering traces of the tremolo figurations (Example 1.5). The off-tonic (G minor) ending, with three chords descending through the registers, bars 452–53, suggests the finality of the death knell, fused with the sound of the grave that lives on. Its bolts remain closed, 'rigid and eternal' ('starr und ewig'), while ambiguous as to what lies beyond their confines.

---

[22] Personal correspondence with Susan Youens.

[23] Johnson, *The Complete Songs*, Vol. 2, 148.

Example 1.5. Schubert, 'Leichenfantasie', D 7, bars 431–53.
Franz Schubert. *Lieder*, volume 5, high voice (BA 9105), editor: Walther Dürr.
© 2011 Bärenreiter-Verlag Karl Vötterle GmbH & Co KG, Kassel.

—(continued)

Example 1.5—concluded

The Beautiful Dead

Where Schubert's 'Leichenfantasie' embodies the gothic through the disturbing facets of graveyard imagery, the songs discussed next fluctuate between the eeriness of a silent grave and the beguiling apparitions that transpire from it. Devices such as textural sparsity, octave doubling, and rhythmic patterns of death are refashioned with economy of means, devoid of the overt disruptions heard in Examples 1.2 and 1.4. Collectively they broaden the sonic associations between the gothic and graveyard imagery, while highlighting the permeability of a shared vocabulary.

One such song is Schubert's 'Grablied für die Mutter', D 616, composed in 1818 to a text whose author remains unidentified. It was penned – as a 'spontaneous expression of fellow-feeling' – following the death of Maria Anna Streinsberg, mother of Schubert's friend Josef Ludwig von Streinsberg (six years after the death of his own mother).[24] Echoes of 'Leichenfantasie', as the father stands at the 'gloomy graveside', brush shoulders here with the mother's 'beautiful, pure, angelic soul' that sleeps in the grave:

Hauche milder, Abendluft,	Breathe more gently, evening breeze;
Klage sanfter, Philomele,	Lament more softly, Philomel;
Eine schöne, engelreine Seele	A beautiful, pure, angelic soul
Schläft in dieser Gruft.	Sleeps in this grave.

[24] Johnson, *The Complete Songs*, Vol. 1, 775.

Bleich und stumm, am düstern Rand,	The father stands, pale and silent,
Steht der Vater mit dem Sohne,	With his son at the gloomy graveside;
Denen ihres Lebens schönste Krone	With her the fairest crown of their lives
Schnell mit ihr verschwand.	Has suddenly vanished.
Und sie weinen in die Gruft,	And they weep upon the grave.
Aber ihrer Liebe Zähren	But their tears of love
Werden sich zum Perlenkranz verklären	Shall be transfigured to a wreath of pearls
Wenn der Engel ruft.	When the angel calls.[25]

Schubert's setting captures the silence of the grave, its gentle breezes, through a soundscape that remains muted throughout (except for a momentary swell to *forte* for the words 'schnell mit ihr verschwand', suggesting acute despair as the mother vanishes). Subtle shifts and reductions in dynamics highlight here how the gothic lingers in silence as much as in sound. One example occurs in stanza 3, bars 14–21, where the resonance with 'Leichenfantasie', of father and son standing 'pale and silent' at the 'gloomy graveside', sends a shiver through the depiction of the mother's spirit in stanza 1. The withdrawal to *pianissimo*, together with fragmented chordal interjections, and a vocal line hovering around repeated pitches in quasi-recitative style, recalls the association between a silent grave and eerie sonorities in 'Leichenfantasie'. Such writing disturbs the gentle lullaby with the realities of confronting the mother's sudden disappearance.

Another song that channels the sound of the grave through extreme dynamic and textural concentration is Schubert's setting of Franz von Bruchmann's 'Schwestergruss', D 762 (1822). Where his 'Grablied für die Mutter' revolves around a maternal spirit, 'Schwestergruss', by contrast, conjures that of Bruchmann's sister, Sybilla, who died in 1820 aged twenty-one. The nexus of poet–composer relations here – not only of Schubert's connections with Franz and Sybilla, but also their mother Justine von Bruchmann, to whom he dedicated his Op. 20 'Frühlingsglaube', D 686/2 (1823) – further complicates the reading of death as real and imagined. In contrast to his graveyard songs where the protagonists remain anonymous, 'Schwestergruss' draws a specific individual into a web of ghostly presences that extend into the world of gothic ideas.

What prevails throughout 'Schwestergruss', writes Richard Kramer, is 'muted grief', its soundworlds steeped in the '*Geisterhauch*', ghostly tones, of a silent grave:[26]

Im Mondenschein	In the moonlight
Wall' ich auf und ab,	I wander up and down
Seh' Totenbein'	Seeing dead bones
Und stilles Grab.	And a silent grave.

---

[25] Johnson, *The Complete Songs*, Vol. 1, 774.

[26] Richard Kramer, 'Against the Grain: The Sonata in G (D. 894) and a Hermeneutics of Late Style', in *Schubert's Late Music*, 117–21.

Im Geisterhauch	In the ghostly breeze
Vorüber bebt's,	Something floats past,
Wie Flamm' und Rauch	Flickering
Vorüber schwebt's;	Like flame and smoke.
Aus Nebeltrug	From the deluding mists
Steigt eine Gestalt,	A figure rises,
Ohn' Sünd' und Lug	Without sin or falsehood,
Vorüber wallt,	And drifts past.
Das Aug' so blau,	Such blue eyes,
Der Blick so gross	Such a noble gaze,
Wie in Himmelsau,	As in the fields of heaven,
Wie in Gottes Schoss;	As in the lap of God.
Ein weiss Gewand	A white garment
Bedeckt das Bild,	Covers the apparition.
In zarter Hand	From its delicate hand
Eine Lilie quillt.	Springs a lily.[27]

Schubert's setting crystallizes around the tolling dactyls in the introduction, bars 1–6 (Example 1.6) – at times capturing the silence of the grave, in other moments depicting the spirit of Sybilla that rises in stanza 2. Octave doubling, by now a recurring feature in Schubert's graveyard songs, blurs the boundaries between harmonies implied yet texturally empty. The effect of these octave iterations, each displacing the previous, comes into sharper focus through the restless dactylic pattern, that emblem of death in Schubert's music (cf. the slow movement in the 'Death and the Maiden' Quartet, D 810). Subtle rhythmic swells, a stressed downbeat followed by two unstressed utterances, create movement amid stasis, in keeping with the circularity of the protagonist's trajectory in stanza 1.

The fixation on a single sonority throughout 'Schwestergruss' resonates with themes of circularity, of sounds appearing, undergoing change, then looping back on themselves, common to gothic discourse. One example occurs in the transformation of texture in bars 6–16, set to the words 'in the moonlight / I wander up and down / seeing dead bones / and a silent grave' ('Im Mondenschein / Wall' ich auf und ab, / Seh' Totenbein' / Und stilles Grab') (Example 1.7). The sustained C sharp octaves resurface, in fractured form, within a constellation of death-related symbols, from the repeated triplets, resembling the opening of the 'Death and the Maiden' Quartet, to the stepwise descent in the upper octave of the right hand, bars 8–10, a faint echo of lament long associated with the descending tetrachord.

---

[27] Johnson, *The Complete Songs*, Vol. 3, 81–83.

Example 1.6. Schubert, 'Schwestergruss', D 762, bars 1–6.
Franz Schubert. *Lieder*, volume 13 (BA 5535), editor: Walther Dürr.
© 1988 Bärenreiter-Verlag Karl Vötterle GmbH & Co KG, Kassel.

Semitonal inflections throughout bars 11–20 similarly unsettle the ghostly tones, their sliding between pitches feeding into the doubling of material in both music and words. These features encapsulate the eeriness of a grave that is both silent and audible.

Another instance of sounds returning in strange contexts occurs in stanza 6 of 'Schwestergruss', where the silence of the grave gives way to Sybilla's ghostly whispers:

Im Geisterhauch	In a ghostly whisper
Sie zu mir spricht:	She speaks to me:
'Ich wand're schon	'Already I walk
Im reinen Licht.'	In the pure light.'[28]

The turn to C sharp major, bars 41 ff., reflecting the 'pure light' ('reinen Licht'), gives new life to the tolling C sharps as they merge with spread, harp-like sonorities (Example 1.8). Sybilla's identity – her blue eyes, the noble gaze, the delicate hand from which springs a lily – shines through in the brightening of the soundscape, yet the slippage from one tonal realm, in tandem with the shift to the upper registers, also highlights the unreal nature of her presence vis-à-vis the surrounding material. The image of the beautiful dead is thus both part of and distanced from the graveyard scenery.[29]

---

[28] Johnson, *The Complete Songs*, Vol. 3, 82.

[29] On notions of the beautiful dead in relation to the gothic, see Elisabeth Bronfen, *Over her Dead Body: Death, Femininity and the Aesthetic* (Manchester: Manchester University Press, 1992); and more widely, see Matthew Head, 'Cultural Meanings for Women Composers: Charlotte ("Minna") Brandes and the Beautiful Dead in the German Enlightenment', *Journal of the American Musicological Society* 57/2 (2004), 231–84.

Example 1.7. Schubert, 'Schwestergruss', D 762, bars 6–20.
Franz Schubert. *Lieder*, volume 13 (BA 5535), editor: Walther Dürr.
© 1988 Bärenreiter-Verlag Karl Vötterle GmbH & Co KG, Kassel.

—(continued)

Example 1.7—*concluded*

Example 1.8. Schubert, 'Schwestergruss', D 762, bars 41–48.
Franz Schubert. *Lieder*, volume 13 (BA 5535), editor: Walther Dürr.
© 1988 Bärenreiter-Verlag Karl Vötterle GmbH & Co KG, Kassel.

The depiction of ghostly voices in 'Schwestergruss' draws into its web of references earlier portrayals of such writing, among them Schubert's second setting of Schiller's 'Thekla: Eine Geisterstimme', D 595 (1817). Here, as the G major tonality of the first setting, D 73 (1813), gives way to C minor in the second version, traces of 'Schwestergruss' are foreshadowed tonally and texturally.[30] Ghostly presences, while less explicit than in 'Schwestergruss' or 'Leichenfantasie', are implied through the disappearance of a 'fleeting shade', and depicted musically through semitonal inflections that cast shadows over the octave doubling in the vocal line and piano part. The blend of stasis and restlessness in the opening of 'Schwestergruss' is pre-empted here through the undulating left-hand accompaniment and the fixation on sustained sonorities, C and B natural, in the opening lines (Example 1.9): 'You ask where I am, where I turned to / When my fleeting shade disappeared' ('Wo ich sei, und wo mich hingewendet / Als mein flücht'ger Schatte dir entschwebt?').[31] Even closer in spirit to 'Schwestergruss' is the shift from C minor to C major, from *pianissimo* to triple *piano*, from bar 15 ff. of D 595: 'Have I not finished, reached my end? / Have I not loved and lived?' ('Hab' ich nicht beschlossen und geendet? / Hab' ich nicht geliebet und gelebt?') (Example 1.10).[32] This tonal shift, as in 'Schwestergruss', binds life and death as the original pitches are retraced in the parallel major. The distance between the two is a matter of semitonal slippage, their boundaries coalescing as minor gives way to major.

Much of 'Schwestergruss', with its inward intensity, sits uneasily with ideas of the gothic as outwardly transgressive or disruptive. Its ghostly presences, muted throughout, disturb instead through textural shifts, moments of withdrawal, or through registral transformations at odds with the surrounding material. Yet, despite these differences, 'Schwestergruss' can be heard as forming dialogues with the graveyard songs explored here, particularly through the writing that depicts Sybilla's spirit. This transformation complicates a dualistic understanding of major and minor, life and death, by rendering traces of C minor increasingly terror-laden as they merge with the sharpened pitches of the major mode. The blurring of beauty and terror carries forward to the piano postlude through the turn to the parallel (F sharp) major, the tolling dactyls transferred there to the bass, before coming to rest on a sustained

---

[30] The two versions of 'Thekla' further reinforce the ambiguity of ghostliness in Schubert's music. The earlier version, D 73, penned in 1813 – two years after 'Leichenfantasie' – captures the 'Geisterstimme' in the gaps between recitative and the lyricism reserved for reminiscences. Restlessness in the vocal line mirrors the fleeting shades depicted in the text and the voice of the spirit. It was not uncommon for Schubert to produce multiple settings of a text, among them his two versions of 'Gruppe aus dem Tartarus', D 396 (1816) and D 583 (1817), the former an 'ambitious fragment', the latter a full-fledged essay in *ombra* style: 'music of the dark shadows where demons, furies, and malevolent deities lurk'. Youens, 'Reentering Mozart's Hell', 171 and 180.

[31] Johnson, *The Complete Songs*, Vol. 3, 327.

[32] Johnson, *The Complete Songs*, Vol. 3, 327.

Example 1.9. Schubert, 'Thekla: Eine Geisterstimme', D 595, bars 7–10. Franz Schubert. *Lieder*, volume 3, high voice (BA 9103), editor: Walther Dürr. © 2008 Bärenreiter-Verlag Karl Vötterle GmbH & Co KG, Kassel.

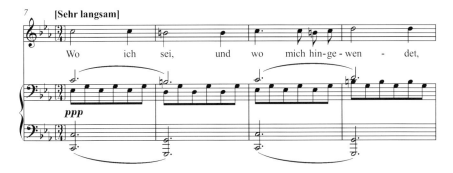

Example 1.10. Schubert, 'Thekla: Eine Geisterstimme', D 595, bars 15–18. Franz Schubert. *Lieder*, volume 3, high voice (BA 9103), editor: Walther Dürr. © 2008 Bärenreiter-Verlag Karl Vötterle GmbH & Co KG, Kassel.

chord of indefinite length.[33] This tonal shift captures the dissolution of pain and grief in the penultimate stanza, as Sybilla's spirit floats up,[34] while recalling the metamorphosis from B minor to B major in the closing section of Schubert's 'Grablied für die Mutter' as tears turn into pearl wreathes. Both instances, exuding (tonal) distance from their surroundings, are at the same time intricately connected to the prevailing soundworlds. Eeriness, these endings suggest, stems as much from textural sparsity and octave doubling as in those brighter moments seemingly at odds with the poetic frames of reference.

---

[33] For wider context on beauty infused with terror, see Scott Burnham, *Mozart's Grace* (Princeton, NJ: Princeton University Press, 2013).

[34] 'She floats up / In pure flame, / Without pain or grief, / To the choir of angels ('In reiner Flamm' / Schwebt sie empor, / Ohne Schmerz und Harm, / Zu der Engel Chor'). Johnson, *The Complete Songs*, Vol. 3, 82.

'Into the Grave, Deep Down!'

Schubert's setting of J.N. Craigher's 'Totengräbers Heimweh', D 842 (1825), adds further psychological depth to the portrayal of the gothic discussed thus far. Its processional style looks back to his earlier graveyard settings, among them his 'Grablied', D 218, a modest thirteen bars of music penned ten years earlier in the same key, while standing apart in its approach to death. The text of that earlier song, written in 1813 by Schubert's friend Josef Kenner, tells of the death of a soldier, its content steeped in the realities of warfare:

Er fiel den Tod für's Vaterland,	He met his death for the Fatherland,
Den süssen der Befreiungsschlacht;	A sweet death in the battle for freedom.
Wir graben ihm mit treuer Hand,	With loyal hands we bury him
Tief, tief den schwarzen Ruheschacht.	Deep in the dark tomb of peace.[35]

Schubert's setting, a sombre funeral march, is marked by its rhythmic regularity and processional poise (Example 1.11), divorced from the horror-inducing elements of songs such as 'Leichenfantasie'. The textural reduction in bars 5–7, underscored by a *pianissimo* dynamic marking (that hallmark of Schubertian ghostliness), initiates the descent 'deep in[to] the dark tomb of peace' that is completed as the piano postlude withdraws into the depth of its register.

'Totengräbers Heimweh', while retaining the key of F minor, distorts the processional style of Schubert's 'Grablied', and inverts its ending through two gothic images: the desperation of the protagonist's circumstances (mirroring those of the 'unglücksel'ger' Atlas in Schubert's eponymous song, D 957/8) and death as a means by which to escape the oppressions of life. Standing alone at the edge of the grave, the protagonist yearns for someone to lay him to rest. In the final stanza those wishes are granted as an eternal light binds his soul to the homeland of peace, the Land of the blessed:

O Menschheit – O Leben! –	O mankind, O life!
Was soll's? – o was soll's?!	To what purpose? To what purpose?
Grabe aus – scharre zu!	Dig out, fill in!
Tag und Nacht keine Ruh'! –	No rest, day and night!
Das Triebn, das Drängen –	This urgency, this haste,
Wohin? o wohin? – –	Where does it lead? Where?
'Ins Grab – tief hinab!' –	'Into the grave, deep down!'
O Schicksal – o traurige Pflicht –	O fate, O sad duty,
Ich trag's länger nicht! – –	I can bear it no longer!
Wann wirst du mir schlagen,	When will you strike for me,

---

[35] Johnson, *The Complete Songs*, Vol. 1, 770.

O stunde der Ruh?! –	Hour of peace?!
O Tod! Komm und drücke	O death, come and close
Die Augen mir zu! – –	My eyes!
Im Leben da ist's ach! so schwül! –	Life, alas is so sultry, so oppressive!
Im Grabe – so friedlich, so kühl!	The grave is so peaceful, so cool!
Doch ach, wer legt mich hinein? –	But, ah, who will lay me there?
Ich stehe allein! – so ganz allein! –	I stand alone, quite alone!
Von allen verlassen,	By all forsaken,
Dem Tod nur verwandt,	Kin to death alone,
Verweil' ich am Rande –	I tarry on the brink,
Das Kreuz in der Hand,	Cross in hand,
Und starre mit sehnendem Blick,	Staring longingly down
Hinab, ins tiefe Grab! –	Into the deep grave!
O Heimat des Friedens,	O homeland of peace,
Der Seligen Land!	Land of the blessed!
An dich knüpft die Seele	A magic bond
Ein magisches Band. –	Binds my soul to you.
Du winkst mir von ferne,	You beckon to me from afar,
Du ewiges Licht: –	Eternal light;
Es schwinden die Sterne –	The stars vanish,
Das Auge schon bricht! – –	My eyes already grow dim.
Ich sinke – ich sinke! – Ihr Lieben –	I am sinking, I am sinking! Loved ones –
Ich komme! – – –	I come! – – –[36]

The distance between the deep grave and eternal light beckoning the protagonist from afar offers a contrasting perspective on death to that of the graveyard settings explored previously. Whereas 'Leichenfantasie' emphasizes the finality of death through the securing of the grave's bolts, the closing imagery of 'Totengräbers Heimweh' calls to mind Edward Young's observation that 'Life makes the soul dependent on the dust; Death gives her wings to mount about the spheres'.[37] 'Death but entombs the body, life the soul.'[38] Death, for Young, represented an opportunity to rise beyond finite existence, as is the case for the gravedigger in 'Totengräbers Heimweh'.

---

[36] Johnson, *The Complete Songs*, Vol. 3, 368–69.

[37] Quoted in Smith, *Gothic Death*, 22; see also Edward Young, *Night Thoughts on Life, Death and Immortality* [1742–45] (London: Baynes and Son, 1824), III, 61–62; and Edward Young, *Klagen, oder Nachtgedanken über Leben, Tod, und Unsterblichkeit*, trans. J.A. Ebert (Leipzig, 1790–94). Further on ideas of death as a release, together with application of Young's ideas, see chapter 3, 'Songs of the Night'.

[38] Quoted in Smith, *Gothic Death*, 22.

Example 1.11. Schubert, 'Grablied', D 218, bars 1–13.
Franz Schubert. *Lieder*, volume 12 (BA 5543), editor: Walther Dürr.
© 1996 Bärenreiter-Verlag Karl Vötterle GmbH & Co KG, Kassel.

Songs of the Grave

Such thinking shifts the emphasis towards Romantic conceptions of dying as a 'gradual sink[ing] into death'.[39] There is, as Paul Fry observes, a 'turning away, a gesture that expresses [...] a complex register of emotions': 'exhaustion, despair of recovery tempered by indifference to life, and embarrassment in the presence of those onlookers who must be left behind with the pain of loss'.[40] This approach to death, evident throughout 'Totengräbers Heimweh', is highlighted through comparison with its treatment in Schubert's 'Totengräberweise', D 869, a setting of a text by Franz Schlechta, composed one year later (1826). Here, the idea of death as release is replaced with a focus on earthly concerns – from the dead body falling prey to worms in stanza 2, to the closing call for sleep 'until bodies rise from the grave to new life'. Hints of the supernatural, suggesting a connection with Schubert's earlier graveyard settings, are undermined by the imagery throughout: the heart living on, 'even as dust', the sound of the trumpet in the closing lines (seemingly more ceremonial than the death tolls elsewhere in this chapter), and that final image of dead bodies returning. These songs position the figure of the gravedigger at either ends of gothic necropoetics: 'Totengräbers Heimweh' affords an experience of life beyond death, while 'Totengräberweise' reverses the trajectory with the gravedigger finding grim pleasure in the relentlessness of a task with no apparent endpoint.[41]

Schubert's setting of 'Totengräbers Heimweh' fluctuates between barely audible sounds and the 'claustrophobic sense of enclosure in space', another characteristic feature of the gothic.[42] The impression of packing much into a small space is palpable in the opening material, where physical unrest ('Unruhige Bewegung') is depicted through constant sound and saturation of texture (Example 1.12). Its churning piano accompaniment – trapped in an unending cycle – captures the monotony of gravedigging, while mirroring the protagonist's inner turmoil through its dense chordal textures and angstladen octaves. An amalgam of song and recitative in the vocal part intensifies the restlessness, notably at the words 'dig out, fill in' (bars 6–7), where the repeated Cs (a distorted echo of the tolling octaves in 'Schwestergruss') convey the terror of confronting the grave. The fluctuations between C minor and A flat major further hint at the life–death duality central to the gothic, without affirming what lies ahead.

The haunting side of gothic necropoetics rises up in stanza 3 of 'Totengräbers Heimweh' – 'by all forsaken, / kin to death alone' ('Von allen verlassen, / Dem Tod nur verwandt') – through the modulation to C minor, the textural reduction to bare octaves, and the chant-like vocal line, its message conveyed in whispered tones (Example 1.13). Death's pull is felt in melodic lines that sink ever lower, coming to

---

[39] Paul H. Fry, 'Disposing of the Body: The Romantic Moment of Dying', *Southwest Review* 71/1 (1986), 8–26, at 12. See also Trowbridge, 'Past, Present, and Future in the Gothic Graveyard'.

[40] Fry, 'Disposing of the Body', 12–13.

[41] On ideas of 'cyclicity and constancy', 'life turn[ing] to death which turns to new life in eternity', as they pertain to 'Totengräberweise', D 869, see Susan Youens, *Schubert's Late Lieder: Beyond the Song-Cycles* (Cambridge: Cambridge University Press, 2002), 352–62.

[42] Chris Baldick (ed.), *The Oxford Book of Gothic Tales* (Oxford: Oxford University Press, 2009), xix.

Example 1.12. Schubert, 'Totengräbers Heimweh', D 842, bars 1–9.
Franz Schubert. *Lieder*, volume 13 (BA 5535), editor: Walther Dürr.
© 1996 Bärenreiter-Verlag Karl Vötterle GmbH & Co KG, Kassel.

Example 1.13 Schubert, 'Totengräbers Heimweh', D 842, bars 40–48.
Franz Schubert. *Lieder*, volume 13 (BA 5535), editor: Walther Dürr.
© 1996 Bärenreiter-Verlag Karl Vötterle GmbH & Co KG, Kassel.

rest on a single pitch, A, in the depths of the piano and voice, for the words 'deep grave'. The low tessitura and empty textures frame this encounter with death as a point from which there is no return.

The threshold between life and death is crossed in one of those enigmatic moments where the music changes around a fixed pitch (Example 1.14). Bare octave As, evading tonal grounding, metamorphose into an A major chord akin to the light that beckons the protagonist, while the accompaniment dissipates into a dance-like lilt around the dactylic rhythms – a gentle dance of death – in the upper regions of the texture. The reaching into otherworldly dimensions is reflected in the leap up a major ninth for 'a magic bond' ('ein magisches Band'), and in the repetition of 'you beckon to me from afar, eternal light' ('Du winkst mir von ferne, / Du ewiges Licht'). Here, as the music circles around D major and F major, the darkness of the grave is eclipsed by the world that lies beyond.

The ending of 'Totengräbers Heimweh' presents life and death as 'contained within one another, two sides of existence's coin'.[43] Its closing lines foreground the tensions between sinking (into the grave) and rising (into eternal light): 'You beckon to me from afar, / Eternal light: / – The stars vanish – / My eyes already grow dim' ('Du winkst mir von ferne, / Du ewiges Licht: / Es schwinden die Sterne – / Das Auge schon bricht! – –'). 'I am sinking' ('Ich sinke'), declaims the singer to a descending diminished fifth, while the words 'I am sinking! – Loved ones – I come' ('Ich sinke! / – Ihr Lieben – / Ich komme!') rise to the music initially set to 'a magical bond' (Example 1.15). The protagonist sinks and rises, his destination unknown, as traces of the grave linger in the tolling bells in the piano postlude. The shift to F major, while mirroring the journey from darkness to light depicted in the text, resists linearity, of one state leading smoothly to another, through its proximity to the ghostly sounds of bars 41–49. That earlier music and the song's ending coalesce in the gaps between life and death depicted in the text. The postlude thus sounds both hopeful and unreal in light of the sudden turn to music seemingly at odds with its surroundings.

---

43 Youens, 'Reentering Mozart's Hell', 184.

Example 1.14 Schubert, 'Totengräbers Heimweh', D 842, bars 49–62.
Franz Schubert. *Lieder*, volume 13 (BA 5535), editor: Walther Dürr.
© 1996 Bärenreiter-Verlag Karl Vötterle GmbH & Co KG, Kassel.

Example 1.15 Schubert, 'Totengräbers Heimweh', D 842, bars 82–86.
Franz Schubert. *Lieder*, volume 13 (BA 5535), editor: Walther Dürr.
© 1996 Bärenreiter-Verlag Karl Vötterle GmbH & Co KG, Kassel.

Beyond the Grave

The songs discussed here establish a backdrop against which to hear the gothic imagination in the chapters that follow. Their vocabulary – whether associated with the finality of the grave, or with an imaginary realm beyond the living – puts pressure on the life–death duality and its connections with the macabre and the supernatural. These songs, even when their texts may appear steeped in ghostly presences or other such allusions to the undead, reveal deeper meanings through the fusion of words and music: sometimes in an affirmative relationship, other times with critical distance from the subject matter, or through stylistic references at odds with those of the text. Across all examples, the graveyard offers a space within which to reimagine the sound of death as part of the constellation of tropes – doubles, apparitions, the returning dead – surrounding gothic necropoetics.

2

Doubles and Distortions

'Leute, die sich selber sehen' (*'People who see themselves'*)

—Jean Paul Friedrich Richter, *Siebenkäs*[1]

The finale of Schubert's Piano Trio in E flat, D 929, composed in 1827, encapsulates the doubling that permeates the soundworlds of this chapter. The funereal theme from the Andante, cast initially in C minor, re-emerges in curious locations – first in B minor at bar 279, then in E flat minor at bar 795 – moments before the end of the piece (Example 2.1). In both instances, the theme, detached from its processional accompaniment, skims a texture of pizzicato chordal interjections in the upper range of the violin part and étude-like figurations in the piano part. Such reconfigurations position the funereal music, seemingly of the past, as returning in the present.[2]

On first hearing, these repetitions may not sound out of the ordinary. Yet tracing their roots back to the theme's initial presentation in the Andante unsettles ideas of the Finale bringing about 'resolution and closure'.[3] Its first appearance in the upper registers of the cello (bars 1–21) carries signs of the disjuncture to follow, as it soars above the accompaniment, rooted in the dactylic pattern of death in Schubert's music, while confined by its restricted melodic compass (Example 2.2). Mournful

---

[1]   Jean Paul, *Siebenkäs*, ed. Klaus Pauler (Munich, 1991), 92, note 15. For wider perspectives, see Andrew J. Webber, 'Life, Death, and Birth of the *Doppelgänger* in Jean Paul', in *The Doppelgänger: Double Visions in German Literature* (Oxford: Oxford University Press, 1996), 56–112; Erika Reiman, '"Seldom Satisfied, But Always Delighted": Jean Paul and his Novels', in *Schumann's Piano Cycles and the Novels of Jean Paul* (Rochester, NY: University of Rochester Press, 2004), 1–8; and Anchit Sathi, 'The (Queer) Aesthetics of Jean Paul's *Siebenkäs*', *German Life and Letters* 76/2 (2023), 198–221.

[2]   Further on the past in Schubert's music, with contrasting emphases to the strange, often disturbing distortions discussed here, see Walter Frisch, '"You Must Remember This": Memory and Structure in Schubert's String Quartet in G Major, D. 887', *Musical Quarterly* 84/4 (2000), 582–603, at 588. See also Anne M. Hyland, 'In Search of Liberated Time, or Schubert's Quartet in G Major, D. 887: Once More between Sonata and Variation', *Music Theory Spectrum* 38/1 (2016), 85–108; Carl Dahlhaus, 'Sonata Form in Schubert: The First Movement of the G-Major String Quartet, Op. 161 (D. 887)', in *Schubert: Critical and Analytical Studies*, ed. Walter Frisch, trans. Thilo Reinhard (Lincoln, NB: University of Nebraska Press, 1986), 1–12; and Scott Burnham, 'Landscape as Music, Landscape as Truth: Schubert and the Burden of Repetition', *19th-Century Music* 29 (2005), 31–41.

[3]   Lawrence Kramer, *Franz Schubert: Sexuality, Subjectivity, Song* (Cambridge: Cambridge University Press, 1998), 157.

Example 2.1. Schubert, Piano Trio in E flat major, D 929, IV, bars 273–86. Franz Schubert. Trio for Piano, Violin and Violincello in E flat major op. 100 D 929 (BA 5610), editor: Arnold Feil. © 1975 Bärenreiter-Verlag Karl Vötterle GmbH & Co KG, Kassel.

Example 2.2. Schubert, Piano Trio in E flat major, D 929, II, bars 1–21. Franz Schubert. Trio for Piano, Violin and Violincello in E flat major op. 100 D 929 (BA 5610), editor: Arnold Feil. © 1975 Bärenreiter-Verlag Karl Vötterle GmbH & Co KG, Kassel.

on the surface, replete with disruptive undercurrents, the theme distorts the regularity of the funeral march through the accent on the second half of the bar (cf. bars 4 and 5), the dotted rhythmic motion, and emphasis on the minor iv.[4] Here, as in all of Schubert's music, surface details run deep. Thus, when the texture is inverted in bars 21–40, the theme doubled in the upper ranges of the piano, the impression of hovering at the boundaries is intensified through the withdrawal from *piano* to *pianissimo*.

Returns of this kind, connected to and detached from their earlier incarnations, provide a backdrop against which to hear the doubles and distortions across the main case studies of this chapter: the *Grande Marche Funèbre*, D 859, the C minor

---

[4] Apposite here is Benedict Taylor's observation that 'Schubert's trudging figures give the sense of an unrelenting movement towards a preordained goal, inevitable and implacable – eliding physical motion with a fatalistic temporal sense'. Taylor, 'Schubert and the Construction of Memory: The String Quartet in A Minor, D. 804 ("Rosamunde")', *Journal of the Royal Musical Association* 139/1 (2014), 74–75.

56   *The Gothic Imagination in the Music of Franz Schubert*

Impromptu, D 899/1, and the F minor Fantasy for four hands, D 940. These pieces form a constellation around funereal elements, voices from the past, and blurred boundaries between life and death characteristic of the graveyard imagery discussed in chapter 1. The recurrence of stylistic features – from fleeting disturbances, a rhythmic shudder or a tremolo figuration, to prolonged outbursts and distortions – speaks to a shared vocabulary in the absence of textual cues. The case studies, as with those in chapter 4, move away from direct transference between song and instrumental music towards dialogues that work in both directions.

Biographical readings of the pieces discussed here are numerous. Christopher Gibbs, identifying Beethoven as the 'ghost' haunting the E flat Trio, characterizes the piece as Schubert's '*tombeau de Beethoven*'.[5] Gibbs bases this idea on affinities with the *marcia funebre* of Beethoven's 'Eroica' Symphony, Op. 55 – through key, rhythm, affect, and melodic contour. These, in tandem with the allusions to the Swedish folksong 'Se solen junker', notably the falling octave leaps (set in the song to the words 'Farewell, Farewell'), lead Gibbs to view the piece as a 'conscious homage' to the memory of Beethoven.[6] For Charles Fisk, Schubert's C minor Impromptu, which 'shares its mood' with 'Gute Nacht' and 'Der Wegweiser' from *Winterreise*, D 911, infused with echoes of 'Der Wanderer', D 489, conveys the 'fulfillment of finding a "Heimat" – a homeland, or an inner sense of peace' (denied of the protagonist in *Winterreise*, but made a possibility in instrumental genres, he suggests, through 'musical resolution and a return to life').[7] Fisk traces these themes beyond musical dialogues to consideration of Schubert's own experience of estrangement and impending mortality. The F minor Fantasy has similarly prompted biographical connections, while opening up wider pathways between sound and hermeneutic thought, as in Susan Wollenberg's observation: 'whatever we interpret those final bars of D 940 as representing – death, resignation, grandeur, or sorrow (Atlas with his unending misery) – they, together with the closing passage as a whole, speak with a largeness of spirit and depth of experience' of a 'composer steeped in poetic expression throughout his creative life'.[8]

The gothic, with its emphasis on dislocations and the returning past, offers a framework for recontextualizing death and doubles beyond the realm of biography and exploring further the evocation of poetic tropes within instrumental genres. Doubles carry associations with the phenomenon of the Doppelgänger – a trope bound up

---

5   Christopher H. Gibbs, 'Schubert's *Tombeau de Beethoven*: Decrypting the Piano Trio in E-flat Major, Op. 100', in *Franz Schubert and his World*, ed. Gibbs and Morten Solvik (Princeton, NJ: Princeton University Press, 2014), 241–98.

6   Gibbs, 'Schubert's *Tombeau de Beethoven*', 274.

7   Charles Fisk, *Returning Cycles: Contexts for the Interpretation of Schubert's Impromptus and Last Sonatas* (Berkeley: University of California Press, 2001), 72; on Fisk's approach, see reviews by Harald Krebs, *Music Theory Spectrum* 25/2 (2003), 388–400; and Scott Burnham, 'Music Therapy', *19th-Century Music* 26/2 (2002), 178–91.

8   Susan Wollenberg, 'From Song to Instrumental Style: Some Schubert Fingerprints', in *Rethinking Schubert*, 71–72.

Doubles and Distortions 57

with Romanticism and the mirror image revealing the inner depths of the psyche, as in Jean Paul's coinage quoted in the epigraph above, but also germane to the gothic imagination: from the doubling of sound associated with graveyard imagery, to ghostly occurrences that disrupt the present.[9] The double, Andrew Webber writes, is 'not in any simple sense a Romantic figure', for it 'resists categorical literary-historical definition', 'stepping out of time and then stepping back in'.[10] It 'appears as an interloper, an unwanted guest, out of place in the texts it visits', Webber continues, while simultaneously at 'home in the Gothic scenery of Romantic fiction'.[11]

The readings offered here are situated between these notions of the double, sometimes looking back to the death-related tropes of chapter 1, at other times grappling with the implications of distorted themes akin to the Romantic Doppelgänger. Doubles are traced across the separate case studies, as well as 'intertextually from one to the other', as Webber puts it, their 'performances repeat[ing] both [their] host subject and its own previous appearance'.[12] These dialogues feed into the nexus of gothic tropes in Schubert's music, closely aligned with the soundworlds of his *Schauerballaden*, that are refashioned across generic boundaries.

The dedication of Schubert's *Grande Marche Funèbre* to Alexander I – Emperor of Russia from 1801, the first King of Congress Poland from 1815, and the Grand Duke of Finland from 1809 to his death in 1825 – widens the lens, albeit curiously, for understanding death vis-à-vis the socio-cultural climate of the time. Alexander I had little to do with Schubert's music, but mention of his reign, which swayed between the liberal and the autocratic,[13] brings into focus the political landscape of Schubert's Vienna between the French Revolution (1789) and the Napoleonic wars (1803–15).[14] That period, full of suffering and violence, ushered in new approaches to death and

---

9   On gothic doubles, see Christine Berthin, *Gothic Hauntings: Melancholy Crypts and Textual Ghosts* (London: Palgrave Macmillan, 2010), 58–88; Eugenia C. DeLamotte, *Perils of the Night: A Feminist Study of Nineteenth-Century Gothic* (Oxford: Oxford University Press, 1990), 94–96. Further on ghostliness in nineteenth-century music, see Lawrence Kramer, 'Ghost Stories: Cultural Memory, Mourning, and the Myth of Originality', in *Musical Meaning: Toward a Critical History* (Berkeley: University of California, Press, 2001), 258–87; Wayne C. Petty, 'Chopin and the Ghost of Beethoven', *19th-Century Music* 22 (1999), 281–99; and Ewelina Boczkowska, 'Chopin's Ghosts', *19th-Century Music* 35/3 (2012), 204–23.

10 Webber, *The Doppelgänger*, 9–10.

11 Webber, *The Doppelgänger*, 8.

12 Webber, *The Doppelgänger*, 6.

13 For biographical context, see Marie-Pierre Rey, *Alexander I: The Tsar Who Defeated Napoleon*, trans. Susan Emanuel (Dekalb, IL: Northern Illinois University Press, 2016).

14 For general context, see Ernst Hilmar, *Franz Schubert in seiner Zeit* (Vienna: Hermann Böhlaus Nachf., 1985); trans. Reinhard G. Pauly as *Franz Schubert in his Time* (Portland, OR: Amadeus Press, 1988); Raymond Erickson (ed.), *Schubert's Vienna* (New Haven and London: Yale University Press, 1997); and Christopher H. Gibbs and Morten Solvik (eds), *Franz Schubert and his World* (Princeton, NJ: Princeton University Press, 2014).

58   *The Gothic Imagination in the Music of Franz Schubert*

the afterlife, censorship, and the boundaries between revolutionary thinking and the curtailment of liberatory ideals in the public domain.[15]

It is a small step from this backdrop, opened up through the dedication of Schubert's *Grande Marche Funèbre*, to ideas of the gothic as a space for confronting themes with wider socio-cultural resonances,[16] either implicitly or directly (as in the subject matter of Schubert's setting of Kenner's 'Grablied', discussed in chapter 1), and for giving voice to that which was concealed or all too palpable in everyday life. The gothic, as David Punter observes, 'deals in opposition to rules, resistance to regulations', 'transgression against human norms', and 'with that which is not strictly within the human realm'.[17] There is 'terror', Punter continues, 'a looking down into the abyss, a confrontation with death', but also 'the possibility of return' ('benign or malignant').[18] Such thinking, beyond its traces that Punter locates in literature, finds a sonic outlet in the case studies that follow, where gothic ambivalence reverberates through the gaps between surface-level audibility and that which is latent beneath.[19]

---

[15]   See Friedrich Schlegel's description of the French Revolution in his 1798 *Athenaeum* as 'an almost universal earthquake, an immeasurable flood in the political world; or as a prototype of revolutions, as the absolute revolution per se. These are the usual points of view. But one can also see it as [...] where all its paradoxes are thrust together; as the most frightful grotesque of the age, where the most profound prejudices and their most brutal punishments are mixed up in a fearful chaos and woven as bizarrely as possible into a monstrous human tragicomedy.' Fragment 424, quoted in Friedrich Schlegel, *Philosophical Fragments*, trans. Peter Firchow (Minneapolis: University of Minnesota Press, 1991), 86. See also Sophie Rosenfeld, 'The French Revolution in Cultural History', *Journal of Social History* 52/3 (2019), 555–65; Timothy Tackett, *The Coming of the Terror in the French Revolution* (Cambridge, MA, and London: Belknap Press of Harvard University Press, 2015), esp. 1–69; and Alexander Mikaberidze, *The Napoleonic Wars: A Global History* (Oxford: Oxford University Press, 2020). On the power of music and arts in times of socio-political change, see Andrea Lindmayr-Brandl, 'Music and Culture in Schubert's Vienna', in *The Cambridge Companion to Schubert's 'Winterreise'*, ed. Marjorie W. Hirsch and Lisa Feurzeig (Cambridge: Cambridge University Press, 2021), 11–23; Leon Botstein, 'Realism Transformed: Franz Schubert and Vienna', in *The Cambridge Companion to Schubert*, ed. Christopher H. Gibbs (Cambridge: Cambridge University Press, 1997), 13–35; Lisa Feurzeig, *Schubert's Lieder and the Philosophy of Early German Romanticism* (Farnham: Ashgate, 2014); Kristina Muxfeldt, *Vanishing Sensibilities: Schubert, Beethoven, Schumann* (New York: Oxford University Press, 2011); Susan Youens, 'Of Dwarves, Perversion, and Patriotism: Schubert's "Der Zwerg", D. 771', *19th-Century Music* 21/2 (1997), 177–207.

[16]   See Robert Miles, 'Political Gothic Fiction', in *Romantic Gothic: An Edinburgh Companion*, ed. Angela Wright and Dale Townshend (Edinburgh: Edinburgh University Press, 2015), 129–46; Nick Groom, *The Gothic: A Very Short Introduction* (Oxford: Oxford University Press, 2012), esp. chapter 6, 'Gothic Whiggery'; Crystal B. Lake, 'Bloody Records: Manuscripts and Politics in *The Castle of Otranto*', *Modern Philology* 110/4 (2013), 489–512.

[17]   David Punter, 'Introduction', in *The Edinburgh Companion to Gothic and the Arts*, ed. Punter (Edinburgh: Edinburgh University Press, 2019), 2.

[18]   Punter, 'Introduction', 2.

[19]   Further on ideas of latency in Schubert's music, see Xavier Hascher, 'Narrative Dislocations in the First Movement of Schubert's "Unfinished" Symphony', in *Rethinking Schubert*, 127–46, at 137.

Hearing Doubles, Contextualizing Distortions

I. Eerie Beginnings

Beginnings – where things originate, how they unfold – are a primary locus for hearing how the gothic conceals as much as it reveals. Sounds emanate from afar, as in 'Leichenfantasie' and 'Schwestergruss', discussed in chapter 1, or they rear up *ex nihilo*, sudden disturbances that carry implications for what follows. Both these approaches surface in the opening of Schubert's *Grande Marche Funèbre*,[20] its soundscape appearing 'indefinite, overladen, smothered with ornament', to borrow Goethe's description of the gothic design of Strasbourg cathedral (Example 2.3).[21] Doubling arises not only through octave figures in both parts, but also at the level of stylistic categories, in the gaps between historical periods (a theme that resurfaces throughout the chapter). A reference to French overture, suggested through the double-dotted rhythmic profile, summons the world of the Baroque, the heyday of this stylistic zone. Here, however, intimations of the majestic or the ceremonial – as in the Overture to J.S. Bach's Partita in D major, BWV 828 – are replaced by the disjunctive style of the funeral march. This process of distortion takes place through abrupt harmonic shifts, octave unisons fluctuating between the declamatory (bars 1–2) and the ephemeral (bars 3–4),[22] trills that destabilize the musical surface, and densely packed chords pushing at registral and dynamic extremes (Example 2.4). The overarching impression is of (misshapen) music from the past that disrupts the present.

The main theme of Schubert's C minor Impromptu (bars 1–33),[23] initiated by the forcefully struck, double octave unison figure, unfolds within this lexicon of

---

[20] On Schubert's marches, see Scott Messing, *Marching to the Canon: The Life of Schubert's 'Marche Militaire'* (Rochester, NY: University of Rochester Press, 2014).

[21] Johann Wolfgang von Goethe, 'On German Architecture', in *Goethe on Art*, ed. and trans. John Gage (London: Scholar Press, 1980), 106–7; for his full description, see the Introduction. On earlier models, particularly Mozart's Fantasie in F Minor for clockwork organ, K 608, which similarly profiles a distorted past, see Annette Richards, 'Automatic Genius: Mozart and the Mechanical Sublime', *Music & Letters* 80/3 (1999), 336–89.

[22] On the semiotic properties of octave unison passages, see Janet Levy, 'Texture as a Sign in Classic and Early Romantic Music', *Journal of the American Musicological Society* 35/3 (1982), 482–531, at 507: 'It does not appear to occur in nature, to happen naturally. It must, in some sense, be organized, preordained – imposed. On the one hand, it is an authority given by human ritual or ceremony – as in the intoning of chant, patriotic and work songs, heraldic fanfares. On the other hand, it is an authority that seems to rest in compulsions that inhabit the deepest reaches of the psyche or in forces outside man's nature (the demonic, the supernatural).'

[23] The readings offered here focus on soundbites, the ways in which the gothic is suggested through texture, topic, dynamic, and register, those elusive parameters that connect sound to poetic imagery. For formal analyses, with an emphasis on its structural hybridity, see Brian Black, 'Lyricism and the Dramatic Unity of Schubert's Instrumental Music: The Impromptu in C Minor, D. 899/1', in *Drama in the Music of Franz Schubert*, 233–56; Fisk,

Example 2.3. Schubert, *Grand Marche Funèbre* in C minor for four hands, D 859, bars 1–6. Franz Schubert. Works for piano duet, volume 4: Marches and Dances (BA 5507), editor: Christa Landon. © 1972 Bärenreiter-Verlag Karl Vötterle GmbH & Co KG, Kassel.

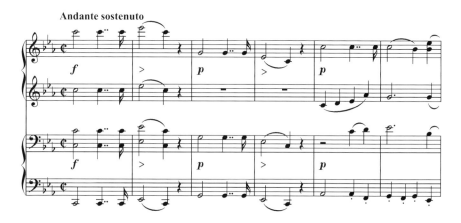

sounds doubled and split into multiple layers: not only those of the opening of the *Grande Marche Funèbre*, but also the octave unison figures in the slow introductions to Schubert's Fantasy in G minor, D 9, penned in the same year as 'Leichenfantasie', 1811, and his Fantasy in C minor, D 48, composed two years later (Examples 2.5, 2.6, and 2.7).[24] These examples, as with the Impromptu, enmesh octave unisons with references to the past – interwoven with ornaments (notably turn figures) and echoes of a lament bass in D 9, and in D 48 similarly interlaced with a descending tetrachord, followed by fugal writing in the Allegro section. Such allusions weave their way around the funereal main theme of the Impromptu, implicitly in the unaccompanied opening and explicitly in the fuller texture that follows (the latter resonating with the main theme in the Trio's Andante, Example 2.2). Technical precision – evident through the intricate mix of staccato and legato markings – meets with the sonic ambivalence of material that continually loops around its starting point. Each iteration of the theme reveals further layers, especially in the variation of bars 17–32, where diminished sevenths, thicker textures, harsher dynamics, and octave doubling (a lingering trace of the opening figure) hint at darker forces beneath the surface.

Returning Cycles, 25–29; Susan McClary, 'Pitches, Expression, Ideology: An Exercise in Mediation', *Enclitic* 7 (1983), 76–86, repr. in *Reading Music: Selected Essays* (Farnham: Ashgate, 2007), 3–14; and David Damschroder, *Harmony in Schubert* (Cambridge: Cambridge University Press, 2010), 201–11.

[24] On D 9 and D 48, see Barbara Strahan, '(De)Constructing Paradigms of Genre: Aesthetics, Identity and Form in Franz Schubert's Four-Hand Fantasias' (PhD dissertation, Maynooth University, 2013).

Example 2.4. Schubert, *Grande Marche Funèbre* in C minor for four hands, D 859, bars 15–28. Franz Schubert. Works for piano duet, volume 4: Marches and Dances (BA 5507), editor: Christa Landon. © 1972 Bärenreiter-Verlag Karl Vötterle GmbH & Co KG, Kassel.

Example 2.5. Schubert, Impromptu in C minor, D 899/1, bars 1–17. Franz Schubert. Impromptus op. 90 D 899, op. post. 142 D 935 (BA 9648), editor: Walther Dürr. © 2011 Bärenreiter-Verlag Karl Vötterle GmbH & Co KG, Kassel.

Example 2.6. Schubert, Fantasy in G minor for four hands, D 9, bars 1–7. Franz Schubert. Works for piano duet, volume 1 (BA 5558), editor: Walburga Litschauer. © 2007 Bärenreiter-Verlag Karl Vötterle GmbH & Co KG, Kassel.

Example 2.7. Schubert, Fantasy in C minor for four hands, D 48, bars 1–4. Franz Schubert. Works for piano duet, volume 1 (BA 5558), editor: Walburga Litschauer. © 2007 Bärenreiter-Verlag Karl Vötterle GmbH & Co KG, Kassel.

Schubert's Impromptu belongs to a nexus of pieces that evoke gothic tensions between (physical) presence and (textural) absence, prominent among them the Andante of his Piano Sonata in A minor, D 784 (1823).[25] The persistent turn figures here, creeping around semitonal inflections, reveal the eerie nature of music that is barely audible: their presence is palpable, returning in exact repetition in bars 4, 8, and 15, displaced at the octave in bar 18, and sonically elusive in all instances (Example 2.8).[26] These figures, coupled with the doubling of the main theme in the tenor voice, a mirror of its upper contours, draw attention to the ways in which writing with gothic connotations can surface in contexts that seem otherwise not to carry its traces. The origins of these interjections can be traced back to the skeletal texture of the opening movement of D 784 – where the main theme rises from tonic to dominant, pivoting around a semitonal inflection, before falling to the tonic an octave below its starting point (Example 2.9). These features, marked *pianissimo* in the gaps between sound and silence, are accentuated through the processional tone of the left-hand figures from bar 9 and the distorted return of the theme in bar 26, doubled at the octave in both hands and prefigured by tremolo figurations.[27]

Echoes of the writing in the slow movement of D 784 extend beyond their immediate context to the opening movement of Schubert's later A minor Piano Sonata, D 845 (1825), with its turn-like contours embedded there in a phrase oscillating among mediant, supertonic, and displaced octaves (Example 2.10). Their return in curious places, notably in C minor at bar 63, foreshadows the textural and thematic profile of Schubert's C minor Impromptu, while also recalling the music of the grave in 'Totengräbers Heimweh', 'By all forsaken, kin to death alone', penned one month earlier and discussed in chapter 1 (cf. Example 1.13). Death lingers in skeletal textures or figurations reminiscent of Schubert's graveyard settings. In all cases, as in the C minor Impromptu, eeriness is heightened through muted sounds that carry meanings beneath their almost inaudible surfaces.

---

[25] I acknowledge here the imaginative work of Emily Jones, whose Senior Thesis, '"There were frequent and violent alterations …".: Gothic Terror in Schubert's Sonata D.784', I had the pleasure of supervising at the University of California, Irvine, 2022–23.

[26] For alternative readings of D 784 and D 845, see Robert S. Hatten, *Interpreting Musical Gestures, Topics, and Tropes: Mozart, Beethoven, Schubert* (Bloomington: Indiana University Press, 2004), 187–200.

[27] The unleashing of qualities latent from the outset of this movement becomes ever more prominent as the sighing figures, no longer connected via slurs, erupt as chordal outbursts through the development section, especially bars 110–19. The sonic force of the chordal interjections, in tandem with the silence that lingers between the bars, suggests both proximity and distance from those earlier tremors in low register (cf. bar 22 ff.).

Example 2.8. Schubert, Piano Sonata in A minor, D 784, II, bars 1–8.
Franz Schubert. Piano Sonatas, volume 2 (BA 5541), editor: Walburga Litschauer.
© 2003 Bärenreiter-Verlag Karl Vötterle GmbH & Co KG, Kassel.

Example 2.9. Schubert, Piano Sonata in A minor, D 784, I, bars 1–22.
Franz Schubert. Piano Sonatas, volume 2 (BA 5541), editor: Walburga Litschauer.
© 2003 Bärenreiter-Verlag Karl Vötterle GmbH & Co KG, Kassel.

Example 2.10. Schubert, Piano Sonata in A minor, D 845, I, bars 1–10.
Franz Schubert. Piano Sonatas, volume 2 (BA 5541), editor: Walburga Litschauer.
© 2003 Bärenreiter-Verlag Karl Vötterle GmbH & Co KG, Kassel.

II. Distortions

Schubert's C minor Impromptu captures the sound of the gothic from the eeriness of the main theme to its visceral, powerfully charged return, bars 95–124, adorned with recurrent iterations of the dominant (G) in the bass and a dissonant voice in the inner part of the texture (Example 2.11). The boundaries between the opening octave figure and the theme are ruptured here as the former becomes enmeshed with the latter, now fractured into repeated triplets (a harbinger of death in Schubert's music). This effect is taken further in bars 111–18, where the sound of dragging down, as in 'Totengräbers Heimweh', is juxtaposed with stabbing C minor chords throughout bars 113–17. These chordal interjections – recalling the rupture in bar 62 of the 'Unfinished' Symphony, D 759, I (1822), a 'catastrophe', in Glenn Stanley's words[28] – their expansive textures, and the dissonant language, with

---

[28] Glenn Stanley, 'Schubert Hearing *Don Giovanni*: Mozartian Death Music in the "Unfinished" Symphony', in *Schubert's Late Music*, 193–218. Stanley locates traces of 'death' in the first movement's topical and structural fabric, notably in the development section, where he identifies allusions to the second-act finale of Mozart's *Don Giovanni*, a scene in which the death of the Don is staged, and a stylistic idiom that recalls the *ombra* topic (see especially 205–8), the *lingua franca* of operatic supernaturalism. Further on ideas of rupture in D 759, see Davies, 'Interpreting the Expressive Worlds of Schubert's Late Instrumental Works' (DPhil dissertation, University of Oxford, 2018), chapter 3; Barbara Barry, 'A Shouting Silence: Further Thoughts about Schubert's "Unfinished"', *Musical Times* 151 (2010), 39–52; John Gingerich, 'Unfinished Considerations: Schubert's "Unfinished" Symphony in the Context of his Beethoven Project', *19th-Century Music* 31/2 (2007), 99–112; and Xavier Hascher, 'Narrative Dislocations in the First Movement of Schubert's "Unfinished" Symphony', in *Rethinking Schubert*, 127–46.

Example 2.11. Schubert, Impromptu in C minor, D 899/1, bars 95–118. Franz Schubert. Impromptus op. 90 D 899, op. post. 142 D 935 (BA 9648), editor: Walther Dürr.
© 2011 Bärenreiter-Verlag Karl Vötterle GmbH & Co KG, Kassel.

—(continued)

Example 2.11—*concluded*

clashes between the hands, distort the funereal frame of reference with an outpouring of harsh sounds and densely wrought textures.

Such distortion brings to mind the intertextual dialogues across song and instrumental music central to the gothic worlds explored here. One such piece is the 'Death and the Maiden' Quartet in D minor, D 810 (1824), particularly the treatment of the slow movement's main theme, derived from 'Der Tod und das Mädchen', D 531.[29] The theme's features – rhythmic fixity, enshrined in dactylic patterns, replete with surface fragility, hushed dynamic markings, confined melodic contours, and textural concentration – are subject to increasing distortion across the variations (Example 2.12). The processional style of the opening is first derailed in variation 3 by the warping of its rhythmic profile, with compressed dactylic patterns filtering through in all parts, and through the alternation of *fortissimo-sforzando* interjections (Example 2.13). The penultimate variation is further distorted through repeated tremolo figurations, triple *forte* dynamic markings, and writing that pushes at the extremes of the instruments (Example 2.14). These alterations render the theme unfamiliar as its initial qualities give way to disruption of the kind heard throughout this chapter's case studies.

The return of the funereal theme in Schubert's C minor Impromptu not only recalls the vocabulary of the slow movement of the 'Death and the Maiden' Quartet, its rhythmic properties and tremolo-based textures, but also the world of *ombra*, a central site of the gothic, from his *Schauerballaden*.[30] The angular melodic lines, pervasive dissonance, and chromaticism coupled with disjunct bass movement, repeated pedal points, and tremolo figurations align with the soundworlds of such songs as 'Gruppe aus dem Tartarus', D 583, whose invocation of *ombra* music portrays, in Marjorie Hirsch's words, the 'torments suffered by damned souls in hell'.[31]

---

[29] Christoph Wolff, 'Schubert's "Der Tod und das Mädchen": Analytical and Explanatory Notes on the Song D 531 and the Quartet D 810', in *Schubert Studies: Problems of Style and Chronology*, ed. Eva Badura-Skoda and Peter Branscombe (Cambridge: Cambridge University Press, 1982), 143–71; and John Gingerich, 'Songs of Death and the Chamber Music of 1824', in *Schubert's Beethoven Project*, 85–104.

[30] On *ombra* music, see the Introduction of this book.

[31] Marjorie Hirsch, 'Schubert's Reconciliation of Gothic and Classical Influences', in *Schubert's Late Music*, 159. See also Susan Youens, 'Reentering Mozart's Hell: Schubert's "Gruppe aus dem Tartarus", D. 538', in *Drama in the Music of Franz Schubert*, 171–204.

Example 2.12. Schubert, String Quartet in D minor, D 810, II, bars 1–8. Franz Schubert. String Quartet in D minor D 810 'Death and the Maiden' (TP 301), editor: Werner Aderhold. © 1989 Bärenreiter-Verlag Karl Vötterle GmbH & Co KG, Kassel.

Example 2.13. Schubert, String Quartet in D minor, D 810, II, bars 73–75. Franz Schubert. String Quartet in D minor D 810 'Death and the Maiden' (TP 301), editor: Werner Aderhold. © 1989 Bärenreiter-Verlag Karl Vötterle GmbH & Co KG, Kassel.

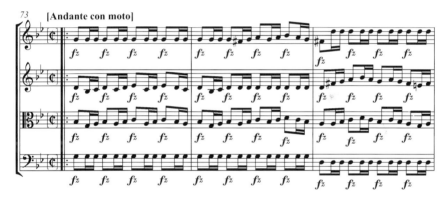

Similarly lurking in the shadows are traces of the obsessive accompaniment in 'Der Zwerg', D 771, together with echoes of the boy's shrieks in 'Erlkönig', D 328, suggested through the clashing ninths (here between the A flat in the inner part and the G in the bass in bars 99 and 107) central to both.[32]

Further parallels can be drawn here with the distortion of the funereal theme in the Andante of the E flat Trio, bars 104–28, discussed above. Both case studies blur the boundaries between discrete sections, from the chordal interruptions in D 899/1, to the tremolando figure that derails the funereal theme at bar 104 of D 929, II (Example 2.15). Stylistic categories are destabilized, especially from bar 114 where

---

[32] I thank Susan Wollenberg for bringing this shared intervallic pattern to mind (personal correspondence).

Example 2.14. Schubert, String Quartet in D minor, D 810, II, bars 81–92. Franz Schubert. String Quartet in D minor D 810 'Death and the Maiden' (TP 301), editor: Werner Aderhold. © 1989 Bärenreiter-Verlag Karl Vötterle GmbH & Co KG, Kassel.

Example 2.15. Schubert, Piano Trio in E flat major, D 929, II, bars 104–14.
Franz Schubert. Trio for Piano, Violin and Violincello in E flat major op. 100 D 929
(BA 5610), editor: Arnold Feil. © 1975 Bärenreiter-Verlag
Karl Vötterle GmbH & Co KG, Kassel.

—(continued)

Example 2.15—concluded

the expansion in volume and texture, the chromatic layering, and the sonic twists and turns resemble the pianistic depiction of Hell in his 'Gruppe aus dem Tartarus', D 583. All traces of the funereal theme are distorted by material that builds towards triple *forte* by the climax in bar 122 (a soundscape distant from that of the opening).

❦ ❦ ❦

Traces of the gothic in the pieces explored here extend beyond the distortion of funereal music (as in his graveyard songs discussed in chapter 1), to the implied blurring of boundaries between life and death. In each, the processional themes give way to a contrasting reality, as is customary in funeral marches (cf. the *marcia funebre* of Beethoven's 'Eroica' Symphony, Op. 55, or the third movement of Chopin's Piano Sonata in B flat Minor, Op. 35). Yet qualities of escapism, intimated through changes in mode, texture, and topic, are subsequently undermined through doubling and proximity to the funereal surroundings.

Distortions of this kind play out in bars 41–73 of the C minor Impromptu, which Fisk describes as an 'echo into a contrasting episode'; the music 'evokes a dream, or perhaps only the memory of a time when dreaming was still possible, in relation to the opening's bleak reality' (Example 2.16).[33] The modulation to the submediant (A flat) major, bar 41, together with the allusion to the

---

[33] Fisk, *Returning Cycles*, 27. The approach to modulation, bars 33–41, underlines the tentative nature of the material that follows: A flat major is intimated first in a quasi-deceptive cadence (bar 34), pulled back to the tonic minor in the following bars (playing out the tonal ambivalence foreshadowed in the primary theme in relation to the relative major), then unlocked via the Neapolitan in the final moments. For wider context, see Susan Wollenberg, 'Schubert's Transitions', in *Schubert Studies*, ed. Newbould, 16–61; and Wollenberg, 'Poetic Transitions', *Schubert's Fingerprints: Studies in the Instrumental Works* (Farnham: Ashgate, 2011), 47–97.

Example 2.16. Schubert, Impromptu in C minor, D 899/1, bars 33–51. Franz Schubert. Impromptus op. 90 D 899, op. post. 142 D 935 (BA 9648), editor: Walther Dürr. © 2011 Bärenreiter-Verlag Karl Vötterle GmbH & Co KG, Kassel.

genre of song without words, contains signs that Schubert's use of the major can be deceptive, as in the case of 'Erlkönig', D 328. Unsettling – or 'uncanny', as Christopher Gibbs observes – is the combination of 'sweetness and terror' in the music associated with the Erlking.[34] That the Erlking speaks in dulcet tones – 'human music' at odds with the figure it depicts – heightens the sinister nature of his actions as he lures the young boy to his death.[35] While no such supernatural beings infiltrate the A flat music in the Impromptu, there are intimations that

[34] Christopher H. Gibbs, '"Komm geh mit mir": Schubert's Uncanny "Erlkönig"', 19th-Century Music 19/2 (1995), 115–35, at 132.
[35] Gibbs, 'Schubert's Uncanny "Erlkönig"', 120.

74   *The Gothic Imagination in the Music of Franz Schubert*

the material is not as idyllic as it first appears. The continued dotted rhythms, in tandem with the modal fluctuations between A flat major and A flat minor in bar 56, bring the funereal profile of the main theme into close contact with this contrasting episode.

Such tensions rise to the surface when the A flat major music is drawn directly into the web of the funereal theme, from bar 124 (Example 2.17). A flat major gives way to G minor and the music unfolds in a perturbed manner, with the bass line's offbeat utterances betraying the influence of the repeated pedal point throughout bars 95–118 (Example 2.11). The power of the octave to distort is striking from bar 138 when the theme is doubled in the left hand, surrounded by dissonant chordal fragments, sequential bass lines, and suspensions; residual traces of the references to the past in D 9 and D 48 (cf. Examples 2.6 and 2.7). The proximity to the funereal theme, particularly its distorted return in Example 2.11, transforms the earlier evocation of an alternate reality into a distant reality.[36]

A further parallel with the Trio's Andante, D 929, can be drawn here with its treatment of thematic material in bars 41–85.[37] At first the modulation to the relative E flat major, bar 41, and the dissipation of the funeral march portray an alternate reality akin to the A flat major music in the Impromptu (Example 2.18). However, bar 67 – with its sudden surge of rhythmic activity, angular fragments of the theme, and diminished harmonies – blurs the relationship between this material and its funereal counterpart (Example 2.19). In contrast to the C minor Impromptu, where the A flat major material undergoes distortion in subsequent sections of the music (cf. Examples 2.16 and 2.17), here the impression of simultaneity is foregrounded immediately. The silence after this outburst, bar 81, consolidates these blurred boundaries. Traces of the funereal theme intermingle with the dissolving bass line in the cello, filled in with embellishment and enveloped by spread, harp-like sonorities in the piano part. The alternate reality slips out of reach as texture and dynamic recede to *pianissimo*.

---

[36] The Trio section of the *Grande Marche Funèbre* (bars 81–124) contains a comparable instance of distortion, notably in bar 91, where the abrupt shift from A flat major to E minor conflates the music of the Trio section with the funereal soundscape of the opening, its associations with escape or an alternate reality rendered untenable.

[37] See James William Sobaskie, 'A Balance Struck: Gesture, Form, and Drama in Schubert's E-flat Major Piano Trio', in *Le style instrumental de Schubert: sources, analyse, évolution*, ed. Xavier Hascher (Paris: Publications de la Sorbonne, 2007), 115–46, at 124.

Example 2.17. Schubert, Impromptu in C minor, D 899/1, bars 124–29. Franz Schubert. Impromptus op. 90 D 899, op. post. 142 D 935 (BA 9648), editor: Walther Dürr. © 2011 Bärenreiter-Verlag Karl Vötterle GmbH & Co KG, Kassel.

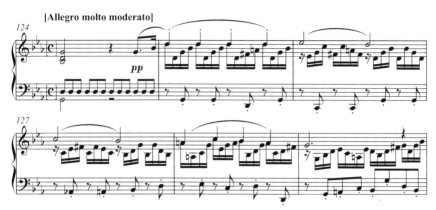

Example 2.18. Schubert, Piano Trio in E flat major, D 929, II, bars 41–44. Franz Schubert. Trio for Piano, Violin and Violincello in E flat major op. 100 D 929 (BA 5610), editor: Arnold Feil. © 1975 Bärenreiter-Verlag Karl Vötterle GmbH & Co KG, Kassel.

Example 2.19. Schubert, Piano Trio in E flat major, D 929, II, bars 67–84. Franz Schubert. Trio for Piano, Violin and Violincello in E flat major op. 100 D 929 (BA 5610), editor: Arnold Feil. © 1975 Bärenreiter-Verlag Karl Vötterle GmbH & Co KG, Kassel.

—(continued)

Example 2.19—*concluded*

III. The Returning Past

Sounds of the gothic – whether through funereal imagery, or textural doubling and stylistic distortion – resurface in Schubert's F minor Fantasy for four hands, D 940 (1828) – a piece not readily apparent in this context but that nevertheless reveals associations by way of a shared vocabulary.[38] The instances explored here, while

---

[38] For contrasting readings of D 940, see Philip Brett, 'Piano Four-Hands: Schubert and the Performance of Gay Male Desire', *19th-Century Music* 21/2 (1997), 149–76; Wollenberg, *Schubert's Fingerprints*, 19–23; Nicholas Rast, 'Une declaration d'amour en code? La Fantaisie en *fa* mineur D940 de Schubert et la comtesse Caroline Esterházy', *Cahiers Franz Schubert* 13 (1998), 5–16; and Robert Samuels, 'Schubert's Instrumental Voice: Vocality in Melodic Construction in the Late Works', in *On Voice*, ed. Walter Bernhart and Lawrence Kramer (Amsterdam: Rodopi, 2014), 161–78. On Schubert's fantasies, see Jeffrey Perrey, 'The Wanderer's Many Returns: Schubert's Variations Reconsidered', *Journal of Musicology* 19/2 (2002), 374–416; Patrick McCreless, 'A Candidate for the Canon? A New Look at Schubert's Fantasie in C major for Violin and Piano',

78   *The Gothic Imagination in the Music of Franz Schubert*

recalling tropes from the Fantasies in G minor, D 9, and C minor, D 48, to the *Grande Marche Funèbre*, D 859, prompt a reimagining of gothic ideas in Schubert's music as a trajectory that cuts across time, genres, and stylistic boundaries. Worlds converge while also diverging. Compositional approaches discussed thus far are deployed in ways that highlight the widening distance from the soundworlds explored in the previous chapter, particularly that of 'Leichenfantasie'. Just as Schubert's graveyard settings range from encounters with the supernatural to depictions of life beyond death, so the treatment of material in D 940 similarly suggests shifting associations with the gothic. Direct links with death (its funereal rhythms pervasive throughout) combine with implicit doubles and distortions, as in the evocation of the past in the second and fourth movements.

Intertextual dialogues are evident from the outset. In the opening bars, as the main theme undulates against the weighty, march-like tread of the accompaniment, echoes of the funereal theme from the Trio's Andante filter through in its outlining of a perfect fourth, C–F, together with traces of the octave signal from the opening of the C minor Impromptu (Example 2.20). These dialogues are heard also in the theme's malleability, particularly in the octave layering of bars 12–23 (cf. the textural doubling in Examples 2.8–2.10). Here in D 940, as in the Trio and Impromptu, the fluidity between eeriness and disruption becomes more pronounced later in the movement, most markedly at bars 37–65. Those shifts between C minor and A major in 'Totengräbers Heimweh' – life and death representing sides of the same coin – are close to hand (albeit in a different tonal context) as tonic minor gives way to parallel major, in a shift that eclipses the funereal associations still prevalent in the secondo part.[39] The proximity to the minor mode, its presence lingering on an unresolved dominant seventh, is underlined by the emergence of the major-mode incarnation out of silence – without thematic or tonal preparation. The idea of displaced sonorities returning in strange contexts extends in the opposite direction at bar 48, where the theme resurfaces amid a texture of percussive chordal interjections and disjunctive passagework.[40] These transformations imbue the funereal theme with ambiguity – the sound of eeriness

---

19th-Century Music 20 (1997), 205–30; and Su Yin Mak, 'Formal Ambiguity and Generic Reinterpretation in the Late Instrumental Music', in *Schubert's Late Music*, 282–306.

[39] A parallel is seen here with Haydn's F minor Variations, a piece which, in Nancy November's words, juxtaposes a main theme based on a 'pervasive funereal dotted-note motive' in the minor mode with a 'more lyrical, thematically and rhythmically freer theme in the tonic major'. See Nancy November, 'Haydn's Melancholy Voice: Lost Dialectics in his Late Chamber Music and English Songs', *Eighteenth-Century Music* 4/1 (2007), 71–106, at 100.

[40] See William Kinderman, 'Schubert's Piano Music: Probing the Human Condition', in *The Cambridge Companion to Schubert*, ed. Christopher H. Gibbs (Cambridge: Cambridge University Press, 1997), 171, who describes the transformation, 'utterly opposed to the opening theme', as a 'related but more energetic form' of the dactylic pattern of death in 'Der Tod und das Mädchen'.

Example 2.20. Schubert, Fantasy in F minor for four hands, D 940 I, bars 1–8. Franz Schubert. Works for piano duet, volume 3 (BA 9645), editors: Walburga Litschauer, Werner Aderhold. © 2013 Bärenreiter-Verlag Karl Vötterle GmbH & Co KG, Kassel.

and distortion combined, yet capable of giving rise to an alternate reality when its pitches are recast in the major mode, comparable to the contrasting (tonal) faces of the grave in 'Schwestergruss' and 'Totengräbers Heimweh'.

Signs of the gothic in the Largo of Schubert's D 940 are bound up with the treatment of Baroque-inspired styles.[41] Goethe's description of the gothic as 'indefinite, unnatural, smothered with ornament', invoked in relation to Schubert's *Grande Marche Funèbre*, is equally apt here (Example 2.21). The double- and triple-dotted rhythms, bars 121–32, recall the fusion of funeral march and French overture in that earlier duet. The two speak to one another through the distortion of historical styles – now rendered even more disruptive. Dense chordal textures, angular bass lines, frequent pauses, and dynamic extremities conjure the sound of the past as stylistically remote, viscerally present. Further doubling is suggested in bars 149–63 of D 940, II, when the overture style returns *pianissimo* and encrusted with additional trills. This muted return distills the past as a distant shudder – that quality of being familiar yet unfamiliar first encountered in the returns of the funereal theme throughout the E flat Trio.

[41] The writing here encapsulates the imprints of the past surfacing in the *Quartettsatz*, D 703 (1820), there in the form of a descending tetrachord that weaves a contrapuntal texture in tremolo figuration; and through the distorted overture style in the first movement of the String Quartet in G major, D 887 (1826). See Barbara Barry, 'Schubert's *Quartettsatz*: A Case Study in Confrontation', *Musical Times* 155 (2014), 31–49; Su Yin Mak, 'Et in Arcadia Ego: The Elegiac Structure of Schubert's *Quartettsatz* in C Minor (D. 703)', in *The Unknown Schubert*, ed. Barbara M. Reul and Lorraine Byrne Bodley (Farnham: Ashgate, 2008), 145–53; Hali Fieldman, 'Schubert's *Quartettsatz* and Sonata Form's New Way', *Journal of Musicological Research* 12/1–2 (2002), 99–146; and Wollenberg, *Schubert's Fingerprints*, 36–40, 56–57, and 207–8.

Example 2.21. Schubert, Fantasy in F minor for four hands, D 940, II, bars 121–32. Franz Schubert. Works for piano duet, volume 3 (BA 9645), editors: Walburga Litschauer, Werner Aderhold. © 2013 Bärenreiter-Verlag Karl Vötterle GmbH & Co KG, Kassel.

The entwining in the finale of D 940 of fugue and fantasy – the former rooted in ideas of the learned style, the latter foregrounding abrupt twists and turns, with juxtaposition as an underlying premise – offers further ground for hearing doubles and distortions.[42] The conflation of the two recalls the slippages between the improvisatory and the learned central to organ music[43] – from J.S. Bach's Toccata and Fugue in D minor, BWV 565, to Schubert's Fugue in D minor, D 13 (1813), and his Fugue in E minor, D 952 (1828), penned for a performance with Franz Lachner on the organ in Heiligenkreuz. Fugue, a remnant of a bygone era, serves as vessel through which to double material at the level of individual voices, with the contours of the subject and countersubject mirroring one another, and in terms of wider stylistic-historical categories.

The fugal writing in D 940, IV, recalls the weight of the past from the first movement through the return of the opening theme, while also projecting echoes of J.S. Bach's Fugue in F minor from Book I of the *Well-Tempered Clavier*, their pathways intersecting around the shared compass of the perfect fourth (Example 2.22).[44] Ideas of gothic ruins, as in Goethe's description of Strasbourg cathedral, extend from the misshapen French overture style in the slow movement to the disintegration of fugal devices from bar 513 of the finale. The return of the split-octave triplets, a flashback to their disruptive presence in the first movement, shifts the pendulum from the learned style to music that distorts all stylistic references.

---

[42] On Schubert's engagement with Baroque styles, particularly his acquaintance with the music of Bach and Handel through Raphael Kiesewetter's salons, see Walther Dürr, 'Über Schuberts Verhältnis zu Bach', in *Johann Sebastian Bach: Beiträge zur Wirkungsgeschichte* (Vienna: Kongressbericht Wien, 1992), 69–79; Michael Kube, 'Zur Satztechnik in Schuberts Sonate für Klavier, Violine und Violoncello, B-Dur D 28 (Triosatz)', in *Bach und Schubert: Beiträge zur Musikforschung* (Munich: Katzbichler [Jahrbuch der Bachwochen Dill], 1999), 15–22; and Lorraine Byrne Bodley, *Franz Schubert: A Musical Wayfarer* (New Haven: Yale University Press, 2023), chapter 7, esp. the discussion of Pergolesi's and Bach's influence in Schubert's Stabat Mater in F minor, D 383, aria no. 6, 'Ach, was hätten wir empfunden'.

[43] I thank Natasha Loges for this reference to organ music.

[44] See Matthew Dirst, *Engaging Bach: The Keyboard Legacy from Marpurg to Mendelssohn* (Cambridge: Cambridge University Press, 2012), 25.

Example 2.22. Schubert, Fantasy in F minor for fours hands, D 940, IV, bars 474–81. Franz Schubert. Works for piano duet, volume 3 (BA 9645), editors: Walburga Litschauer, Werner Aderhold. © 2013 Bärenreiter-Verlag Karl Vötterle GmbH & Co KG, Kassel.

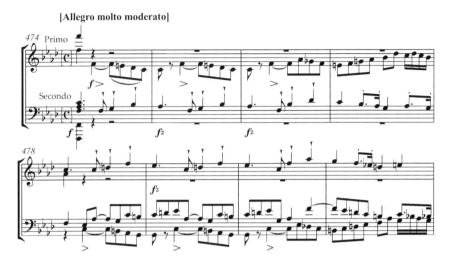

IV. Ambivalent Endings

The gothic prioritizes open-endedness, a blurring of where things begin and close. Sounds undergo change, lingering in curious places. Such is the case in the endings of the pieces discussed here, for they withhold a finite conclusion through held sonorities or traces of the earlier disruptions that reverberate beyond the final bar line.[45]

The coda of the Impromptu, bars 193–204, incorporates these ideas at the level of thematic recall and tonal trajectory (Example 2.23).[46] Its closing bars offer an ambivalent stance on the *ad astra* archetype, defined by its trajectory of darkness to light, or, in Reinhold Brinkmann's words, as 'the resolution of a conflict of ideas through an inner formal process aimed toward a liberating ending – in a nutshell, the "positive" overcoming of a "negative" principle'.[47] Here, major and minor entwine as the tonic minor pivots to the parallel major. These fluctuations parallel those in

---

[45] Further on disturbed endings, see chapter 4, 'Grotesquerie', particularly in relation to the slow movements of Schubert's String Quintet in C major, D 956, and A major Piano Sonata, D 959.

[46] For an alternative reading of the ending, see Fisk, *Returning Cycles*, 133: 'even here, at the end of the impromptu, the major never regains a complete phrase of its own. Instead, it emerges these last times from the minor, like the image of a freedom or fulfilment never achieved, or of a love that can still be born only of pain.'

[47] Reinhold Brinkmann, *Late Idyll: The Second Symphony of Johannes Brahms*, trans. P. Palmer (Cambridge, MA: Harvard University Press, 1995), 34.

Example 2.23. Schubert, Impromptu in C minor, D 899/1, bars 193–204. Franz Schubert. Impromptus op. 90 D 899, op. post. 142 D 935 (BA 9648), editor: Walther Dürr. © 2011 Bärenreiter-Verlag Karl Vötterle GmbH & Co KG, Kassel.

Example 2.5, where the intimation of the relative major in the theme's varied restatement (bars 9–11) is subsequently negated by the return to C minor in bar 17. As the major takes hold, there is a glimpse of a theme never fully realized – a suggestion of 'fragility', through the pared-down texture and gradual dissipation of the funereal rhythms, that was 'evident at the (hesitant) start of the piece'.[48] The piece closes in a space between presence and absence, its echoing chain of cadences commingling with the eeriness heard at the outset.

The abridged return of the main theme in the closing bars of the Trio's Andante, bars 196–212 (Example 2.24), similarly suggests a resistance to closure. Slippages between eeriness and disruption remain until the closing bars – through remnants of the preceding outburst resurfacing in the chromatic bass line of the piano part (bars 204–8) and the rapid scalar flourish redolent of the passagework discussed above. These elements, coupled with the repeated falling octaves in the final three bars, fuse echoes of the funereal theme with its haunting reappearances in the Finale.

Schubert's F minor Fantasy offers a further perspective on ambivalent endings. Out of silence the opening theme returns in bar 556, with its initial contours now increasingly weighed down by the past (Example 2.25). However, the chordal

[48] Quoted from personal correspondence with Susan Wollenberg.

Example 2.24. Schubert, Piano Trio in E flat major, D 929, II, bars 196–212. Franz Schubert. Trio for Piano, Violin and Violincello in E flat major op. 100 D 929 (BA 5610), editor: Arnold Feil. © 1975 Bärenreiter-Verlag Karl Vötterle GmbH & Co KG, Kassel.

Example 2.25. Schubert, Fantasy in F minor for four hands, D 940, IV, bars 556–70. Franz Schubert. Works for piano duet, volume 3 (BA 9645), editors: Walburga Litschauer, Werner Aderhold. © 2013 Bärenreiter-Verlag Karl Vötterle GmbH & Co KG, Kassel.

86   *The Gothic Imagination in the Music of Franz Schubert*

breakthrough in bar 563 – recalling the transformation of the theme in bar 48 of the first movement – throws the music off course moments before the end. Traces of that earlier disruption suffuse this final distortion of the theme, not least through the accented textures and *fortissimo* dynamic marking. The funereal music lingers in the gaps, with the sudden withdrawal from *fffz* to *piano* in the final bar looping back to the muted soundscape of the opening movement.

Beyond Doubles

The case studies of this chapter evade definitive categorization of the intersections between death and the gothic. The shadowy contours of their main themes, particularly in the C minor Impromptu, resonate with the spectral emanations in the graveyard songs of chapter 1, or those in the gothic novels quoted in the Introduction, while pointing beyond the finality of death's traces. As Isabella van Elferen puts it, ghostly sounds 'suggest physical presence but [are] disconnected from it like a phantom doppelgänger of its former self, temporally removed from it and therefore fundamentally out of joint'.[49] Tensions of this kind permeate the Impromptu's opening material, with its juxtaposition of octave unisons and the skeletal theme that follows in their shadows, or the distorted echoes of the unison passages in the *Grande Marche Funèbre*. The reappearance of such material, as happens to the Andante's funereal theme in the E flat Trio, reinforces the idea of displacement, both stylistic and temporal.

One context in which to interpret these distorted returns is that of the uncanny. Pertinent here is Friedrich Schelling's description of 'everything that should remain in secrecy, in concealment, in latency' rising to the surface.[50] Or, as Sigmund Freud later defined it, 'that class of the frightening which leads back to what is known of old and long familiar: it arises when something familiar undergoes repression and returns in a strangely unfamiliar guise'.[51] These definitions are apt to describe the thematic transformations in the Impromptu and the Andante of the Trio – from the recurrent iterations of the dominant and the harsh chordal interjections in Example

---

[49] Isabella van Elferen, *Gothic Music: The Sounds of the Uncanny* (Cardiff: University of Wales Press, 2012), 25.

[50] Quoted in Amanda Lalonde, 'Flowers over the Abyss: A Musical Uncanny in Nineteenth-Century Criticism', *19th-Century Music* 41/2 (2017), 95–120, at 101: 'Unheimlichen nennt man alles, was im Geheimnis, im Verborgnen, in der Latenz bleiben sollte und hervorgetreten ist.' Friedrich Wilhelm Joseph von Schelling, 'Achtundzwanzigste Vorlesung: Qualitativer Unterschied zwischen dem Charakter der griechischen Religion und dem der früheren Religionen', *Philosophie der Mythologie. Erstes Buch: Der Monotheismus*, in *Sämtliche Werke*, vol. II (Stuttgart and Augsburg: J.G. Cotta'scher Verlag, 1857), 649.

[51] Sigmund Freud, 'The "Uncanny"', in *The Standard Edition of the Complete Psychological Works of Sigmund Freud*, ed. J. Strachey (London: Hogarth, 1955), vol. 17: *An Infantile Neurosis and Other Works* [1917–19], 220. On the Freudian uncanny, described as a 'sort of phantom', see Terry Castle, *The Female Thermometer: Eighteenth-Century Culture and the Invention of the Uncanny* (New York: Oxford University Press, 1995), 7.

Doubles and Distortions

2.11 of the former piece, to the repeated tremolos and frenetic textures in Example 2.15 of the latter movement – and outwards to the evocation of a distorted past, bristling with ornate detail, in the Largo of the F minor Fantasy.[52] At the same time, however, these pieces point beyond the uncanny through their continual reconfiguration of musical material. It is 'more than an uncanny repetition', writes Kramer apropos the first return of the funereal theme in the finale of the E flat Trio: 'it is an uncanny repetition of the uncanny'.[53] This kind of multiplicity – with repetitions resisting categorization and sounds displacing one another – provides a connective tissue from the uncanny to the ambivalence of gothic necropoetics.

Mention of uncanniness, readily evoking 'Der Doppelgänger', D 957/13,[54] picks up the thread of gothic and Romantic tropes as interrelated in Schubert's music. The uncanny – at home in the worlds of Schubert's *Schauerballaden* – may be suggested through textual associations between death and the supernatural, or through strange occurrences that emanate from the grave, as in the songs explored in chapter 1. Signs of the gothic in the pieces discussed throughout this chapter intersect with ideas of 'double vision' – of mirrors distorting reality and the imagination – central to Romantic notions of the Doppelgänger.[55] Their soundworlds, whether steeped in a remote past, or twisting the profiles of themes, portray dislocation of the kind encountered as the protagonist in Schubert's 'Der Doppelgänger' sees his double: 'A man stands there too, staring up, / And wringing his hands in anguish; / I shudder when I see his face – / The moon shows me my own form!' ('Da steht auch ein Mensch und starrt in die Höhe, / Und ringt die Hände, vor Schmerzensgewalt; / Mir graust es, wenn ich sein Antlitz sehe, / – / Der Mond zeigt mir meine eigne Gestalt').[56] As in that song, there is less a

---

[52] See also Nicholas Marston, 'Schubert's Homecoming', *Journal of the Royal Musical Association* 125/2 (2000), 248–70; and Michael L. Klein, 'Bloom, Freud, and Riffaterre: Influence and Intertext as Signs of the Uncanny', in *Intertextuality in Western Art Music* (Bloomington: Indiana University Press, 2004), 77–107.

[53] Kramer, *Sexuality, Subjectivity, Song*, 160.

[54] See Benjamin Binder, 'Disability, Self-Critique, and Failure in Schubert's "Der Doppelgänger"', in *Rethinking Schubert*, 418–36; David Ferris, 'Dissociation and Declamation in Schubert's Heine Songs', in *Rethinking Schubert*, 383–403; Richard Kurth, 'Music and Poetry, A Wilderness of Doubles: Heine–Nietzsche–Schubert–Derrida', *19th-Century Music* 21/1 (1997), 3–37; David Code, 'Listening for Schubert's "Doppelgängers"', *Music Theory Online* 1/4 (1995), 218–28; Susan Youens, 'Echoes of the Wounded Self: Schubert's "Ihr Bild"', in *Goethe and Schubert: Across the Divide*, ed. Lorraine Byrne and Dan Farrelly (Dublin: Carysfort Press, 2003), 1–18; Youens, *Heinrich Heine and the Lied* (Cambridge: Cambridge University Press, 2007), 22–34; David Bretherton, 'In Search of Schubert's Doppelgänger', *Musical Times* 144 (2003), 45–50; and Robert Samuels, 'The Double Articulation of Schubert: Reflections on *Der Doppelgänger*', *Musical Quarterly* 93/1 (2010), 192–233.

[55] See Webber, 'Theories and Practices of the *Doppelgänger*', in *The Doppelgänger*, 1–55; and Eran Dorfman, *Double Trouble: The Doppelgänger from Romanticism to Postmodernism* (New York: Routledge, 2021).

[56] Johnson, *The Complete Songs*, Vol. 3, 59.

distinct separation between gothic and Romantic conceptions of doubling than an interconnection characteristic of the Romantic gothic.

The boundaries move in all directions. At times the case studies appear close in spirit to the soundworlds of Schubert's *Schauerballaden,* as in the distorted returns of the main theme in the C minor Impromptu; in other instances, such as the recurring funereal theme in the E flat Trio, they resemble the idea of mirror images, or 'double vision', bound up with Romantic thought. Such thinking complicates ideas of doubling, and of where its traces are located, across all the examples discussed here. In the end, these pieces evoke the gothic in ambivalent terms, for they move beyond literal depictions of death and doubles towards an indeterminate space where musical material takes shape in the destabilizing of fixed foundations – in that 'terrible, hallowed place where we remember what we are'.[57]

[57] Scott Burnham, 'Schubert and the Sound of Memory', *Musical Quarterly* 84/4 (2000), 655–63, at 663.

3
Songs of the Night

Darkness has more Divinity for me;
it strikes Thought inward,
it drives back the Soul
To settle on Herself, our Point supreme!

Life makes the soul dependent on the dust; Death gives her wings to mount about the
spheres.

—Edward Young, *Night Thoughts*[1]

Leben ist der Anfang des Todes. Das Leben ist um des Todes willen.
Life is the beginning of death. Life is there for the sake of death.

—Georg Friedrich Philipp von Hardenberg (Novalis), *Blütenstaub*[2]

Envisioning the Night

Schubert's songs of the night are poised between gothic and Romantic tropes.[3] The gothic looms large in the graveyard settings discussed in chapter 1, notably 'Leichenfantasie', where darkness spotlights spectral presences in the moon's faint rays: 'with dim light the moon shines over the death-still groves; / sighing, the night spirit skims through the air – / mist-clouds lament, pale stars shine down mournfully / like lamps in a vault.' The idea of night revealing things beyond the realm of the living, implied in 'Leichenfantasie' through the 'Nachtgeist', is rendered explicit in the opening stanza of Schubert's 'Die Nacht', D 534, the last of his Ossian settings: 'Night is dull and dark. / The clouds rest on the hills. / No star with green trembling

---

[1] Edward Young, *Night Thoughts on Life, Death and Immortality* [1742–45] (London: Baynes and Son, 1824), III. II. 61–62 and III. I. 470. Further on Young, see the discussion of 'Der Unglückliche', D 713, in this chapter.

[2] Paul Kluckhohn and Richard Samuel (eds), *Novalis Schriften: Die Werke Friedrich von Hardenbergs*, 5 Vols (Stuttgart: W. Kohlhammer, 1983), II, 417.

[3] On these associations, see (among others) Eric Parisot, 'Gothic and Graveyard Poetry: Imagining the Dead (of Night)', in *The Edinburgh Companion to Gothic and the Arts*, ed. David Punter (Edinburgh: Edinburgh University Press, 2019), 245–58; Joseph Crawford, '"Every Night, The Same Routine": Recurring Nightmares and the Repetition Compulsion in Gothic Fiction', *Moveable Type* 6 (2010), 1–9.

beam; / no moon looks from the sky. / I hear the blast in the wood; but I hear it distant far. / The stream of the valley murmurs; but its murmur is sullen and sad.'[4] Such features – distant tremors and sudden blasts of sound – extend to a view of the night as not only revealing but also concealing supernatural beings, as in 'Erlkönig', D 328, where the son experiences the Erlking as all too real, the father dismissing his presence as a 'streak of mist'. Night as a mix of the supernatural and the corporeal is pronounced in the opening stanza of 'Schwestergruss', with traces of the moon's rays but no sound: 'In the moonlight / I wander up and down / Seeing dead bones / And a silent grave.' These songs – distant in chronology, close in spirit – all point to the night as a backdrop to strange happenings brought about by darkness: ghostly presences, funeral processions, and eeriness as sound and silence combined. Death lingers in the shadows – 'It is a ghost! It fades, it flies', to quote from Ossian's 'Die Nacht'.

Night as eerie or tied to the supernatural is counterpointed in the early Romantic imagination with ideas of the night as release from life, associated with rapture or ecstasy, and experiences of unity between self and cosmos.[5] Such thinking, to which Georg Friedrich Philipp von Hardenberg (Novalis) was central,[6] underpins Schubert's setting of his 'Nachthymne', D 687 (1820), where night is lit with fire and death a force of rejuvenation:

Hinüber wall' ich	I shall pass over,
Und jede Pein	And all pain
Wird einst ein Stachel	Will be a stab
Der Wollust sein.	Of pleasure.
[…]	[…]
Unendliches Leben	Eternal life
Wogt mächtig in mir,	Will surge powerfully within me;
Ich schaue von oben	I shall gaze down on you
Herunter nach dir.	From above.
[…]	[…]
Ich fühle des Todes	I feel the rejuvenating
Verjüngender Flut,	Tide of death,
Zu Balsam und Äther	My blood is changed

---

4 See James Porter, *Beyond Fingal's Cave: Ossian in the Musical Imagination* (Rochester, NY: University of Rochester Press, 2019), esp. 123–45; Walther Dürr, 'Schuberts Ossian-Gesänge. Vom Lied zur Szene', in *Schubert: Interpretationen*, ed. Ivana Rentsch and Klaus Pietschmann (Stuttgart: Franz Steiner, 2014), 11–26. Further on Ossian and the gothic, see note 56 in the Introduction of this book.

5 Lisa Feurzeig, *Schubert's Lieder and the Philosophy of Early German Romanticism* (Farnham: Ashgate, 2014).

6 See for example Li Sui Gwee, 'Night in Novalis, Schelling, and Hegel', *Studies in Romanticism* 50/1 (2011), 105–24; and Ricarda Schmidt, 'From Early to Late Romanticism', in *The Cambridge Companion to German Romanticism*, ed. Nicholas Saul (Cambridge: Cambridge University Press, 2009), 21–40.

Verwandelt mein Blut –	To balm and ether.
Ich lebe bei Tage	By day I live
Voll Glauben und Mut,	Full of faith and courage;
Und sterbe die Nächte	At night I die
In heiliger Glut.	In the sacred fire.[7]

The trajectory here – with pain dissolving into pleasure, eternal life surging powerfully within, followed by sleep turning to the rejuvenating tide of death – moves from the nocturnal as a scenic backdrop to the night as a locus for contemplation of inner thoughts and feelings.

Schubert's setting charts this journey tonally and texturally. The piano prelude mixes the semantic weight of pain with the brighter D major tonality and hymnal connotations of its texture. Life surging within binds these contrasts through the return of *schauerlicher* devices: minor-mode tremolando textures – rising up in force and volume – now divorced from earlier associations with the soundscapes of chapter 1 and tinged with the power of death as temporary, life as eternal. The idea of musical devices representing two sides of existence gains further traction when the texture morphs into arpeggiated *pianissimo* triplet figurations, marked by the return to D major, for the depiction of death[8] – a texture that mirrors being uplifted from life's earthly pull as it rises through the upper registers of the piano postlude.

Further examples of song with the power to transfigure death into an experience of harmony and restoration range from Schubert's second setting of his friend Franz von Schober's 'Todesmusik', D 758, to 'Die Nacht', the final song of his *Vier Gesänge* for four-part male voices, D 983/4, with text by Friedrich Adolf Krummacher. Both add contrasting perspectives to the associations of the night that are central to what follows.

Schober's 'Todesmusik', while perhaps not reaching the semantic or metaphysical heights of Novalis's 'Nachthymne', shares with it musical devices that transfigure the protagonist's anguished soul into waves of joy by the close of the poem:

In des Todes Feierstunde,	In the solemn hour of death,
Wenn ich einst von hinnen scheide,	When one day I depart hence
Und den Kampf, den letzten leide,	And suffer my last battle,
Senke, heilige Kamöne,	Then, sacred muse, let your tranquil songs
Noch einmal die stillen Lieder,	And pure tones
Noch einmal die reinen Töne	Descend one more time
Auf die tiefe Abschiedswunde	To heal the deep wound of parting
Meines Busens heilend nieder.	within my heart.
Hebe aus dem ird'schen Ringen	Raise my pure, anguished soul
Die bedrängte reine Seele	From this earthly struggle;

---

[7] Graham Johnson, *Franz Schubert: The Complete Songs*, 3 vols (New Haven and London: Yale University Press, 2014), Vol. 2, 429–30.

[8] Such writing foreshadows the accompaniment of 'Der Lindenbaum', *Winterreise*, D 911/5, where joy and sorrow likewise intermingle in the dead of night ('in tiefer Nacht').

Trage sie auf deinen Schwingen:	Bear it on your wings
Dass sie sich dem Licht vermähle. –	To be united with light. –[9]

A mix of features – tremolo textures, a sudden stripping away of texture, and reconfigurations of triplet rhythms – positions Schubert's 'Todesmusik' between depictions of the night explored at the outset of this chapter and that of his 'Nachthymne'. Textural details capture the contrast between the hour of death bringing about suffering and the pure tones of the sacred music. The opening hymn-like texture recalls that of his 'Nachthymne', while the reduction to bare octaves (doubled in the voice and right hand of the piano part) for the deep wound of parting ('die tiefe Abschiedswunde') looks back to the soundscapes traced in chapter 1. Signs of the latter phenomena, transferred to the piano alone in the three-bar interlude that follows, represent a threshold between parting and the rising of the anguished soul: first as an ascending three-figure pattern echoing (and inverting) the descending 'farewell' motif in Beethoven's Sonata in E flat major, Op. 81a (1809–10), 'Les Adieux', followed by a trilled, turn-like figure in the bass, reminiscent of the murmuring interjections in the Andante of Schubert's A minor Piano Sonata, D 784, discussed in chapter 2. The transformation of pulsating textures similarly feeds into these changing associations of night and death – from the full-texture tremolando passages at the mention of terror ('schrecklichen Minuten'), to the dissolving of repeated chords to triple *piano* over an oscillating drone bass for the transfiguration of perishing in bliss, engulfed by waves of joy ('So in Wonne werd' ich untergehen, Süss verschlungen von der Freude Fluten').

Schubert's 'Die Nacht', D 983/4, smooths over the eeriness of his 'Todesmusik' with music and text in harmony: 'how beautiful are you, friendly stillness, heavenly peace!' ('wie schön bist du, Freundliche Stille, himmlische Ruh!'). Such sentiments, recalling the peacefulness of 'Du bist die Ruh', D 776, or the vanishing world in 'Die Götter Griechenlands', D 677 – 'Schöne Welt, wo bist du?' – are conveyed through a four-part texture, similar in tone to the pianistic figurations of 'Nachthymne' and 'Todesmusik'.[10] Sustained sonorities, interspersed with dactylic rhythms, are ruffled by minor-mode inflections on 'Stille', as if momentarily casting doubt over the nocturnal imagery, without undermining the prevailing mood.

Night, as these songs intimate, reveals experiences beyond the realm of daylight; it listens, and becomes a conduit of unspoken feelings: 'You alone shall know / What rapture overcomes me' ('Dir allein sei mitbewusst, / Welch Vergnügen mich berausche'), to quote from Schubert's setting of Johann Peter Uz's 'Die Nacht', D 358.[11] The

---

9   Johnson, *The Complete Songs*, Vol. 3, 348–49.

10 On Schubert's setting of 'Die Götter Griechenlands', see Su Yin Mak, 'Schubert as Schiller's Sentimental Poet', *Eighteenth-Century Music* 4/2 (2007), 251–63.

11 Johnson, *The Complete Songs*, Vol. 2, 413. On the surface Schubert's setting of 'Die Nacht', D 358, cast in A flat major, sends a gentle radiance through the texture, akin to the vision of ecstasy in Uz's text (penned between 1750 and 1754) – while the turn

Songs of the Night

night's murmurs, whether tranquil or intense, contain within them the power to overwhelm the senses as the oppressions of life intertwine with the sounds of death as joyful or rapturous.[12]

These representations of the night chime with wider philosophical deliberations in the late eighteenth and early nineteenth centuries – at times concerned with concealment, a process of rendering things difficult to discern, in other moments connected to ideas of transfiguration alluded to in the songs discussed above.[13] As Friedrich Schiller observed:

> Darkness is frightful, and for this reason suitable for the sublime. But it is not in itself frightful[;] rather because it conceals [...] objects [...] and therefore hands over to us the full sway of the imaginative power. As soon as the danger is clear, a great part of the fear disappears. The organ of sight, the first guardian of our existence, fails to work for us in the darkness, and we feel ourselves defenselessly exposed to hidden danger. For this reason, superstition places all ghostly phenomena in the midnight hour, and the realm of the dead is conceived as a realm of eternal night.[14]

Several connective threads to gothic necropoetics can be teased out of Schiller's thinking, most markedly in terms of the night, whether ghostly or eternal, as stimulating the realm of imagination.

---

to F minor on the word 'darkness' in bar 3 suggests a literal 'darkening' of the mood together with suggestions of what lies beneath the music's apparent tranquility. The boundaries between life and death, it transpires here and throughout this chapter, are a matter of sharpening or flattening pitches. On modal mixture, see Wollenberg, '"His Favourite Device": Schubert's Major–Minor Nuances', *Schubert's Fingerprints: Studies in the Instrumental Works* (Farnham: Ashgate, 2011), 15–46.

[12] For wider context, see Marjorie W. Hirsch, 'Sleep and Death in Schubert's Lullabies', in *Romantic Lieder and the Search for Lost Paradise* (Cambridge: Cambridge University Press, 2007), 111–39.

[13] Further on musical connections between the night and the sublime, see E.T.A. Hoffmann's review of Beethoven's Fifth Symphony: 'Beethoven's instrumental music unveils before us the realm of the mighty and the immeasurable. Here shining rays of light shoot through the darkness of night, and we become aware of giant shadows swaying back and forth, moving ever closer around us and destroying within us all feeling but the pain of infinite yearning, in which every desire, leaping up in sounds of exultation, sinks back and disappears.' *E.T.A. Hoffmann's Musical Writings: 'Kreisleriana', 'The Poet and the Composer', Music Criticism*, ed. David Charlton, trans. Martyn Clarke (Cambridge: Cambridge University Press, 1989), 238; see also Mark Evan Bonds, *Music as Thought: Listening to the Symphony in the Age of Beethoven* (Princeton, NJ: Princeton University Press, 2006), 44–62; and Abigail Chantler, *E.T.A. Hoffmann's Musical Aesthetics* (Farnham: Ashgate, 2006), 51–78.

[14] Friedrich Schiller, 'Of the Sublime: Towards the Further Realization of Some Kantian Ideas (1793)', trans. in *Fidelio* [The Schiller Institute] 13/1–2 (2004), 90–99, at 98. On Schiller's 'Vom Erhabenen' (published in his periodical *Neue Thalia*, 1793), see 'On the Sublime (Toward the Further Development of Some Kantian Ideas)', in *The Sublime Reader*, ed. Robert R. Clewis (London: Bloomsbury Academic, 2019), 149–61.

A counterpoint to Schiller's conception of the night is found in Novalis's *Hymnen an die Nacht*, a combination of prose and strophic verse, published in 1800.[15] Here, as Jonathan Monroe observes, 'prose, the way the world is, and poetry, the way it might, could or should be, are set against each other.'[16] This approach provides the framework for the night, or death, as an entry into a higher realm (as in his 'Nachthymne') bound up with a reunion with the beloved (in Novalis's case Sophie von Kühn, who died in 1795, one year after their meeting) and with the universe as a whole. Such sentiments come to the fore in the final poem, 'Sehnsucht nach dem Tode', with its portrayal of longing, central to the Romantic imagination, tinged with pain and pleasure (discussed further in what follows): 'Down below, in the shafts of earth, / Far removed from the reach of light, / The rage and wild push of pain / Are the sign of a happy flight' ('Hinunter in der Erde Schooß, / Weg aus des Lichtes Reichen, / Der Schmerzen Wuth und wilder Stoß / Ist froher Abfahrt Zeichen'). The night for Novalis, as conveyed later in the poem, is 'infinite and mysterious': 'Sweet showers through us course – a distant echo of our grief, it seems, / Rings out from an unknown source' ('Unendlich und geheimnißvoll / Durchströmt uns süßer Schauer – / Mir däucht, aus tiefen Fernen scholl / Ein Echo unsrer Trauer').[17]

Depictions of the night find wider contextualization in ideas of the sublime, as defined by Edmund Burke, Immanuel Kant, and Schiller.[18] For Burke, 'pain', 'danger', 'obscurity', and 'whatever is in any sort terrible' were all key ingredients:[19] 'Everyone will be sensible of this', Burke observed, when 'consider[ing] how greatly

---

[15] See Novalis, *Hymnen an die Nacht*, English and German, trans. Dick Higgins (2nd edn, Kingston, NY: McPherson, 1984).

[16] Jonathan Monroe, 'Novalis' *Hymnen an die Nacht* and the Prose Poem *avant la lettre*', in *The Edinburgh Companion to the Prose Poem*, ed. Mary Ann Caws and Michel Delville (Edinburgh: Edinburgh University Press, 2011), 36.

[17] For text and translation by Justin E.H. Smith, see https://www.berfrois.com/2013/11/longing-for-death-novalis/.

[18] See Vijay Mishra, *The Gothic Sublime* (Albany, NY: State University of New York Press, 1994); Andrew Smith, 'The Gothic and the Sublime', in *Gothic Radicalism: Literature, Philosophy, and Psychoanalysis in the Nineteenth Century* (London: Palgrave Macmillan, 2020), 11–37; and David B. Morris, 'Gothic Sublimity', in 'The Sublime and the Beautiful: Reconsiderations', *New Literary History* 16/2 (1985), 299–319.

[19] Edmund Burke, *A Philosophical Enquiry into the Origin of our Ideas of the Sublime and Beautiful* (London: R. and J. Dodsley, 1757), 14. For wider context, see Emily Brady, 'The Romantic Sublime', in *The Sublime in Modern Philosophy: Aesthetics, Ethics, and Nature* (Cambridge: Cambridge University Press, 2013), 24, where she observes that Burke carved out a 'new direction for the sublime as a fully fledged philosophical and psychological study in aesthetics which begins with a strong emphasis on our emotions and the physical effects of the sublime'. See also Frances Ferguson, 'Reflections on Burke, Kant, and Solitude and the Sublime', *European Romantic Review* 23/3 (2012), 316; Ferguson, 'Burke to Kant: A Judgement Outside Comparison', in *Solitude and the Sublime: Romanticism and the Aesthetics of Individuation* (New York: Routledge, 1992), 55–96; and Christine Battersby, *The Sublime: Terror and Human Difference* (New York: Routledge, 2007).

night adds to our dread. In Milton's description of death [in the second book of *Paradise Lost*] all is dark, uncertain, confused, terrible and sublime to the last degree.'[20] These descriptions call up views of the night as dull and dark, or replete with strange sounds and unknown presences, explored in chapter 1.

Further connections are suggested through Kant's framing of the sublime in terms of the 'mathematical' ('that which makes everything seem small in comparison with it') and the 'dynamical' (associated with power or force and the fear of nature).[21] For Kant, a key aspect of the sublime was its capacity to 'elevate powers of [the] soul above their normal state' in service to the 'apparent omnipotence of nature'.[22] Here, too, the night as overwhelming or boundless elicits ideas of the sublime as concealing or rendering things small, an experience simultaneously desirable at a point of remove.

The sublime as alternately full of dread yet enticing, or grounded in the dialectics of pain and pleasure, finds resonance in Schiller's conception of a 'mixed feeling' – of '*woefulness*, which expresses itself in its highest degree as a shudder, and of *joyfulness*, which can rise up to enrapture'. 'We refer it', Schiller continued, 'either to our *power of comprehension*, and succumb in the attempt to form for ourselves an image or a concept of it; or we refer it to our *vital power*, and consider it as a power before which those of ours vanish into nothing.' Central here is the dichotomy of the 'sensuous-infinite', defined by Schiller as the capacity to 'snatch [the] mind away from the narrow sphere of the real and the oppressive imprisonment of physical life'.[23]

Notions of the sublime – of woefulness and joyfulness combined, or of intimations of the sensuous-infinite – provide a pathway between the shifting associations of nocturnal imagery and the gothic imagination.[24] The sounds of the night are inter-

---

[20] Burke, *A Philosophical Enquiry*, 44.

[21] See Immanuel Kant, 'Analytic of the Sublime' [1790], in *Kritik der Urteilskraft*, ed. Gerhard Lehmann (Stuttgart, 1966), Part 1, Book 2; trans. in James Day and Peter Le Huray (eds), *Music and Aesthetics in the Eighteenth and Early Nineteenth Centuries* (Cambridge: Cambridge University Press, 1981), 223–30.

[22] Kant, quoted in *Music and Aesthetics*, 224–25.

[23] Quoted excerpts are drawn from Schiller's later essay, 'Concerning the Sublime' ('Über das Erhabene'), 1801, briefer than the earlier version and less overtly Kantian. Trans. William F. Wertz, Jr, *The Schiller Institute*, https://archive.schillerinstitute.com/transl/trans_on_sublime.html.

[24] On Schubert and the sublime, see Davies, 'Interpreting the Expressive Worlds of Schubert's Late Instrumental Works' (DPhil dissertation, University of Oxford, 2018), chapter 3, '"Too Vast and Significant, Too Strange and Wonderful": The Poetics of the Schubertian Sublime'; Marjorie Hirsch, 'Schubert's Reconciliation of Gothic and Classical Influences', in *Schubert's Late Music*, 170; Michael Spitzer, 'Mapping the Human Heart: A Holistic Analysis of Fear in Schubert', *Music Analysis* 29/1–3 (2010), 149–213; Lorraine Byrne Bodley, *Franz Schubert: A Musical Wayfarer* (New Haven: Yale University Press, 2023), esp. 381–91, 446–48, and 466; and Leo Black, *Franz Schubert: Music and Belief* (Woodbridge: Boydell & Brewer, 2003), 114–47. See also Sarah Hibberd and Miranda Stanyon (eds), *Music and the Sonorous Sublime in European Culture, 1680–1880* (Cambridge: Cambridge University Press, 2020); Stephen Downes, 'Beautiful

96 *The Gothic Imagination in the Music of Franz Schubert*

woven with tropes explored throughout the book, particularly graveyard imagery, while forming a category of the gothic that encompasses Romantic tropes of wandering and longing. The approach adopted here, building on that of chapter 1, moves between poetic imagery (how the night is depicted through words) and musical features (how it is rendered through stylistic vocabulary). Text and music are at times mutually reinforcing, while in other instances conveying disjuncture between textual portrayals of the night and their musical manifestations.

The Nocturnal Sublime

I. Eternal Sleep

Schubert's setting of Johann Mayrhofer's 'Nachtstück', D 672 (1825),[25] summons the worlds of the Romantic wanderer, combined with the sound of the gothic:[26]

Wenn über Berge sich der Nebel breitet,	When the mists spread over the mountains,
Und Luna mit Gewölken kämpft,	And the moon battles with the clouds,
So nimmt der Alte seine Harfe, und schreitet,	The old man takes his harp, and walks
Und singt waldeinwärts und gedämpft:	Towards the wood, singing in muffled tones:
'Du heilge Nacht!	'Holy night,
Bald ist's vollbracht.	Soon it will be done.
Bald schlaf ich ihn	Soon I shall sleep
Den langen Schlummer,	The long sleep
Der mich erlöst	Which will free me
Von allem Kummer.'	From all the grief.'
Die grünne Bäume rauschen dann,	Then the green trees rustle:
'Schlaf süss, du guter, alter Mann';	'Sleep sweetly, good old man';
Die Gräser lispeln wankend fort,	And the swaying grasses whisper:
'Wir decken seinen Ruheort';	'We shall cover his resting place'.

---

and Sublime', in *Aesthetics of Music: Musicological Perspectives*, ed. Downes (New York: Routledge, 2014), 84–110; and Keith Chapin, 'Sublime Experience and Ironic Action: E.T.A. Hoffmann and the Use of Music for Life', in *Musical Meaning and Human Values*, ed. Chapin and Lawrence Kramer (New York: Fordham University Press, 2009), 32–58.

[25] On Schubert and Mayrhofer, see Blake Howe, 'The Allure of Dissolution: Bodies, Forces, and Cyclicity in Schubert's Final Mayrhofer Settings', *Journal of the American Musicological Society* 62/2 (2009), 271–322; and Susan Youens, 'Chromatic Melancholy: Johann Mayrhofer and Schubert', in *Schubert's Poets and the Making of Lieder* (Cambridge: Cambridge University Press, 1996), 151–227.

[26] On Schubert's wanderer settings, see Lorraine Byrne Bodley, 'In Pursuit of a Single Flame? On Schubert's Settings of Goethe's Poems', *Nineteenth-Century Music Review* 13/2 (2016), 11–33; Byrne Bodley, 'Music of the Orphaned Self? Schubert and Concepts of Late Style', in *Schubert's Late Music*, 331–56; Lauri Suurpää, *Death in Winterreise: Music-Poetic Associations in Schubert's Song Cycle* (Bloomington: Indiana University Press, 2014); and Susan Youens, *Retracing a Winter's Journey: Schubert's 'Winterreise'* (Ithaca, NY: Cornell University Press, 1991).

Und mancher liebe Vogel ruft:	And many a sweet bird calls:
'O last ihn ruhn in Rasengruft!'	'Let him rest in his grassy grave!'
Der Alte horcht, der Alte schweigt –	The old man listens, the old man is silent.
Der Tod hat sich zu ihm geneigt.	Death has inclined towards him.[27]

The moonlit landscape of Schubert's second setting of Ludwig Christoph Heinrich Hölty's 'An den Mond', D 193, shines through in the shadows here, especially as depicted in the final stanza: 'Then, beloved moon, take your veil once more / And mourn for your friend. / Weep down through the hazy clouds, / as I, forsaken, weep' ('Dann, lieber Mond, dann nimm den / Schleier wieder, / Und traur um deinen Freund, / Und weine durch den Wolkenflor hernieder, / Wie dein Verlassner weint!').[28] Traces of Schubert's setting of Georg Schmidt von Lübeck's 'Der Wanderer', D 489, similarly suffuse this landscape, its tonality (C sharp) only a semitonal inflection from that of the later song (C minor). The image of the protagonist wandering silent and joyless ('still, bin wenig froh'), his sighs forever asking where – 'wo?' – finds a companion in the wanderer who walks towards the woods in 'Nachtstück', singing in muffled tones. References to Schubert's wanderers look both back and forward, with their promise of sweet, long sleep foreshadowing the peace that beckons in his setting of Goethe's 'Wanderers Nachtlied II', D 768: 'Wait, soon you will rest too' ('Warte nur, balde ruhest du auch').[29]

Mayrhofer's setting of 'Nachtstück' extends outward from these associations with Schubert's wanderer settings to the themes of Caspar David Friedrich's 'Abbey in an Oak Forest', Figure 0.1, discussed in the Introduction.[30] Darkness illuminates

---

[27] Johnson, *The Complete Songs*, Vol. 2, 435–36.

[28] Johnson, *The Complete Songs*, Vol. 1, 147. In D 193 as the protagonist addresses the beloved moon ('lieber Mond'), subtle shifts between fantasies and dream-like images ('Phantasien und Traumgestalten') are depicted musically through modal mixture. The opening cast in F minor, with the triplet accompaniment recalling that of Beethoven's 'Moonlight' Sonata in C sharp minor, Op. 27, No. 2, gives way to the relative (A flat) major as the text slips into dreams and reflections on the past. In Schubert's setting of Goethe's 'An den Mond', D 259, the moon's glow similarly offers solace as the protagonist contemplates the dialectics of joy and sorrow: 'Once more you silently fill wood and vale / with your hazy gleam / and at last set my soul quite free' (stanza 1); 'My heart feels every echo / of times both glad and gloomy. / I hover between joy and sorrow / in my solitude' ('Füllest wieder Busch und Tal / Still mit Nebelglanz, / Lösest endlich auch einmal / Meine Seele ganz. / Jeden Nachklang fühlt mein Herz / Froh- und trüber Zeit, / Wandle zwischen Freud und Schmerz / In der Einsamkeit'). See Lorraine Byrne Bodley, *Schubert's Goethe Settings* (Farnham: Ashgate, 2003).

[29] See Byrne Bodley, 'In Pursuit of a Single Flame?'.

[30] On references to Schubert and Caspar David Friedrich, see Scott Burnham, 'Thresholds Between, Worlds Apart', in 'Schubert's String Quintet in C major, D. 956', ed. William Drabkin, special issue, *Music Analysis* 33/2 (2014), 156–67, at 156, where he detects an

signs of death in both song and painting. The mists spreading over the mountains are close in ethos to Friedrich's blurring of day and night as the procession carries the coffin towards the derelict abbey. Traces of human presence blend into the nocturnal backdrop – sounds emanate from afar, with the promise of death slipping in and out of focus.

Despite these intertextual dialogues, or the kinship of Schubert's first setting of 'Nachtstück' to 'Der Wanderer' through their shared key of C sharp minor, his second setting, published as Op. 36, No. 2 in 1825, is closer in spirit to his graveyard settings discussed in chapter 1 (Example 3.1).[31] The sound of a distorted past filters through the descending bass lines, imbued with echoes of earlier usages, as in 'Hagars Klage', D 5 (1811), and dotted rhythms that slip between French overture and funeral march (cf. those discussed in chapter 2). Past and future coalesce as the semiquaver shudders pre-empt the acciaccatura figures in 'Der Leiermann', D 911/24, with which 'Nachtstück' shares the figure of a wanderer seeking death. Night weighs down heavier through the repetition of this material in the lower regions of the piano as the singer enters: 'when the mists spread over the mountains / And the moon battles with the clouds' ('Wenn über Berge sich der Nebel breitet, / Und Luna mit Gewölken kämpft'). Further distortions, sounds that are both full and devoid of life, are heard as 'the old man takes his harp, and walks / towards the wood, singing in muffled tones' ('So nimmt der Alte seine Harfe, und schreitet, / Und singt waldeinwärts und gedämpft'); the walking bass line, reduced to single pitches in bars 11–12, pre-empts the music to the words 'by all forsaken, kin to death alone' in 'Totengräbers Heimweh'. There is inclination towards death, without confirmation of what lies beyond.

In contrast to the opening material, the music of the 'holy night' ('heilge Nacht') brings forth the 'sensuous-infinite' divide that Schiller located as a source of the sublime (Example 3.2). The meanings of sleep are thrown into doubt here: 'Soon it will be done. / Soon I shall sleep / the long sleep / which will free me / from all the grief' ('Bald ist's vollbracht. / Bald schlaf' ich ihn / Der mich erlöst / Von allem Kummer').[32] This imagery, mirroring the mixture of joy and grief ('Lust und Schmerz') in 'Du bist die Ruh', D 776, awakens the night as a release from life, temporarily (during sleep) and permanently (in death). Past joy turns to escaping the grief of daily life, of seeking pleasure in what lies beyond the realm of the living. The spectrum between 'succumbing' to and 'vanishing into nothing', to draw on

---

affinity between the opening of D 956, II, and *The Monk by the Sea*; and Edward Michael Hafer, 'The Wanderer Archetype in the Music of Franz Schubert and the Paintings of Caspar David Friedrich' (PhD dissertation, University of Illinois, 2006).

[31] On the two settings, see Johnson, *The Complete Songs*, Vol. 2, 435–39.

[32] On the transience of Schubertian surfaces, see Brian Black, 'The Sensuous as a Constructive Force in Schubert's Late Works', in *Rethinking Schubert*, 77–108; and Scott Burnham, 'Beethoven, Schubert and the Movement of Phenomena', in *Schubert's Late Music*, 35–51.

Example 3.1. Schubert, 'Nachtstück', D 672, bars 1–10.
Franz Schubert. *Lieder*, volume 2, high voice (BA 9102), editor: Walther Dürr.
© 2006 Bärenreiter-Verlag Karl Vötterle GmbH & Co KG, Kassel.

Example 3.2. Schubert, 'Nachtstück', D 672, bars 17–29.
Franz Schubert. *Lieder*, volume 2, high voice (BA 9102), editor: Walther Dürr.
© 2006 Bärenreiter-Verlag Karl Vötterle GmbH & Co KG, Kassel.

—(continued)

Example 3.2—concluded

Schillerian imagery, tilts towards the latter as the music of sleep eclipses that of the opening section. Continuous semiquavers flowing through the accompaniment portray sound as ephemeral, while the sustained vocal line possesses expansiveness of the kind associated with the sublime. The widening registral gulf between voice and piano contributes further to the portrayal of the sublime as that which envelops and vanishes in the gaps between sleep and death.

Schubert's 'Nachtstück' captures in microcosm the fusion of gothic and Romantic elements that runs through his nocturnal settings. Its poetic imagery of a wanderer seeking release from life, underscored by night's promise offering (eternal) sleep, elides with a musical vocabulary that looks to the past through its stylistic references and textural configurations, while at the same time projecting the associations between the night and the sublime central to Schillerian poetics. The two worlds collide in the depiction of the holy night as a source of release, shrouded in muted textures in the piano accompaniment. This mixing of Romantic tropes with the soundworlds of Schubert's earlier graveyard settings, the one inseparable from the other, forms a central thread across this chapter's case studies. The pendulum tilts in all directions – leaning further to the past in some instances, while in others juxtaposing or dissolving the boundaries between the gothic and Romantic facets of the night.

II. The Enigmas of Night

Where Schubert's 'Nachtstück' combines the gothic with imagery of the Romantic wanderer, his setting of Franz Grillparzer's 'Bertas Lied in der Nacht', D 653 (1819), conjures the night in contradictory terms – seemingly peaceful, but ambiguous as to what sleep represents musically and textually:

Nacht umhüllt	With fluttering wings
Mit wehendem Flügel	Night envelops
Täler und Hügel	Valley and hill,
Ladend zur Ruh'.	Bidding them rest.

Und dem Schlummer	And to sleep,
Dem lieblichen Kinde,	That sweet child,
Leise und linde	She whispers
Flüstert sie zu:	Softly and gently:
'Weisst du ein Auge,	'If you know of an eye
Wachend im Kummer,	That stays awake, grieving,
Lieblicher Schlummer,	sweet Sleep,
Drücke mir's zu!'	Close it for me!'
Fühlst du sein Nahen?	Do you feel him draw near?
Ahnest du Ruh?	Do you have a presentiment of peace?
Alles deckt der Schlummer,	Sleep makes all things well;
Schlumm're du, schlumm're auch du.	Then sleep also.[33]

At first glance, the text of 'Bertas Lied' recalls that of Schubert's earlier songs of the night, particularly his setting of Goethe's 'Nachtgesang', D 119 (1814). Both depict sleep as consoling – encapsulated in the opening stanza of D 119: 'O lend, from your soft pillow, / Dreaming, but half an ear! / To the music of my strings / Sleep! What more do you desire?' ('O gib, vom weichen Pfühle, / Träumend, ein halb Gehör! / Bei meinem Saitenspiele / Schlafe! was willst du mehr?').[34] And both indulge muted senses – 'an eye' in 'Bertas Lied', 'half an ear' in 'Nachtgesang'. The night renders things hazy to see, difficult to hear, while all too clear, as intimated in the penultimate stanza of D 119: 'you spellbind me to this coolness' ('Bannst mich in diese Kühle').[35] Parallels emerge also between 'Bertas Lied' and Schubert's setting of Ludwig Kosegarten's 'Nachtgesang', D 314 (c.1816), both revolving around the power of the night to 'envelop every being' ('Umsäuselt alles Sein!'). Their resonances extend to the slippages between the real and the beautiful dream ('deinem schönsten Traum') in D 314, the promise of 'golden slumber' ('Goldner Schlummer') and 'ineffable peace' ('namenloser Friede'), tinged with 'wakeful sorrow' ('Wacher Kummer').[36]

Despite these intertextual connections, 'Bertas Lied' stands apart from those earlier songs through its distortion of nocturnal imagery. Mention of the 'soft pillow' is replaced by the valley and hill, a foreboding landscape that engulfs inner consciousness. The emphasis on 'an eye that stays awake, grieving', with its implications of seeing things that are visible only at night, throws into sharp relief the image of sleep as comforting. The rhetorical questions in the final stanza introduce further

---

[33] Johnson, *The Complete Songs*, Vol. 1, 297.

[34] Johnson, *The Complete Songs*, Vol. 2, 423.

[35] Johnson, *The Complete Songs*, Vol. 2, 423.

[36] Johnson, *The Complete Songs*, Vol. 2, 425.

ambiguity. Sleep draws nearer, making 'all things well', without clear indication of its meanings or implications.

One context in which to ponder the enigmas of 'Bertas Lied in der Nacht', Susan Youens proposes, is that of Franz Seraphicus Grillparzer's drama *Die Ahnfrau* (The Ancestress), premiered on 31 January 1817 at the Theater an der Wien, a year prior to the publication of 'Bertas Lied', first in the literary periodical *Janus*, followed by the setting from 1819 under discussion here.[37] Connections, Youens suggests, stem from the song's incorporation of the drama's 'most singular features – doublings of many kinds, unnatural relationships, the relentless unfolding of deterministic Fate, things that appear/sound the same and yet are not the same, the living and the dead inhabiting the same stage – into the architecture of the music he composed to words taken from outside the play'.[38] Music, Youens continues, 'is the medium to tell of wordless but very real presence'.[39] These features speak less to the night as offering transfiguration or release, as in the Romantic conception, than as a backdrop for distortions and strange happenings central to the gothic as it developed across the eighteenth century.

Mention of the sweet child in stanza 2 brings further gothic references into the fold, namely of death and the supernatural, as depicted by Goethe in 'Erlkönig', D 328 (1815), and Matthias Claudius in 'Der Tod und das Mädchen', D 531 (1817). The pairing of the 'sweet child' and sleep's gentle utterances recalls (albeit in a contrasting nocturnal setting) the Erlking luring the boy into the realm of nightly dances, with the promise of his daughters singing him to sleep.[40] The voice of death in 'Der Tod und das Mädchen' similarly comes to mind: 'Give me your hand, you lovely, tender creature. / I am your friend, and come not to chastise. / Be of good courage, I am not cruel; / you shall sleep softly in my arms' ('Gib deine Hand, du schön und zart Gebild! / Bin Freund und komme nicht zu strafen. / Sei gutes Muts! Ich bin nicht wild, / Sollst sanft in meinen Armen schlafen!').[41]

The shifting associations of nocturnal imagery in Schubert's songs can be gleaned through a comparison of 'Bertas Lied in der Nacht' with his settings of Goethe's 'Nachtgesang', D 119 (1814), and Ludwig Kosegarten's 'Nachtgesang', D 314 (first setting 1815, the second *c.*1816). His setting of Goethe in D 119, cast in A flat major, foregrounds the unreal aspects of sleep through slippages between the topos of a

---

[37] Susan Youens, 'Fate, Doubling, and Displacement in a Schubert Song: "Bertha's Lied in der Nacht", D. 653' (forthcoming). I am grateful to Professor Youens for sharing a copy prior to publication.

[38] Youens, 'Fate, Doubling, and Displacement'.

[39] Youens, 'Fate, Doubling, and Displacement'.

[40] 'Willst, feiner Knabe, du mit mir gehn? / Meine Töchter sollen dich warten schön; / Meine Töchter führen den nächtlichen Reihn /Und wiegen und tanzen und singen dich ein'. Johnson, *The Complete Songs*, Vol. 1, 518.

[41] Johnson, *The Complete Songs*, Vol. 3, 343. See Christoph Wolff, 'Schubert's "Der Tod und das Mädchen": Analytical and Explanatory Notes on the Song D 531 and the Quartet D 810', in *Schubert Studies: Problems of Style and Chronology*, ed. Eva Badura-Skoda and Peter Branscombe (Cambridge: Cambridge University Press, 1982), 143–71.

lullaby and a dreamworld. The rising, turn-like figure and dotted rhythms in the vocal line (bars 1–3) suggest an affinity here with the night spirits in 'Geistertanz', D 116. In Schubert's second setting of Kosegarten's 'Nachtgesang', by contrast, the night slips from the lulling qualities of D 119, now with a weightier piano texture, to the eeriness of bars 9–12, reduced to bare octaves for the words 'dim and dull and weary / this life slumbers, and indescribable peace rustles around all beings.' Peacefulness gives way to a foreshadowing of the writing in 'Bertas Lied in der Nacht'.

Nothing about Schubert's approach to 'Bertas Lied' suggests that night is comforting, or at least not audibly so. Its opening bar, replete with octave unisons, turn-like figures, double- and triple-dotted rhythms, strikes a tone akin to depictions of the grave discussed in chapter 1 (Example 3.3). Night as that which both flutters and envelops is captured in the filling in of registral space as the piano part ascends via a chain of semitones, a 'warped scalewise crawl', their rhythmic profile (four semi-quavers) injecting restlessness at odds with the gravity of the overture style of beat 1.[42] Traces of a lullaby style (implied by the title and text) are distorted through the doubling of pitches, sounds splitting into multiple layers through bars 3–8 as the piano mirrors the chant-like vocal line. The music rises and falls, its tonal destination unknown, despite the pausing on G flat major in bars 7–8 for the depiction of rest.

The fusion of woefulness (expressed as a shudder) and joyfulness (rising to rapture) at the heart of the Schillerian sublime can be sensed in stanzas 2 and 3 of 'Bertas Lied' through a disjuncture between music and text (Example 3.4). Schubert's setting of Grillparzer's ostensibly peaceful call to sleep – 'and to sleep / that sweet child, / she whispers / softly and gently' ('Und dem Schlummer / Dem lieblichen Kinde, / Leise und linde / Flüstert sie zu') – sends a shudder through the texture with a modulation to C sharp major and tolling octaves that foreshadow the music of Sybilla's spirit in 'Schwestergruss' (cf. Example 1.8). These slippages from minor to major, central to the gothic soundworlds explored here, create disjuncture between what is audible and that which lies beneath the semantics of the night. Sleep and death converge in a way that unsettles the promise of peacefulness. The quietude of night fluctuates between dread (recalling the spectres of death in 'Erlkönig' and 'Der Tod und das Mädchen') and an illusory reality, hinted at but never confirmed.

The apparent peacefulness of the final two stanzas, marked triple *piano* for the words 'sleep makes all things well; / Then sleep also' ('Alles deckt der Schlummer, / Schlumm're du, schlumm're auch du'), is disturbed at a deeper level through the compression of funereal rhythms and French overture style in the vocal line. So, too, is the piano accompaniment, with its lulling outer voices unsettled by the iterations of a short–long–short pattern in the inner voices. This reversal of rhythmic emphasis from the dactylic vocal line creates further dissonance with the image of sleep as 'making all things well'.

---

[42] Youens, 'Fate, Doubling, and Displacement'.

Example 3.3 Schubert, 'Bertas Lied in der Nacht', D 653, bars 1–8.
Franz Schubert. *Lieder*, volume 12 (BA 5543), editor: Walther Dürr.
© 1996 Bärenreiter-Verlag Karl Vötterle GmbH & Co KG, Kassel.

Example 3.4. Schubert, 'Bertas Lied in der Nacht', D 653, bars 8–15.
Franz Schubert. *Lieder*, volume 12 (BA 5543), editor: Walther Dürr.
© 1996 Bärenreiter-Verlag Karl Vötterle GmbH & Co KG, Kassel.

Songs of the Night 107

Schubert's setting reinforces the textual enigmas of 'Bertas Lied' through an approach of the past, its stylistic idiom harking back to the Baroque, while being strangely prescient, with its nascent traces of the tolling octaves in 'Schwestergruss'. The idea of night as that which flutters, enveloping valley and hill, collides with the awe-inspiring power of nature as a source of the sublime noted by Burke, Kant, and Schiller. At a musical level, sounds of the sublime blend with the panoply of devices associated with the life–death duality in Schubert's graveyard songs. Eerie sonorities in the depths of the piano, infused with chromatic meandering, then doubled in the vocal line, convey, as in those earlier songs, the fear-inducing side of music that is barely audible, its tonal and style references inferred through association rather than firmly established. The night in this song falls between the depictions at the outset of this chapter – from the dull and dark, to the visionary or restorative. Associations with the gothic lie in those moments where ideas are doubly distorted through text and sound – implied, concealed, ambivalent in all contexts.

III. Pain and Pleasure Combined

The final case study here, Schubert's second setting of Caroline Pichler's 'Der Unglückliche', D 713 (1821),[43] foregrounds the gothic within a nexus of longing, isolation, *Sehnsucht* and *Einsamkeit*,[44] those perennial preoccupations among the Romantics, and pain and pleasure combined.[45] Pichler's poem (1801–2), form-

---

[43] For details of Schubert's first setting of Pichler's text, titled 'Die Nacht' / 'Der Unglückliche I' (H 463), see Johnson, *The Complete Songs*, Vol. 2, 410–11.

[44] On Schubert and *Einsamkeit*, see Susan Youens, 'The "Problem of Solitude" and Critique in Song: Schubert's Loneliness', in *Schubert's Late Music*, 309–30; and Youens, 'A Gauntlet Thrown: Schubert's "Einsamkeit", D 620, and Beethoven's *An die ferne Geliebte*', in *Rethinking Schubert*, 456–84. On Schubert and *Sehnsucht*, see Lauri Suurpää, 'Longing for the Unattainable: The Second Movement of the "Great" C major Symphony', in *Schubert's Late Music*, 219–40; and Barbara Barry, '"Sehnsucht" and Melancholy: Explorations of Time and Structure in Schubert's *Winterreise*', in *The Philosopher's Stone: Essays in the Transformation of Musical Structure* (Hillsdale, NY: Pendragon Press, 2000), 181–202. For wider reference, see Frances Ferguson, *Solitude and the Sublime* (London: Routledge, 1992); and Kiene Wurth, 'Sehnsucht, Music, and the Sublime', in *Musically Sublime: Indeterminacy, Infinity, Irresolvability* (New York: Fordham University Press, 2009), 47–71.

[45] Schubert's evocation of the dialectics of pain and pleasure can be gleaned from his writings, among them an entry in his notebook dated 25 March 1824: 'pain sharpens the understanding and strengthens the mind, whereas joy seldom troubles about the former and softens the latter or makes it frivolous.' Quoted in Otto Erich Deutsch, *Schubert: A Documentary Biography*, trans. Eric Blom (London: J.M. Dent & Sons, 1947), 336. He expressed similar sentiments in 'Mein Traum': 'For many a year I sang songs. Whenever I attempted to sing of love, it turned to pain. And again, when I tried to sing of pain, it turned to love' ('Lieder sang ich nun lange lange Jahre. Wollte ich Liebe singen, ward sie mir zum Schmerz. Und wollte ich wieder Schmerz nur singen, war er mir zur Liebe'). Quoted in Deutsch, *A Documentary Biography*, 226–28. See also Schubert's letter to his friend Franz von Schober (21 September 1824): 'And what ever should we do with happiness, misery being the only stimulant left to us? If only we were together, you, Schwind, Kuppel [Kuppelwieser] and I, and misfortune would seem to be but a light matter; but here we are, separated, each in a different corner, and that is

ing part of her novella *Olivier* (1803), tells of the 'unfortunate one' who has yet to recover from the untimely loss of a beloved.[46] These reflections on lost happiness unfold against the pleasures derived from nocturnal contemplation.

Worlds collide here with Schillerian imagery – depths of grief, sorrows, sweet delight – and the spirit of Edward Young's *Night Thoughts*, quoted in the epigraph above, of contemplating a world beyond death that exists only within the mind:[47]

Die Nacht bricht an, mit leisen Lüften sinket	Night falls, descending with light breezes
Sie auf die müden Sterblichen herab.	Upon weary mortals.
Der sanfte Schlaf, des Todes Bruder, winket,	Gentle sleep, death's brother, beckons,
Und legt sie freundlich in ihr täglich Grab.	And lays them fondly in their daily graves.
Jetzt wachet auf der lichtberaubten Erde	Now only malice and pain
Vielleicht nur noch die Arglist und der Schmerz,	Perchance watch over the earth, robbed of light;
Und jetzt, da ich durch nichts gestöret werde,	And now, since nothing may disturb me,
Lass deine Wunden bluten, armes Herz!	Let your wounds bleed, poor heart.
Versenke dich in deines Kummers Tiefen,	Plunge to the depths of your grief,
Und wenn vielleicht in der zerrissnen Brust	And if perchance half-forgotten sorrows
Halb verjährte Leiden schliefen,	Have slept in your anguished heart,
So wecke sie mit grausam süsser Lust!	Awaken them with cruelly sweet delight!
Berechne die verlornen Seligkeiten,	Consider your lost happiness,
Zähl' alle, alle Blumen in dem Paradies,	Count all the flowers in paradise,
Woraus in deiner Jugend goldnen Zeiten	From which, in the golden days of your youth,

---

what makes my wretchedness. I want to exclaim with Goethe: "Who will bring me back just an hour of that sweet time!" ["Ach! Wer bringt nur eine Stunde jener holden Zeit zurück!"] That time when we sat so snugly together and each disclosed the children of his art to the others with motherly shyness, not without dread expecting the judgment to be pronounced by affection and truth; that time when one inspired the other and thus united striving after the highest beauty enlivened us all.' Quoted in Deutsch, *A Documentary Biography*, 363.

46 For context on Pichler (1769–1843), see Ritchie Robertson, 'The Complexities of Caroline Pichler: *Die Schweden in Prag* (1827)', in *Enlightenment and Religion in German and Austrian Literature* (Barnsley: Legenda, 2018), 251–62; and Susanne Kord, '"Und drinnen waltet die züchtige Hausfrau?" Caroline Pichler's Fictional Auto/Biographies', *Women in German Yearbook* 8 (1992), 141–58.

47 On these associations and Schubert's connection with Pichler, see Susan Youens, '"Der Mensch ist zur Geselligkeit geboren": Salon Culture, Night Thoughts and a Schubert Song', in *Musical Salon Culture in the Long Nineteenth Century*, ed. Anja Bunzel and Natasha Loges (Woodbridge: Boydell & Brewer, 2019), 167–84. On Pichler's engagement with Young, see Caroline Pichler, *Denkwürdigkeiten aus meinem Leben*, ed. E.K. Blümml (Munich: Georg Müller, 1914, orig. pub. Vienna: A. Pichlers Witwe, 1844), 129; and J. Barnstorff, *Youngs Nachtgedanken und ihr Einfluss auf die deutsche Litteratur* (Bamberg, 1895).

Die harte Hand des Schicksals dich verstiess!	The harsh hand of fate banished you!
Du hast geliebt, du hast das Glück empfunden,	You have loved, you have experienced a happiness
Dem jede Seligkeit der Erde weicht.	Which eclipses all earthly bliss.
Du hast ein Herz, das dich verstand, gefunden,	You have found a heart that understands you,
Der kühnsten Hoffnung schönes Ziel erreicht.	Your wildest hopes have attained their fair goal.
Da stürzte dich ein grausam Machtwort nieder,	Then the cruel decree of authority dashed you down
Aus deinen Himmeln nieder, und dein stilles Glück,	From your heaven, and your tranquil happiness,
Dein allzuschönes Traumbild kehrte wieder	Your all-too-lovely dream vision, returned
Zur besser'n Welt, aus der es kam, zurück.	To the better world from which it came.
Zerrissen sind nun alle süssen Bande,	Now all the sweet bonds are torn asunder;
Mir schlägt kein Herz mehr auf der weiten Welt!	no heart now beats for me in the whole world![48]

Night, death, sleep, and loss form a strange amalgam of ideas in Pichler's poem. The imagery of stanza 1 – with night descending through light breezes – recalls the cool breezes and gentle darkness of 'Die Nacht', D 358. The 'mother of gentle darkness' in that earlier setting finds a counterpart here in the depiction of 'gentle sleep' as 'death's brother'. Yet as early as line 2 the nightly breezes are weighed down by 'weary mortals', and two lines later by the 'daily graves'. This text, it transpires, is anything but a peaceful meditation on the night. The tensions between the eerie and the joyful (encapsulated by the last line of the opening stanza) represent a shifting spectrum throughout the poem. In stanza 2, night robs the earth of light, an image far removed from its promise of sleep in 'Bertas Lied' and 'Nachtstück', followed by the plunging into the depths of grief in stanza 3: 'awaken the [half-forgotten sorrows] with cruelly sweet delight' ('So wecke sie mit grausam süsser Lust'). In stanzas 4–6, night becomes the conduit for loss literal and figurative, tied up not only with past love and happiness, but also with the cruel hand of fate that has rendered hope an impossibility. The closing imagery – with hearts no longer beating, sweet bonds torn asunder – leads to the realization that night and solitude, *Einsamkeit*, are one and the same.

The contrasting faces of night in stanza 1, its gentle breezes weighed down by weary souls, are seen through music similar in ethos to Schubert's 'Grablied für die Mutter', D 616, with which it shares its B minor tonality, infused with traces of the repeated three-note figures that dominate the texture of 'Schwestergruss' (Example 3.5). Musical details bring out the dialectical representation of night discussed above, notably in bars 7–11, where the vocal line ascends for the words 'night falls' ('Die

---

[48] Johnson, *The Complete Songs*, Vol. 3, 439.

Example 3.5. Schubert, 'Der Unglückliche', D 713, bars 1–30.
Franz Schubert. *Lieder*, volume 4 (BA 5516), editor: Walther Dürr.
© 1979 Bärenreiter-Verlag Karl Vötterle GmbH & Co KG, Kassel.

—(continued)

Example 3.5—concluded

Nacht bricht an'). The weary souls are similarly characterized by music brighter than the text implies – a turn to the relative, D major – while the depiction of 'daily graves' ('täglich Grab') in bars 24–30 ushers in B major. This harmonic brightening, possibly suggesting a disjuncture between music and text, has the opposite effect of capturing cruelly sweet delight as sonically intertwined.

The music of stanzas 2 and 3 elicits the fusion of joyfulness and rapture central to the Schillerian sublime through the sound of pain and pleasure combined. The depiction of bleeding wounds as night robs day of light ushers in a profusion of incessant sound and rhythmic irregularity in bars 31–47 (Example 3.6), recalling the music of 'Der Zwerg', D 771, particularly bars 37–50 (Example 3.7). Sonic force, imminent and immersive, creates a world disparate from the sentiment of 'nothing being able to disturb' that closes stanza 2. The paradoxical rearing up of sound for the plunging into grief in stanza 3 adds a further twist to the promise of sweetness tied to a torturous reality (Example 3.8). Conflicting motion between voice and piano (bars 49–54) – the former descending, the latter rising in jagged octaves – contributes to a claustrophobic soundscape of the kind heard in 'Totengräbers Heimweh'. Pain, sorrow, and sweet delight converge in a chilling reminder of the eternity of the daily grave referenced in stanza 1.

Dialectical tensions between pain and pleasure resurface in the depiction of past happiness in the penultimate stanza of 'Der Unglückliche'. The re-emergence of the tolling octaves in G major, bar 118, appears bittersweet in the aftermath of the preceding four-bar recitative, where harsh chordal interjections and a return of tremolo figurations depict the inevitability of life's sorrows and the dashing of dreams dealt by the cruel hand of fate (Example 3.9). This interjection blurs the distinction between dream and reality. There is resignation that dreams exist only in the imagination – conveyed through musical echoes of the past – but more chillingly a realization that isolation prevails: 'now all the sweet bonds are torn sunder; no heart now beats for me in the whole world' ('Zerrissen sind nun alle süssen Bande, / Mir schlägt kein Herz mehr auf der weiten Welt').

Example 3.6. Schubert, 'Der Unglückliche', D 713, bars 31–47.
Franz Schubert. *Lieder*, volume 4 (BA 5516), editor: Walther Dürr.
© 1979 Bärenreiter-Verlag Karl Vötterle GmbH & Co KG, Kassel.

Example 3.7. Schubert, 'Der Zwerg', D 771, bars 37–50.
Franz Schubert. *Lieder*, volume 1, high voice (BA 9101), editor: Walther Dürr.
© 2005 Bärenreiter-Verlag Karl Vötterle GmbH & Co KG, Kassel.

Example 3.8. Schubert, 'Der Unglückliche', D 713, bars 47–55.
Franz Schubert. *Lieder*, volume 4 (BA 5516), editor: Walther Dürr.
© 1979 Bärenreiter-Verlag Karl Vötterle GmbH & Co KG, Kassel.

Example 3.9. Schubert, 'Der Unglückliche', D 713, bars 114–23.
Franz Schubert. *Lieder*, volume 4 (BA 5516), editor: Walther Dürr.
© 1979 Bärenreiter-Verlag Karl Vötterle GmbH & Co KG, Kassel.

'Come Back, Holy Night: Fair Dreams, Return!'

Heil'ge Nacht, du sinkest nieder;	Holy night, you sink down;
Nieder wallen auch die Träume,	Dreams, too, float down,
Wie dein Mondlicht durch die Räume,	Like your moonlight through space,
Durch der Menschen stille Brust.	Through the silent hearts of men.
Die belauschen sie mit Lust;	They listen with delight,
Rufen, wenn der Tag erwacht:	Crying out when day awakes:
Kehre wieder, heil'ge Nacht!	Come back, holy night!
Holde Träume, kehret wieder!	Fair dreams, return![49]

Schubert's setting of Matthäus von Collin's 'Nacht und Träume', D 827, brings together the contrasting examples of nocturnal imagery examined throughout this chapter.[50] Night as a site for remembering and reliving past happiness, imbued with ephemerality, coalesces in the sentiment that captured Samuel Beckett's attention: 'come back, holy night! / Fair dreams, return!', invoked in the Introduction.[51] Schubert's setting, largely devoid of disturbances, conveys the mutability of night through muted language, fluctuating between *pianissimo* and triple *piano*, and transient pianistic figuration like that of the holy night in 'Nachtstück' (Example 3.10). The pivot to the submediant, G major, bars 14–15, an 'interior dream-world', at the words 'they listen with delight / crying out when day awakes' ('Die belauschen sie mit Lust; / Rufen, wenn der Tag erwacht'), further emphasizes the ephemerality of dreams with music seemingly on the edge of consciousness (Example 3.11).[52]

The intimations of pain and pleasure in 'Nacht und Träume' recall (albeit in a contrasting setting) those that permeate the settings discussed here, particularly 'Der Unglückliche', while the reference to the holy night looks back to that of Schubert's 'Nachtstück', now with an inversion of expressive associations: offering the promise of eternal sleep in that earlier song, linked to the vanishing of dreams in 'Nacht und Träume'. Common to all examples is the fluctuation between the haunting connotations of the night, and a world located between the sublime and the ungraspable. Traces of the night constantly slip in and out of reach, whether by evoking the infinite possibilities offered by sleep, or leaving ambiguity as to what lies beyond the moonlit imagery in the songs of the night.

---

[49] Johnson, *The Complete Songs*, Vol. 2, 420.

[50] For wider reference, see David Bretherton, 'The Musico-Poetics of the Flat Submediant in Schubert's Songs', *Journal of the Royal Musical Association* 144 (2019), 239–86; and Susan Youens, *Schubert's Late Lieder: Beyond the Song-Cycle*s (Cambridge: Cambridge University Press, 2002), ix–xi, 64–69, 84–92.

[51] Samuel Beckett, 'Nacht und Träume', in *Collected Shorter Plays* (New York: Grove, 1984), 303–6. See Paul Lawley, '"The Grim Journey": Beckett Listens to Schubert', *Samuel Beckett Today* 11 (2001), 255–66; Noel Witts, 'Beckett and Schubert', *Performance Research* 12/1 (2007), 138–44; Graley Herren, 'Splitting Images: Samuel Beckett's *Nacht und Träume*', *Modern Drama* 43/2 (2000), 182–91; and Katherine Weiss, 'Deciphering the Dream in Samuel Beckett's *Nacht und Träume*', *Journal of Drama Studies* 1/2 (2007), 51–57.

[52] Brian Black, 'Remembering a Dream: The Tragedy of Romantic Memory in the Modulatory Processes of Schubert's Sonata Forms', *Intersections* 25/1–2 (2005), 202–28, at 204.

Example 3.10. Schubert, 'Nacht und Träume', D 827, bars 1–6.
Franz Schubert. *Lieder*, volume 4 (BA 5516), editor: Walther Dürr.
© 1979 Bärenreiter-Verlag Karl Vötterle GmbH & Co KG, Kassel.

Example 3.11 Schubert, 'Nacht und Träume', D 827, bars 14–21.
Franz Schubert. *Lieder*, volume 4 (BA 5516), editor: Walther Dürr.
© 1979 Bärenreiter-Verlag Karl Vötterle GmbH & Co KG, Kassel.

4

Grotesquerie

Ich wandle still, bin wenig froh,
Und immer fragt der Seufzer – wo? –
Im Geisterhauch tönt's mir zurück.
'Dort, wo du nicht bist, dort ist das Glück!'

I wander, silent and joyless,
And my sighs forever ask: Where?
In a ghostly whisper the answer comes:
'There, where you are not, is happiness!'[1]

The Adagio of Schubert's 'Wanderer' Fantasy in C major, D 760 (1822), forms a bridge between the previous chapter and the sound(s) of the grotesque traced in what follows.[2] Its thematic material takes the disjuncture embodied in his setting of 'Der Wanderer', D 489 (1816), on which the movement is based, to extremes. The music shown in Example 4.1 throws into stark relief the fusion of the silent and joyless (stanza 1) with the vision of dead ones rising (stanza 4).[3] Ghostly whispers in the final stanza, quoted in the epigraph above, serve as a threshold between the passagework that skims the texture in bars 227–30 and the distortions that follow in its pathway. Traces of dreamt-of joy in the song source are shattered by the profusion of harsh sonorities, chromatic warping, and textural density unleashed in bars 231–35. The lack of articulation here between the diaphanous and the distorted, the one flowing seam-

---

[1] Graham Johnson, *Franz Schubert: The Complete Songs*, 3 vols (New Haven and London: Yale University Press, 2014), Vol. 3, 539.

[2] On D 760, II, see Jonathan Dunsby, 'Adorno's Image of Schubert's "Wanderer" Fantasy Multiplied by Ten', *19th-Century Music* 29/1 (2005), 209–36; Theodor Adorno, 'Schubert (1928)', trans. Jonathan Dunsby and Beate Perrey, *19th-Century Music* 2/1 (2005), 3–14; Charles Fisk, *Returning Cycles: Contexts for the Interpretation of Schubert's Impromptus and Last Sonatas* (Berkeley: University of California Press, 2001); and Susan Wollenberg, *Schubert's Fingerprints: Studies in the Instrumental Works* (Farnham: Ashgate, 2011), 94–95.

[3] Stanza 1: 'Ich komme vom Gebirge her / Es dampft das Tal, es braust das Meer. / Ich wandle still, bin wenig froh / Und immer fragt der Seufzer: wo?' ('I come from the mountains; / The valley steams, the ocean roars. / I wander, silent and joyless, / And my sighs for ever ask: Where?'). Stanza 4: 'Wo meine Freunde wandeln geh'n, / Wo meine Toten aufersteh'n, / Das Land, das meine Sprache spricht, / O Land, wo bist du?' ('Where my friends walk, / Where my dead ones rise again, / The land that speaks my tongue, / O land, where are you?'). Johnson, *The Complete Songs*, Vol. 3, 538–39.

Example 4.1. Schubert, 'Wanderer' Fantasy in C major, D 760, II, bars 227–35. Franz Schubert. Fantasy for piano in C major op. 15 D 760 'Wanderer Fantasy' (BA 10870), editor: Walther Dürr. © 2014 Bärenreiter-Verlag Karl Vötterle GmbH & Co KG, Kassel.

—(continued)

Example 4.1—continued

—(continued)

Example 4.1—concluded

Grotesquerie   123

lessly from the other, renders this process of distortion all the more disturbing. The
extremity of such writing tilts the pendulum from the fusion of pain and pleasure
at the heart of the sublime discussed in the previous chapter, to the prising open of
boundaries that defines the grotesque.[4] Tropes explored throughout the book – nocturnal imagery, doubles, and distortions – coincide with the disjuncture studied in this
chapter. Stylistic references are destabilized, their soundworlds subject to rupture or
conflation vis-à-vis the permeable nature of the gothic imagination.[5]

Definitions of the grotesque from the late eighteenth and early nineteenth centuries foreground themes that are central to gothic necropoetics.[6] Pertinent here
is the art historian Johann Fiorillo's attention to its 'horror-inducing' aspects, epit-
omized in his view by the fusion of incongruous elements in Henry Fuseli's 'The
Nightmare' (Figure 4.1).[7] The suggestion of sleep as a gateway to dreaming (recalling themes of the previous chapter) is sharply juxtaposed with the mythical figures
to which it gives rise. The disembodied horse's head, its eyes bulged in terror, the
incubus squatting on the woman's lower torso, and the invitation to peer in on the
inner worlds of her dream all capture the twisted form the gothic can take as death
meets with erotic desire. These elements point, in Maryanne Ward's words, to the
'unspeakable, the horrible, perhaps the surreal, but for the most part the "unreal"'
work of the imagination – captured in ways all too real.[8] The emphasis on things

---

4   The term 'grotesque' derives from the Italian word *grotta* (meaning 'cave') and was
    used to describe an ornamental style of painting discovered during fifteenth-century
    excavations in Rome and other parts of Italy. Such paintings, unnatural in shape and
    appearance, combine incongruous fusions of plants, animals, and human figures. On the
    history of the grotesque, see Justin D. Edwards and Rune Graulund, *Grotesque: The New
    Critical Idiom* (New York: Routledge, 2013); Karlheinz Barack et al. (eds), 'Grotesk', in
    Ästhetische Grundbegriffe: Band 2, Dekadent bis Grotesk (Stuttgart: J.B. Metzler Verlag,
    2001), 880–98; Maria Parrino, 'The Grotesque', in *The Encyclopedia of the Gothic*, ed.
    William Hughes, David Punter, and Andrew Smith, 2 vols (New York: John Wiley &
    Sons, 2015), 307; and Rémi Astruc, *Le Renouveau du grotesque dans le roman du XXe siècle:
    Essai d'anthropologie littéraire* (Paris: Classiques Garnier, 2010).

5   Further on contrasts in Schubert's music, see Benjamin K. Korstvedt, '"The Prerogative
    of Late Style": Thoughts on the Expressive World of Schubert's Late Works', in *Schubert's
    Late Music*, 404–25, esp. 424: 'Schubert's late music is in its own way often most interested
    in creating the impression of disjunction, of disruptive contrasts of all sorts – whether
    visionary, consoling, tragic, uncanny or occasionally even bathetic.'

6   Cf. Möser's *Harlekin, oder Vertheidigung des Groteske-Komischen* (1761); Karl Flögel's
    Geschichte des Groteske-komischen (1788); C.L. Stieglitz's *Über den Gebrauch des Grotesken
    und Arabesken* (1790).

7   Quoted in Frederick Burwick, *The Haunted Eye: Perception and the Grotesque in English
    and German Romanticism* (Heidelberg: Carl Winter Universitätsverlag, 1987), 70:
    'eine Neigung zu Grausen erregenden Gegenständen' ('a tendency towards horror-
    inducing objects'; translation mine). See also J.D. Fiorillo, *Über die Groteske* (Göttingen:
    Rosenbusch, 1791).

8   Maryanne C. Ward, 'A Painting of the Unspeakable: Henry Fuseli's "The Nightmare" and
    the Creation of Mary Shelley's "Frankenstein"', *Journal of the Midwest Modern Language
    Association* 33/1 (2000), 20–31, at 20; see also Martin Myron, 'Henry Fuseli and Gothic
    Spectacle', *Huntington Library Quarterly* 70/2 (2007), 289–310; John Moffitt, 'A Pictorial

Figure 4.1. The Nightmare, 1781 (oil on canvas), Fuseli, Henry (Fussli, Johann Heinrich) (1741–1825) / Detroit Institute of Arts, USA / © Detroit Institute of Arts / Bridgeman Images.

that appear not to belong together, of giving voice to distorted realities, resonates with Friedrich Schlegel's view that the grotesque is defined by its strange 'permutations of form and matter': 'paradoxes are thrust together', 'woven as bizarrely as possible into a monstrous human tragicomedy'.[9] The boundaries between these

Counterpart to "Gothick" Literature: Fuseli's *The Nightmare*', in 'Haunting II', special issue, *Mosaic: An Interdisciplinary Critical Journal* 25/1 (2002), 173–96.

[9] Fragments 305 and 425, in Friedrich Schlegel, *Philosophical Fragments*, trans. Peter Firchow (Minnesota: University of Minnesota Press, 1991), 60 and 86 respectively. On Schlegel's conception of the grotesque, see Frederick Burwick, 'The Grotesque in the Romantic Movement', in *European Romanticism: Literary Cross-Currents, Modes, and Models*, ed. Gerhart Hoffmeister (Detroit: Wayne State University Press, 1989), 45–46; Burwick, 'Grotesque "Bilderwitz": Friedrich Schlegel', in *The Haunted Eye*, 72–92; Anthony Phelan, 'Prose Fiction of the German Romantics', in *The Cambridge Companion to German Romanticism*, ed. Nicholas Saul (Cambridge: Cambridge University Press, 2009), 41–66; and in connection with music, see John Daverio, 'Schumann's "Im Legendenton" and Friedrich Schlegel's "Arabeske"', *19th-Century Music* 11/2 (1987), 150–63. Jean Paul's discussion of 'die vernichtende Idee des Humors' ('the annihilating idea of humour') in his *Vorschule der Ästhetik* (1804) parallels Schlegel's view of the grotesque as a 'monstrous human tragicomedy': here he defines humour as dark, terrible, painful,

Grotesquerie 125

categories shift in all directions. What is bizarre can quickly turn monstrous, as in Fuseli's 'The Nightmare'.

Like Fiorillo and Schlegel, E.T.A. Hoffmann offered imaginative ways of thinking about the grotesque – whether through strange objects (*Der goldne Topf*, 1814), distorted fairy tales (*Nußknacker und Mausekönig*, 1816), and automata (*Die Automate*, 1814, and *Der Sandmann*, 1816), or in his description of the drawings and etchings of Jacques Callot (1592–1635):[10]

> Why can I not see enough of your strange and fantastic pages, most daring of artists! Why can I not get your figures, often suggested merely by a few bold strokes, out of my mind? When I look long at your compositions which overflow with the most heterogeneous elements, then the thousands of figures come to life, and – often from the furthest background, where at first they are hard even to descry – each of them strides powerfully forth in the most natural colour.
>
> – – –
>
> No[one] has known so well as Callot how to assemble together in a small space such an abundance of motifs, emerging beside each other, even within each other, yet without confusing the eye, so that individual elements are seen as such, but still blend with the whole. [...] Callot's grotesque forms, created out of animal and man, reveal to the serious, deeper-seeing observer all the hidden meanings that lie beneath the cloak of absurdity.[11]

Hoffmann's enthusiasm for the synthesis of ideas in Callot's work feeds into the discourse on the grotesque as revolving around hybridity and metamorphosis. The 'overflow of heterogeneous elements', as Hoffmann put it, reveals connections through worlds that otherwise are entirely unrelated.

Scholars have paid close attention to the metamorphic qualities of the grotesque. For the literary scholar Geoffrey Harpham, 'the perception of the grotesque is never a fixed or stable thing, but always a process, a progression':[12]

> All images split, assuming incongruous double functions, and everything is thrown into doubt. These designs are called grotesques [...] because they throw the reader/viewer into that intertextual 'interval'. [...] The interval of the gro-

---

and awe-inspiring – a product of 'inverse sublimity'. See Kathleen Wheeler (ed.), 'Jean Paul Richter, From *School for Aesthetics*', in *German Aesthetic and Literary Criticism: The Romantic Ironists and Goethe* (Cambridge: Cambridge University Press, 1984), 162–98.

[10] See Birgit Röder, *A Study of the Major Novellas of E.T.A. Hoffmann* (Rochester, NY: Camden House, 2003); Andrew J. Webber, 'Hoffmann's Chronic Dualisms', *The Doppelgänger: Double Visions in German Literature* (Oxford: Clarendon Press, 1996), 113–94; and John MacAuslan, *Schumann's Music and E.T.A. Hoffmann's Fiction* (Cambridge: Cambridge University Press, 2016).

[11] *E.T.A. Hoffmann's Musical Writings: 'Kreisleriana', 'The Poet and the Composer', Music Criticism*, ed. David Charlton, trans. Martyn Clarke (Cambridge: Cambridge University Press, 1989), 76–78.

[12] Geoffrey Galt Harpham, *On the Grotesque: Strategies of Contradiction in Art and Literature* (Princeton, NJ: Princeton University Press, 1982), 17.

tesque is the one in which, although we have recognized a number of different forms in the object, we have not yet developed a clear sense of the dominant principle that defines it and organizes its various elements. [...] Looking for unity between center and margin, the interpreter must, whether he finds it or not, pass through the grotesque.[13]

The 'intertextual interval' is viewed (and heard) here in dialogue with the art historian Frances Connelly's definition of the grotesque as a 'catalyst', opening the 'boundaries of two disparate entities', or that exists 'only in the tensions between distinct realities'.[14] 'Whatever the rules or conventions', Connelly concludes, 'the grotesque subverts them, creating a *Spielraum* full of conflict and new possibilities.'[15]

While it would be a stretch to suggest that Schubert was versed in theories of the grotesque, his diary entry of 16 June 1816 nevertheless suggests an awareness of the potential of conflating opposites:[16]

> It must be beautiful for an artist [Salieri] to see all his students gathered around [...] and to hear in [their] compositions the expression of mere nature, free from all the bizarre elements which are common among composers nowadays and owed almost entirely to one of our greatest German artists [Beethoven]; that eccentricity which joins and confuses the tragic with the comic, the agreeable with the repulsive, heroism with howlings and the holiest with harlequinades, without distinction, so as to goad people to madness.[17]

The stylistic fusions that Schubert decried there (while under the influence of his teacher Antonio Salieri) assume a prominent position in the case studies of this chapter, all of which can be heard as speaking to one another through the sounds of the grotesque.

At first glance, the grotesque, particularly as manifested in Fuseli's painting, has little to do with the semantics of Schubert's music as 'shin[ing] with the exaggerated

---

13 Harpham, *On the Grotesque*, 17–19.

14 Frances S. Connelly, *The Grotesque in Western Art and Culture: The Image at Play* (Cambridge: Cambridge University Press, 2012), 8.

15 Connelly, *The Grotesque in Western Art and Culture*, 14–15.

16 It is not improbable that Schubert would have encountered notions of the grotesque (as with the gothic imagination) within his circle of poets and visual artists. For wider discussion of Schubert's cultural milieu, see David Gramit, 'The Intellectual and Aesthetic Tenets of Franz Schubert's Circle: Their Development and Their Influence on His Music' (PhD dissertation, Duke University, 1987); John Gingerich, '"Those of Us Who Found our Life in Art": The Second-Generation Romanticism of the Schubert–Schober Circle, 1820–25', in *Franz Schubert and his World*, ed. Christopher H. Gibbs and Morten Solvik (Princeton, NJ: Princeton University Press 2014), 67–114; and Raymond Erickson (ed.), *Schubert's Vienna* (New Haven, CT: Yale University Press, 1997).

17 Otto Erich Deutsch (ed.), *The Schubert Reader: A Life of Franz Schubert in Letters and Documents*, trans. Eric Blom (New York: W.W. Norton & Co., 1949), 64. On Schubert's changing attitude towards the music of Beethoven vis-à-vis this diary entry, see Marjorie Hirsch, 'Gothic and Classical Influences', in *Schubert's Late Music*, 167–68; and William Kinderman, 'Franz Schubert's "New Style" and the Legacy of Beethoven', in *Rethinking Schubert*, 43–44.

clarity of a dream',[18] or that which appears 'too good, too pure, to be true'[19] – an obvious exception being 'Der Zwerg', discussed in the Introduction.[20] Yet at a conceptual level, its merging of opposites offers a backdrop against which to hear the thresholds between life and death, dream and reality, in the pieces explored in this chapter. The spectrum shifts at times through sudden rupture (as in the Adagio of the String Quintet in C major, D 956), at other times through gradual processes of change (as in the *Klavierstück* in E flat minor, D 946/1, or the Andantino of the Piano Sonata in A major, D 959). These pieces, while distinct in their stylistic approaches, intersect within the intertextual soundworlds of the grotesque.[21]

Sounding the Grotesque

I. Defamiliarization

Signs of the grotesque in the Adagio of the 'Wanderer' Fantasy, D 760, take shape through the defamiliarization of thematic material and expressive imagery. Tensions between estrangement and dreamt-of joy permeate its main theme, bars 189–205, through the combination of processional style (derived from the dactylic rhythms of stanza 2) and a softening of the dotted rhythms and a shift to the relative (E) major (conjuring the alternate reality of stanza 3):

Stanza 2

Die Sonne dünkt mich hier so kalt,	Here the sun seems so cold,
Die Blüte welk, das Leben alt,	the blossom faded, life old,

---

[18] Scott Burnham, 'Schubert and the Sound of Memory', *Musical Quarterly* 84/4 (2000), 655–63, at 663. Further on Schubertian beauty, see Wollenberg, *Schubert's Fingerprints*, 189.

[19] Benedict Taylor, 'Schubert and the Construction of Memory: The String Quartet in A Minor, D. 804 ("Rosamunde")', *Journal of the Royal Musical Association* 139/1 (2014), 60.

[20] See Susan Youens, 'Of Dwarves, Perversion, and Patriotism: Schubert's "Der Zwerg", D. 771', *19th-Century Music* 21/2 (1997), 177–207.

[21] Further on the grotesque in music, see Francesca Brittan, *Music and Fantasy in the Age of Berlioz* (Cambridge: Cambridge University Press, 2017), 136–88; Martin Čurda, '"From the Monkey Mountains": The Body, the Grotesque and Carnival in the Music of Pavel Haas', *Journal of the Royal Musical Association* 141/1 (2016), 61–112; Robert S. Hatten, 'Interpreting the Grotesque in Music', *Semiotics* (2011), 419–26; Yayoi Uno Everett, 'Signification of Parody and the Grotesque in György Ligeti's *Le Grand Macabre*', *Music Theory Spectrum* 31/1 (2009), 26–56; Julie Brown, *Bartók and the Grotesque: Studies in Modernity, the Body and Contradiction in Music* (Farnham: Ashgate, 2007); Elisabeth Le Guin, '"One Says That One Weeps, but One Does Not Weep": *Sensible*, Grotesque, and Mechanical Embodiments in Boccherini's Chamber Music', *Journal of the American Musicological Society* 55/2 (2002), 207–54; Annette Richards, 'Haydn's London Trios and the Rhetoric of the Grotesque', in *Haydn and the Performance of Rhetoric*, ed. Tom Beghin and Sander M. Goldberg (Chicago: University of Chicago Press, 2007), 251–80; and Esti Sheinberg, *Irony, Satire, Parody and the Grotesque in the Music of Shostakovich: A Theory of Musical Incongruities* (Farnham: Ashgate, 2000).

| Und was sie reden, leerer Schall, | and men's words mere hollow noise; |
| Ich bin ein Fremdling überall. | I am a stranger everywhere. |

Stanza 3

Wo bist du, mein geliebtes Land?	Where are you, my beloved land?
Gesucht, geahnt und nie gekannt,	Sought, dreamt of, yet never known!
Das Land, das Land, so hoffnungsgrün,	The land so green with hope,
Das Land, wo meine Rosen blüh'n.	The land where my roses bloom.[22]

The relationship between these ideas – one rooted in reality, the other illusory – constantly changes, at times fused (as in the opening material), and in other moments prised apart or subject to metamorphosis in the ensuing variations.

The first variation, bars 206–26, sets in motion a process of change via the tremolo figuration beneath fragments of the dactylic rhythm in bar 206 (Example 4.2). These rhythmic reverberations, destabilizing the long–short–short–long patterns of the opening, contribute to the unravelling of the theme that follows – or, in Susan Youens's words, 'the trill liquifies the ground underneath the right-hand chords and then sinks into a registral abyss. Both compositional decisions undermine what sounds above.'[23] Qualities of lullaby – initially suggested through the theme's undulating contours (notably in bars 197–99, coupled with the shift to E major), chiming octaves in bars 189–96, and muted dynamics – are displaced by this undoing of thematic material. Syncopated octave interjections in the left hand, weaving in and out of the chords in the right hand, bars 208 ff., offset the stability of the opening through registral expansion and dynamic intensification. The boundaries between thematic ideas break down as the music of the song source gives way to excess and disequilibrium.

The second variation (bars 227–39), shown in Example 4.1, takes this process of change to greater extremes. Scale-based patterns in the upper limits of the piano fill the frame with incessant sound, underpinned by a restless accompaniment unmoored from its dactylic roots. Ideas of estrangement in stanza 2 of 'Der Wanderer' carry across to the distortion of scalar writing from bar 231 onwards. Recognizable patterns morph into sound that winds its way chromatically across the piano's registral compass. The warping of sonorities and stylistic configurations reaches a climax in the *fz* interjections in bar 235, where the dotted rhythmic profile (now powerfully framed) obscures the dactylic rhythms of the main theme. The two iterations coalesce in the gaps opened up by the tremolo figuration in bar 206 and the defamiliarization of scalar writing thereafter.

These approaches – abrupt distortion via single sonorities, or the gradual undoing of thematic material – provide the foundations for hearing the grotesque in the case studies that follow. Each example represents a distinct instance of the grotesque through hybridity, rupture, or metamorphosis, while collectively they contribute to the constellation of gothic tropes around which this book revolves.

---

[22] Johnson, *The Complete Songs*, Vol. 3, 539.

[23] Quoted from personal correspondence with Susan Youens.

Example 4.2. Schubert, 'Wanderer' Fantasy in C major, D 760, II, bars 206–13. Franz Schubert. Fantasy for piano in C major op. 15 D 760 'Wanderer Fantasy' (BA 10870), editor: Walther Dürr. © 2014 Bärenreiter-Verlag Karl Vötterle GmbH & Co KG, Kassel.

II. Hybridity

The genre of *danse macabre* encapsulates the protean nature of the grotesque.[24] Its fusion of the animate (expressed through physical movement) and the inanimate (corpses, spectral presences) paints an image of death as taking on a life of its own. It is physically alive while simultaneously conveying the spirit of *memento mori*, a symbol of the inevitability of death.[25] Such slippages can be heard across Schubert's *Klavierstück* in E flat minor, D 946/1 (1828), a piece that alludes to *danse macabre* through its stylistic vocabulary.[26] The main theme, bars 1–117, combines the airiness of the night spirits in such songs as 'Der Geistertanz' ('Dance of Death'), D 116, with a distorted funeral march, its rhythmic profile whirling rather than processional (Example 4.3). Traces of the tarantella style of the finale of Schubert's 'Death and the Maiden' Quartet, D 810 (1824), with its sudden lurches and continuous triplets, similarly lurk in the fusion of (right-hand) octaves and (left-hand) triplets.[27] The tensions between the jovial and the deathly slip through also in tonal details, such as the fluctuation between E flat minor and B flat major in bars 1–2, the two speaking to the contrasting faces of *danse macabre*.

Two particular passages bring to mind the undoing of boundaries that defines the grotesque, the first occurring in bars 118–28 (Example 4.4). Life as animate, death as inanimate, is inverted here through the slippage to a chorale-like style in B major, a moment of reverie. The chilling nature of this change, what looks and sounds (ostensibly) peaceful on the surface, comes into focus in relation to the use of the major mode in 'Erlkönig', discussed in chapter 2. Similar juxtapositions suffuse the spread chords in bars 120–21 of the *Klavierstück*, both an echo and a compound of sweetness and eeriness in the midst of death.

---

[24] On *danse macabre*, see Steven Bruhm, 'Gothic, Ballet, Dance: The Aesthetics and Kinaesthetics of Death', in *The Edinburgh Companion to Gothic and the Arts*, ed. David Punter (Edinburgh: Edinburgh University Press, 2019), 214–28; Nahid Shahbazi Moghadam, 'The Grotesque in "Danse Macabre"', *Peake Studies* 13/4 (2014), 15–25; and as it pertains to Schubert, see Christoph Wolff, 'Schubert's "Der Tod und das Mädchen": Analytical and Explanatory Notes on the Song D 531 and the Quartet D 810', in *Schubert Studies: Problems of Style and Chronology*, ed. Eva Badura-Skoda and Peter Branscombe (Cambridge: Cambridge University Press, 1982), 143–71.

[25] On *memento mori*, see Carol M. Davison, 'Introduction – The Corpse in the Closet: The Gothic, Death, and Modernity', in *The Gothic and Death*, ed. Davison (Manchester: Manchester University Press, 2017), 1–17.

[26] For wider discussion on the expressive features of D 946, see Ryan McClelland, 'Hypermeter, Phrase Length, and Temporal Disjuncture in Schubert's *Klavierstück* No. 3 (D.946)', in *The Unknown Schubert*, ed. Barbara M. Reul and Lorraine Byrne Bodley (Farnham: Ashgate, 2008), 157–75.

[27] For wider reference, see Julian Rushton, 'Schubert, the Tarantella, and the *Quartettsatz*, D. 703', in *Variations on the Canon: Essays on Music from Bach to Boulez in Honor of Charles Rosen on his Eightieth Birthday*, ed. Robert Curry, David Gable, and Robert L. Marshall (Rochester, NY: University of Rochester Press, 2008), 163–71.

Example 4.3. Schubert, *Klavierstück* in E flat minor, D 946/1, bars 1–8. Franz Schubert. Late piano pieces (BA 9634), editor: Walther Dürr. © 2012 Bärenreiter-Verlag Karl Vötterle GmbH & Co KG, Kassel.

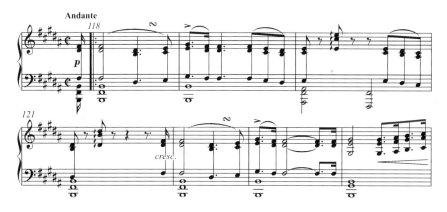

Example 4.4. Schubert, *Klavierstück* in E flat minor, D 946/1, bars 118–24. Franz Schubert. Late piano pieces (BA 9634), editor: Walther Dürr. © 2012 Bärenreiter-Verlag Karl Vötterle GmbH & Co KG, Kassel.

The second passage, bars 129–40, involves the rupturing of boundaries between the opening section and the chorale-like interjection (Example 4.5). Scalar figurations in bars 130 and 132 destabilize the music through their *pianissimo* marking, akin to ghostly emanations from the harmony on which they pause. While their presence is fleeting, the sudden rush of sound and rhythmic motion is arresting – a brief flight into ethereal realms at odds with the music that surrounds this section. A further ingredient in this process of change is the tremolo texture in low register, bar 133, a recurring marker of death throughout this study. The saturation of sound within diminished intervals weighs down the dance of death and the inevitability of life's transience intrinsic to that genre.

Example 4.5. Schubert, *Klavierstück* in E flat minor, D 946/1, bars 129–37. Franz Schubert. Late piano pieces (BA 9634), editor: Walther Dürr. © 2012 Bärenreiter-Verlag Karl Vötterle GmbH & Co KG, Kassel.

Grotesquerie 133

Schubert's *Klavierstück* in E flat major, D 946/2, signifies the grotesque through a shared vocabulary of tremolos and chromatic turn figures associated with death both here and in Schubert's music more broadly (cf. the treatment of the funereal themes in D 899/1 and D 929, II, discussed in chapter 2). Its soundworlds fluctuate between the topos of lullaby, with the physicality of D 946/1 dissolving into a gentle barcarolle (Example 4.6), and a distortion of that style redolent of bars 129–40 in the E flat minor *Klavierstück* – each demonstrating how Schubert could render a lilting barcarolle in major mode not only wistful but also bound up with the gothic imagination. The songs of the night discussed from chapter 3 serve here as a reminder that Schubert's nocturnal imagery (as with Fuseli's 'The Nightmare') often conceals things beneath the surface. Nocturnal imagery provides a backdrop to envisage possibilities beyond the realm of daylight, but it also comes with the inevitability that night and death occupy the same spectrum.

Schlegel's notion of the grotesque as woven with paradox and rooted in strange permutations finds a sonic outlet in bars 30–31 of D 946/2 (Example 4.7). Here the permutation of the lullaby topos is triggered via the semitonal slippage from E flat major to G minor, with the third, B flat, left out and the D doubled three times against the grating dissonance of E flat, while the G minor chord is reduced to open intervals. The two worlds, coalescing around a single harmony, are further conflated through the juxtapositions of tremolo-based textures (marked *pianissimo*) with chordal breakthroughs (marked *ffz* and *fz*) throughout bars 32–44. Adding to the strangeness is the combination of elements within the four-bar phrase: from the chords plus tremolo, to the trilled activation of the harmony in bar 33, followed by a seeming return to the first bar, now twisted into the alternations of *ffz* and *fz* chords in bar 35, those stabbing gestures that further distort the underlying phrase structure. Tremolos in low register at this muted dynamic level, shattered by the chordal entries, are an instance of disruption at the opposite end of the spectrum to that in bar 133 of the E flat minor *Klavierstück*. Quietness renders the *sforzandi* interjections all the more jarring.

Further signs of the grotesque appear in bars 46–59 (Example 4.8) through stylistic juxtapositions and sonorities functioning as markers of change. This approach is suggested texturally, through the dissonant octave- and scale-based combinations, as well as tonally, where in bars 52–54 turn-like figures rise by thirds, from D minor to its dominant, then F minor to its dominant, and finally A flat minor, before descending through chromatic lines.[28] Here, too, lies an emphasis on opposites, especially in bars 56–59, where the theme, after this chromatic meandering, gives way to a major-mode transformation of bar 32, marked triple *piano*. The material is fused in contradictory ways as the initial barcarolle theme undergoes change and resurfaces in these unusual contexts.

---

[28] A parallel can be drawn here with the construction of 'grotesque hellscapes' in Schubert's 'Gruppe aus dem Tartarus', which, as Susan Youens observes, is underpinned by tonal order – chromaticism within chromaticism, tightly structured in the midst of surface-level distortion. Susan Youens, 'Reentering Mozart's Hell: Schubert's "Gruppe aus dem Tartarus", D. 538', in *Drama in the Music of Franz Schubert*, 171–204.

Example 4.6. Schubert, *Klavierstück* in E flat major, D 946/2, bars 1–9. Franz Schubert. Late piano pieces (BA 9634), editor: Walther Dürr. © 2012 Bärenreiter-Verlag Karl Vötterle GmbH & Co KG, Kassel.

Example 4.7. Schubert, *Klavierstück* in E flat major, D 946/2, bars 30–45. Franz Schubert. Late piano pieces (BA 9634), editor: Walther Dürr. © 2012 Bärenreiter-Verlag Karl Vötterle GmbH & Co KG, Kassel.

Example 4.8. Schubert, *Klavierstück* in E flat major, D 946/2, bars 46–59.
Franz Schubert. Late piano pieces (BA 9634), editor: Walther Dürr.
© 2012 Bärenreiter-Verlag Karl Vötterle GmbH & Co KG, Kassel.

136   *The Gothic Imagination in the Music of Franz Schubert*

III. Rupture

The sounds of the grotesque traced thus far – from sudden contrasts to the confla-tion of opposites – coalesce in the Adagio of Schubert's String Quintet in C major, D 956 (1828).[29] Connelly's suggestion that the 'deeper workings' of the grotesque are revealed 'through its changes', when 'the familiar turns strange or shifts unex-pectedly into something else', is brought into sharp focus through the rupture of bar 28 (Example 4.9).[30] Out of nowhere, the music turns strange through trilled unisons twisting cadential closure in E major into jarring sonorities in F minor. The trill, detached from its usage as embellishment or cadential cue, signals a process of disjuncture. Sounds are split into multiple layers and rendered disruptive as they seep through the texture.[31]

The disjuncture of bar 28 calls into question the nature of the opening material, bars 1–27, as a 'static dream tableau' (Example 4.10).[32] There are signs here that Schubert's dream imagery is rarely untroubled.[33] As in 'Nacht und Träume', D 827, so the music

29   On the harmonic and structural properties of D 956, II, see James William Sobaskie, 'The "Problem" of Schubert's String Quintet', *Nineteenth-Century Music Review* 2/1 (2005), 76–79; and Lauri Suurpää, 'The Path from Tonic to Dominant in the Second Movement of Schubert's String Quintet and in Chopin's Fourth Ballade', *Journal of Music Theory* 44/2 (2000), 455–65. On analytical approaches to the Quintet more broadly, see the essays by Scott Burnham, Julian Horton, John Koslovsky, and Nathan John Martin and Steven Vande Moortele in 'Schubert's String Quintet in C major, D. 956', ed. William Drabkin, special issue, *Music Analysis* 33/2 (2014).

30   Connelly, *The Grotesque in Western Art and Culture*, 3. My reading of rupture takes inspiration from Julian Johnson's suggestion (apropos Mahler's music) that 'structural ruptures and stylistic disjunctions [...] take on a metatextual aspect; that is, they reflect on their own conditions as a kind of "writing". They do so through self-conscious intrusions and interpolations.' See Julian Johnson, *Mahler's Voices: Expression and Irony in the Songs and Symphonies* (Oxford: Oxford University Press, 2009), 216–27. See also Michael Spitzer, *Music as Philosophy: Adorno and Beethoven's Late Style* (Bloomington: Indiana University Press, 2006), 71–112.

31   An earlier example of the tonal and textural rupture in bar 28 of D 956, II, occurs in the slow movement of the String Quartet in G major, D 887 (1826), bars 43–48, where the sudden rearing up of angular fragments recalls the distorted French overture topic of the first movement, and through a reference to fantasia in bars 49–53: quasi-improvisatory figurations are combined with extreme tonal, rhythmic, and dynamic flux. On the textural profile of D 887, see Scott Burnham, 'Beethoven, Schubert and the Movement of Phenomena', in *Schubert's Late Music*, 38–41.

32   John Gingerich, 'Remembrance and Consciousness in Schubert's C-Major String Quintet, D. 956', *Musical Quarterly* 84/4 (2000), 619–34, at 621. Cf. Susan Wollenberg, *Schubert's Fingerprints*, 168–70; Xavier Hascher, 'Eine "traumhafte" *barcarola funebre*: Fragmente zu einer Deutung des langsamen Satzes des Streichquintetts D 956', in *Schubert und das Biedermeier, Beiträge zur Musik des frühen 19. Jahrhunderts: Festschrift für Walther Dürr zum 70. Geburtstag*, ed. Michael Kube (Kassel: Bärenreiter, 2002), 127–38; and Peter Gülke, 'In What Respect a Quintet? On the Disposition of Instruments in the String Quintet D 956', in *Schubert Studies*, ed. Badura-Skoda and Branscombe, 173–85.

33   'Frühlingstraum' from *Winterreise*, D 911/11, captures the metamorphic nature of Schubertian dreamworlds in stark terms – triggered in this case by the protagonist's

Example 4.9. Schubert, String Quintet in C major, D 956, II, bars 28–31. Franz Schubert. String Quintet in C major op. post. 163 D 956 (TP 287), editor: Martin Chusid. © 1971 Bärenreiter-Verlag Karl Vötterle GmbH & Co KG, Kassel.

—(continued)

Example 4.9—concluded

Example 4.10. Schubert, String Quintet in C major, D 956, II, bars 1–4. Franz Schubert. String Quintet in C major op. post. 163 D 956 (TP 287), editor: Martin Chusid. © 1971 Bärenreiter-Verlag Karl Vötterle GmbH & Co KG, Kassel.

Grotesquerie

of dreams slips out of reach, its visionary qualities unsettled by the repeated dactylic rhythms – a muted marker of death – in the outer parts (first violin, second cello).[34] At times the music assumes greater urgency, as in bar 7 with the expansion in register and dynamic gradation; at other moments, such as bar 15, it appears increasingly transient through the contraction to triple *piano*.

Dreamworlds come into contact with their opposites in several places through flashbacks to the trills of bar 28. One example occurs in bar 35, where the dynamic marking drops to *piano*, and a series of trilled notes transpires in the upper registers of the first violin and first cello – an echo of the earlier rupture. Another example features in bars 51–54, where the first violin and first cello present 'a shuddering *Zerrbild* – a distorted, grimacing caricature' of the turn-like contour in the opening bars of the movement.[35] This thematic transformation, the former (bar 35) quiet and virtually motionless, the latter instance (bars 51–54) surrounded by rhythmic agitation, captures the mingling of opposites running through the music discussed in this chapter.

Further tensions between dreams prescient at the surface, unsettled at a deeper level, materialize in bars 64–94, where the opening material returns with distorted rhythmic figures (in the first violin and second cello) adorning the inner trio (Example 4.11). The impression of opposites is intensified here through the legato articulation of the inner trio, full of sustained notes, while the first violin and second cello creep around their contours in compressed note values – as if attempting to intrude on the proceedings. That the music is caught between the opening section and the rupture of bar 28, a mix of the two, is affirmed when the trilled note breaks through in the first violin alone at bar 91. Its return, apostrophizing the distortions throughout the movement, leaves an impression of unresolved conflict.[36]

The third movement of Schubert's String Quintet is one such place where the grotesquerie of the Adagio continues to reverberate. Its soundworlds, removed on

---

harsh awakening to reality and the eclipsing of the music of dreams: A major gives way to A minor and the dance fragments into abrupt chordal interjections that foreground harsh sonority over melodic beauty. Even the most enchanting dreams, this song intimates, have the potential to morph into an opposing reality. As Susan Youens put it, '"Frühlingstraum" is a study in contrasts and disjunctions, the silences between sections dramatizing the shocking changes of tempo, voicing, motion, tonal direction, and mood.' See Youens, *Retracing a Winter's Journey*, 211; and Wollenberg, *Schubert's Fingerprints*, 171–74, for discussion of D 911/11 vis-à-vis Schubert's instrumental genres, among them the slow movements of D 956 and D 959.

[34] An earlier example of dream-like fragility fused with visionary breadth is found in the 'A' sections of Schubert's Notturno in E flat major for piano trio, D 897 – a piece that distils the essence of oneiric imagery within its framework.

[35] Burnham, 'Thresholds Between, Worlds Apart', in 'Schubert's String Quintet in C major, D. 956', ed. William Drabkin, special issue, *Music Analysis* 33/2 (2014), 156–67, at 159.

[36] In a private communication Susan Wollenberg suggested that 'an alternative or maybe somehow compatible view is that the horrors of the central section are recalled at a distance and come to terms with finally, now understood in the context of the E major material (whereby V^7/f becomes augmented 6th of E, a recognizable cadential preparation) – peaceful tonic closure is achieved successfully thereafter'.

Example 4.11. Schubert, String Quintet in C major, D 956, II, bars 64–67. Franz Schubert. String Quintet in C major op. post. 163 D 956 (TP 287), editor: Martin Chusid. © 1971 Bärenreiter-Verlag Karl Vötterle GmbH & Co KG, Kassel.

—(continued)

Example 4.11—concluded

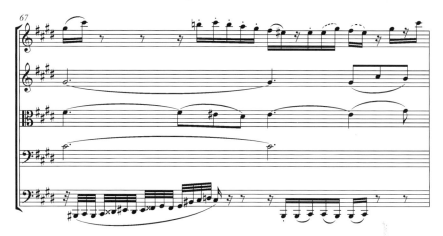

the surface from those of the Adagio, speak to the earlier movement at a deeper level through abrupt semitonal shifts and stylistic juxtaposition.[37] Signs of the grotesque appear in the slippages between the opening section and the central Trio:[38] the former, 'a rough and raucous dance', churns along through full textures and *sforzando* interjections, while the Trio opens up a 'lamenting, valedictory underworld', wherein C major is eclipsed by D flat major and the visceral textures of the opening are suddenly stripped of life.[39] These contrasts arise within an 'ombra scene', a sign that death is never far from reach.[40] Slow, sustained writing, with use of flat keys and dotted rhythms (clipped references to dactylic patterns), coupled with chromaticism and dissonance, intertwines with earlier moments in the Quintet, especially with the turn-like contours and trills (for example bars 219 and 223) that recall those of the Adagio, cast now in a muted texture. The wrenching back to the raucous style of the Scherzo in bar 264, the coalescence of dance and death, creates further ambiguity as to the meaning of such slippages. The boundaries between life

---

[37] On tonal interrelationships in the second and third movements of D 956, see Ryan McClelland, 'Tonal Recollection in Schubert's Late Instrumental Music', in *Schubert's Late Music*, 243–47; and John Gingerich, 'Schubert's *Annus Mirabilis* and the String Quintet', *Schubert's Beethoven Project* (Cambridge: Cambridge University Press, 2014), esp. 318–31.

[38] Further on Schubert's approach to trio sections, 'a retreat into that other world, an internal *Fürsichsein* purged of the antinomies with which Schubert's music must otherwise contend', see Richard Kramer, 'Against the Grain: The Sonata in G (D. 894) and a Hermeneutics of Late Style', in *Schubert's Late Music*, 127.

[39] Burnham, 'Thresholds Between, Worlds Apart', 164.

[40] Quoted in Gingerich, *Schubert's Beethoven Project*, 329; see also Gülke, 'Zum Bilde des späten Schubert: Vorwiegend analytische Betrachtungen zum Streichquintett op. 163', *Musik-Konzepte. Franz Schubert* (Munich: text+kritik, 1979), 114, 159.

142   *The Gothic Imagination in the Music of Franz Schubert*

and death are left unreconciled in the gaps across the scherzo, trio, and the preceding Adagio.

IV. Metamorphosis

Whereas in the Adagio of Schubert's String Quintet the grotesque can be heard through abrupt rupture, in the Andantino of Schubert's Piano Sonata in A major, D 959 (1828), it is suggested through a gradual process of change. The progression from one thing to another, triggered in bars 69–84 via a displacement of the opening theme, picks up on the metamorphic unfolding of ideas in the slow movement of the 'Wanderer' Fantasy, D 760. Both prise open stylistic boundaries through dissociation and disequilibrium. The transformations throughout the Andantino, discussed below, position the main theme,[41] bars 1–59, as not only haunting – its contours rising and falling against the recurrent C sharps in the left hand, redolent of those in 'Schwestergruss', with which it shares its key of F sharp minor – but also intricately entangled with the distortions that follow in its pathway (Example 4.12).

Commentators have pointed to this music (not surprisingly) as something of an anomaly. Robert Winter views it as 'an episode which comes as close to a nervous breakdown as anything in Schubert's output'.[42] In William Kinderman's words, it 'unleashes not just turbulence and foreboding, but chaotic violence';[43] while for Susan Wollenberg, it counts as one of the 'most violent episodes' among his instrumental music.[44] Charles Fisk hears a 'disordering, sense-defying experience';[45] Alfred Brendel a tone of 'feverish paroxysm';[46] Elizabeth McKay an idiom that is 'brutal and despairing, its message cruelly expressed in harsh, ugly sounds'.[47] And where

---

[41] On descriptions of the opening theme as 'plaintive', with qualities of 'lament', 'not merely poignant but desolate', acquiring a 'sinister aura', see respectively Lawrence Kramer, *Music as Cultural Practice, 1800–1900* (Berkeley: University of California Press, 1990), 94; Robert S. Hatten, 'Schubert the Progressive: The Role of Resonance and Gesture in the Piano Sonata in A, D. 959', *Intégral* 7 (1993), 67; Fisk, *Returning Cycles*, 218; and Wollenberg, *Schubert's Fingerprints*, 167.

[42] Robert Winter, 'Schubert', in *The New Grove Dictionary of Music and Musicians*, 683.

[43] William Kinderman, 'Wandering Archetypes in Schubert's Instrumental Music', *19th-Century Music* 21/2 (1997), 218.

[44] Wollenberg, *Schubert's Fingerprints*, 165.

[45] Fisk, *Returning Cycles*, 222–23.

[46] Alfred Brendel, 'Schubert's Piano Sonatas, 1822–1828', in *Musical Thoughts and Afterthoughts* (Princeton, NJ: Princeton University Press, 1976), 67.

[47] Elizabeth Norman McKay, *Schubert: The Piano and Dark Keys* (Tutzing: Schneider, 2009), 120. Among the scholars who have interpreted this music through a biographical lens, McKay argues that the 'disturbing changes of key, including frequent repetitions of unmelodic musical figurations across the entire keyboard, the harsh dynamics and relentless momentum, together suggest that, when he wrote it, the composer was in a state of hellish depression': 'the passage, climaxing in bar 122, might be used as evidence that Schubert's mental health had now, in 1828, deteriorated, in parallel with his physical health, from the milder cyclothymia from which he had almost certainly suffered over the past six years, into the far more serious full-blown manic depression.'

Example 4.12. Schubert, Piano Sonata in A major, D 959, II, bars 1–8. Franz Schubert. Sonata for Piano in A major D 959 (BA 10861), editor: Walburga Litschauer. © 2014 Bärenreiter-Verlag Karl Vötterle GmbH & Co KG, Kassel.

Marjorie Hirsch hears music 'caught up in an unexpected emotional maelstrom, overwhelming any sense of predictability, stability or security',[48] Kiene Brillenburg Wurth observes 'a provocation of shock through the sonorous staging of unbridgeable gaps and irreconcilable frictions'.[49]

The grotesque offers a context in which to rehear the strangeness of Schubert's Andantino and its hybridity as the opening theme turns into diminished sevenths and chromatic bass lines in the style of fantasia (Example 4.13).[50] Robert Schumann's observation that 'apart from Schubert's music, none exists that is so psychologically unusual in the course and connection of its ideas' is apposite here.[51] The metamorphic qualities of the music play out through a thematic profile constantly in flux,

---

[48] Hirsch, 'Gothic and Classical Influences', 152.

[49] Kiene Brillenburg Wurth, *Musically Sublime: Indeterminacy, Infinity, Irresolvability* (New York: Fordham University Press, 2011), 153.

[50] On the stylistic characteristics of fantasia, see Matthew Head, 'Fantasia and Sensibility', in *The Oxford Handbook of Topic Theory*, ed. Danuta Mirka (New York: Oxford University Press, 2014), 259–78, esp. 261, where he defines fantasia as a 'distinctive type of material at home in improvisatory keyboard works and recognizable in other contexts' through 'generic figuration (arpeggiations, scales, broken chords)' or 'abrupt, remote, and evaded modulations', achieved through 'chromaticism, enharmony, and the diminished seventh chord'. For wider reference on the evolution of fantasia in late eighteenth and early nineteenth-century music, see Susan Wollenberg, '"Es lebe die Ordnung und Betriebsamkeit! Was hilft das beste Herz ohne jene!": A New Look at Fantasia Elements in the Keyboard Sonatas of C.P.E. Bach', *Eighteenth-Century Music* 4/1 (2007), 119–28; and Annette Richards, *The Free Fantasia and the Musical Picturesque* (Cambridge: Cambridge University Press, 2001), esp. 1–33.

[51] Quoted in John Daverio, *Crossing Paths: Schubert, Schumann, and Brahms* (New York: Oxford University Press, 2002), 14. For broader context, see Schumann's evocative accounts of the literary dimension of Schubert's music. An aphoristic diary entry from August 1828 is especially revealing: 'Schubert expresses Jean Paul, Novalis, and E.T.A. Hoffmann in tones.' In the following year, Schumann disclosed in a letter to his piano teacher Friedrich Wieck that 'when I play Schubert, it's as if I were reading a novel composed by Jean Paul'. Quoted in Daverio, *Crossing Paths*, 14. Schumann reiterated the parallel between Schubert and Jean Paul in his review of the 'Great' C major Symphony, D 944. 'Consider also the heavenly length of the symphony, like a thick novel in four volumes by Jean Paul, who was also incapable of coming to an end, and to be sure for the best of reasons: to allow the reader, at a later point, to recreate it for himself.' Quoted

Example 4.13 Schubert, Piano Sonata in A major, D 959, II, bars 69–122. Franz Schubert. Sonata for Piano in A major D 959 (BA 10861), editor: Walburga Litschauer. © 2014 Bärenreiter-Verlag Karl Vötterle GmbH & Co KG, Kassel.

—(continued)

Example 4.13—continued

—(continued)

Example 4.13—*concluded*

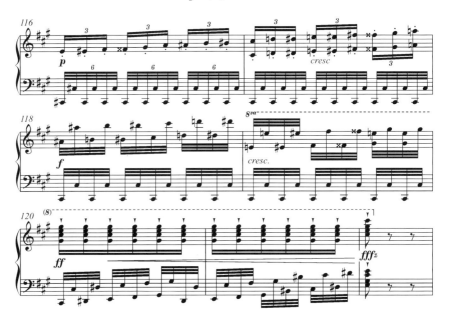

its digressive tonal language – from C minor (bar 85) to C sharp minor (bar 122) – interacting with swirling figurations, dense chordal interjections, and long stretches of trills. Change occurs at myriad levels here, with the series of sighing figures in bars 69–70 morphing into triplet figures in bars 73–74, followed by a descending-by-step sequence of diminished seventh chords – writing that seems improvisatory but rooted in the distortion of established compositional devices. Topical frames of reference, such as the allusion to a two-part invention that Hirsch identifies in bars 85–98, are defamiliarized through their tonal and textural surroundings, as well as through a use of trills that further distorts the musical surface.[52] The transformation of the C sharp pedal point, initially an unsettling presence, similarly plays a role in the evocation of the grotesque. Its disfigured rhythmic profile in bars 92–93 (split between an upper and lower octave) and 101–4 (leading to a four-octave scalar descent) unleashes the disruptive qualities latent in its earlier incarnation. These features, as with the climactic C sharp minor chord in bar 122,[53] conjure a soundscape embroiled in yet dissociated from the opening music.

---

    in Daverio, *Crossing Paths*, 17; the original text is provided in note 26 on p. 255. The full review appears in the *Neue Zeitschrift für Musik* 12 (1840), 82.

52 Hirsch, 'Gothic and Classical Influences', 157.

53 On Schubert's treatment of C sharp minor, the 'Wanderer key', in alienating ways, as in the slow movement of the 'Wanderer' Fantasy, D 760, with its intrusion of C sharp minor

Further conflation of ideas pervades bars 123–58: first, as a fragment of the opening theme, specifically its turn-like figure, returns in a quasi-recitative guise, only to be shattered by a chordal outburst reminiscent of bar 122; then extended as two subsequent fragments of the theme are interrupted by chordal outbursts, with the scalar writing of the second, bar 128, recalling that of bars 85–122.[54] These blurred boundaries extend also to the closing section, bars 159–95, there in the form of rhythmic shudders (repeated C sharp triplets) above the main theme. This represents another instance of material being familiar yet unfamiliar, first met in the returns of the funereal theme in the E flat Trio, chapter 2, as the ending retains traces of the distortions in the central section. Spread chords dissipating into bare octaves, marked triple *piano*, suggest a blurring of beginnings and endings both within this movement and in the wider selection of case studies across the book.[55]

Intertextual Dialogues

'The grotesque is assigned a reality which contradicts reality as we know it, while at the same time being seen as a true reality, a higher reality, even perhaps the reality.'[56]

The idea of the grotesque as emerging in the gaps between stylistic zones, or bound up with conflict and contradiction, plays out here in overlapping ways. While the case studies are distinct in their approaches, their soundworlds intersect through shared vocabulary – from the use of tremolo figures in the Adagio of D 760, where the music of its song source is undone by the disruptions that follow, to the juxtaposition of death and alternate realities in the *Klavierstücke* in E flat minor and E flat major. All three examples highlight the subversive nature of sonorities, whether in terms of scalar flourishes or tremolo interjections, in bringing together contrasting stylistic ideas.

The Adagio of D 956 and Andantino of D 959 converge and diverge within the world of the grotesque.[57] Where the latter movement displays a gradual metamorphosis from lyricism to fantasy through bars 69–122, in the Adagio of D 956 two worlds collide, reminiscent of Fuseli's 'The Nightmare', as the trills in bar 28

---

in the context of C major (recalling the key of 'Der Wanderer', D 489), see Fisk, *Returning Cycles*, 64–78.

[54] On resonances between the treatment of this material and the scene from Gluck's *Orfeo* where Orpheus pleads with the chorus of Furies, see Wollenberg, *Schubert's Fingerprints*, 166.

[55] For contrasting readings, see Gingerich, *Schubert's Beethoven Project*, 308–13; and Hirsch, 'Gothic and Classical Influences', 149–70. Gingerich detects 'gestures of consolation', a form of 'gently redemptive benediction', while in Hirsch's view the ending reconciles the contrasts embodied throughout.

[56] Leonard J. Kent and Elizabeth C. Knight (eds), *Tales of E.T.A. Hoffmann* (Chicago: University of Chicago Press, 1972), xvii.

[57] On intertextual dialogues between the slow movements of D 956 and D 959, in light of their shared 'extremity', see Gingerich, *Schubert's Beethoven Project*, 308.

bring the dream imagery into contact with its opposite. Despite these differing approaches, both movements retain traces of disjuncture until their closing bars, suggested through the dissolution of spread chords in low register in D 959, II, a gradual withdrawal of presence rather than a definitive ending, and by a flashback to the rupture of bar 28 in the closing bars of D 956, II.[58] The music loops back on itself, its frames of reference subject to continual defamiliarization.

The sound of the grotesque, rooted in extremity and contradiction, extends beyond the case studies discussed here to two songs that partake of this vocabulary: 'Der Leiermann' from *Winterreise*, D 911/24, and 'Der Atlas' from *Schwanengesang*, D 957/8, wherein Schubert, as Lorraine Byrne Bodley puts it, 'dared to humanize what was distant and nonhuman'.[59] Juxtapositions of life and death are pronounced in Wilhelm Müller's text of 'Der Leiermann'. Its content, while set apart chronologically, resonates with Schubert's graveyard songs in chapter 1 through repetition and sounds that blur the boundaries between the animate and the inanimate (here between the protagonist and the music of the hurdy-gurdy). The embellishments and turn-like figures in the accompaniment look back to earlier instances of such writing in instrumental genres, notably in the C minor Impromptu, while rendering them grotesque as they converge with the closing imagery: 'Strange old man, / shall I go with you? / Will you turn your hurdy-gurdy / To my songs?' ('Wunderlicher Alter, / Soll ich mit dir gehn? / Willst zu meinen Liedern / Deine Leier drehn?').[60]

Where 'Der Leiermann' conveys the grotesque through economy of means, 'Der Atlas' fills the frame with incessant sound, redolent of the accompaniment to 'Erlkönig' and 'Der Zwerg'.[61] The desperation of the 'unglücksel'ger Atlas' in Heinrich Heine's poem is mirrored in an idiom of harsh timbres, harmonic eccentricities (with diminished sevenths taking centre stage), extreme dynamic contrasts (ranging from *p* to *fff*), and constant use of tremolo (echoing the gestural patterns

---

[58] The finale too incorporates a flashback to bar 28 of the slow movement that casts, in Benedict Taylor's words, an 'uncanny shadow' over the ending. Taylor, 'Schubert and the Construction of Memory', 56.

[59] Byrne Bodley, 'A Place at the Edge: Reflections on Schubert's Late Style', *Oxford German Studies* 44/1 (2015), 18–29, at 27.

[60] Johnson, *The Complete Songs*, Vol. 3, 726. For differing interpretations of the song's enigmatic ending, particularly its displacement of reality and resistance to closure, see Lorraine Byrne Bodley, 'Music of the Orphaned Self? Schubert and Concepts of Late Style', in *Schubert's Late Music*, 331–56; Deborah Stein, 'The End of the Road in Schubert's *Winterreise*: The Contradiction of Coherence and Fragmentation', in *Rethinking Schubert*, 355–82; and Youens, *Retracing a Winter's Journey*, 298–307.

[61] 'Ich unglücksel'ger Atlas! eine Welt, / Die ganze Welt der Schmerzen muss ich tragen. / Ich trage Unerträgliches, und brechen / Will mir das Herz im Leibe' ('I, unhappy Atlas, must bear a world, / The whole world of sorrows. / I bear the unbearable, and my heart / Would break within my body'). 'Du stolzes Herz! du hast es ja gewollt, / Du wolltest glücklich sein, unendlich glücklich / Oder unendlich elend, stolzes Herz, / Und jetzo bist du elend' ('Proud heart, you wished it so! / You wished to be happy, endlessly happy, / Or endlessly wretched, proud heart! / And now you are wretched!'). Johnson, *The Complete Songs*, Vol. 3, 39.

Grotesquerie

found in D 959, II), 'a long-established Schubertian symbol for a mind in turmoil', to borrow Youens's description.[62] The combination of sorrow and wretchedness represents an extreme instance of the tensions in 'Der Wanderer' and in the songs of the night (notably 'Der Unglückliche') explored in the previous chapter. The pendulum shifts from the eeriness with which this book begins to the visceral intensity of the gothic imagination as it slips into the territory of the grotesque.

---

[62] Youens, *Heinrich Heine and the Lied* (Cambridge: Cambridge University Press, 2007), 18. See also David Ferris, 'Dissociation and Declamation in Schubert's Heine Songs', in *Rethinking Schubert*, 383–403; Xavier Hascher, '"In dunklen Traümen": Schubert's Heine-Lieder through the Psychoanalytical Prism', *Nineteenth-Century Music Review* 5/2 (2008), 43–70; Richard Kramer, 'Schubert's Heine', *19th-Century Music* 8/3 (1985), 213–25.

Epilogue

The 'strange procedures' of Schubert's creativity that the publisher detected in 1826, or the critic's mention of 'bizarre, grotesque things' in his early songs, quoted in the Introduction and chapter 1, re-emerge through this book as part of the lexicon of gothic necropoetics that captivated the imagination of the time. Strangeness, whether through sonic signifiers or poetic subject matter, weaves its way in and out of the case studies. Pieces that reflect the dreamworlds of 'Nacht und Träume', such as the Adagio of the String Quintet, give way to extreme disjuncture characteristic of the grotesque. Funereal music undergoes doubling and distortion, as in the Andante of the Piano Trio in E flat and the C minor Impromptu, discussed in chapter 2. And music that is eerie one moment turns sublime in another, as suggested in relation to the dialectics of pain and pleasure in 'Bertas Lied in der Nacht' and 'Der Unglückliche', in chapter 3. The recurrence of tropes (musical and poetic) highlights the fluidity of a vocabulary that is doubled, warped, defamiliarized, and left unreconciled across generic and chronological boundaries.

Prominent amid this continuity of gothic tropes are the ways in which their associations, and the contexts in which they appear, change over time. One such example is the octave doubling present in much of the music discussed here, from the opening stanzas of 'Leichenfantasie', the first case study of chapter 1, to the return of split left-hand octaves in the opening of the Andantino of the A major Piano Sonata, D 959, the final case study of chapter 4. Their recurrence suggests implicit dialogues across the case studies, with blurred boundaries among the contrasting iterations: the latter example, while devoid of the supernatural associations of the former, carries traces of death through its distant echoes of the earlier songs, and is now tinged with the weight of what has come before. Musical material undergoes change, returning in altered contexts, as highlighted by the fusions of funereal and French overture style, or the ways in which themes are distorted in the C minor Impromptu and the Adagio of the E flat Trio. Funereal imagery, as in the wider range of case studies in chapter 2, is devoid of its connotations in Schubert's graveyard settings, while containing echoes of their soundworlds. Past and present continually interact, such that the above instrumental examples, though not bound to the gothic through textual cues, are connected through their shared vocabulary of skeletal textures, muted dynamics, sudden rising up of tremolandos, stylistic disjuncture, and doubles and distortions.

Chronological markers of evolution in Schubert's music – whether 1822, 1824, or 1828 – merge with compositional approaches evident throughout his creative life.[1] One example is the Adagio of the 'Wanderer' Fantasy, D 760, whose writing, while distinct, can be seen as part of the trajectory of strangeness apparent from the earliest of Schubert's music. The extreme contrasts discussed in chapter 4 – from the *Klavierstücke* in E flat major and E flat minor, D 946, to the Andantino of D 959 – can likewise be traced to earlier sources, not only the Adagio of D 760, but extending further back to the reviewer's observation of 'bizarre, grotesque things' in Schubert's early songs. This approach, apparent across the book's case studies, allows the soundworlds of music from his final years to intersect with the stylistic approaches and subject matter of his songs from the 1810s. The criss-crossing of styles and genres shifts away from linear narratives of increasing complexity towards a world wherein tropes continually loop back on themselves, collapsing the boundaries between 'early' and 'late' in all instances.

These readings move beyond the biographical associations of death in Schubert's music invoked at the outset of this study. Death, a preoccupation within Schubert's creative world, as viewed here serves (without dismissing the inevitability of its personal significance) as a springboard for gothic necropoetics – from graveyard imagery, through doubling, connections between the night and the sublime, to grotesquerie and intimations of *memento mori*. Such thinking positions Schubert's own confrontation with mortality as an opportunity for creative engagement with death at the intersection of musical, literary, and visual discourses.

Beyond the gothic, ideas of the sublime and grotesque (from which discussion of his music has been largely absent) provide fresh ways of interpreting the aesthetics of Schubert's music more generally. The sublime, rooted in the dialectics of pain

---

[1] Ian Bostridge asserts that 'everything Schubert wrote after 1823, when he was diagnosed with syphilis and faced the prospect of insanity and death, constitutes late work'. For Benjamin Korstvedt, '"late Schubert" refers to the works he wrote in the final years of his short life, starting in 1823 or 1824'. 'When it concerns Schubert's last [three] piano sonatas [...]', Korstvedt continues, 'the term carries a distinct psycho-biographical charge, particularly since these works feel [...] as if they were written under the star of looming mortality'. Other writers have adopted a more cautious stance, among them Hans-Joachim Hinrichsen, who questions the appropriateness of referring to lateness in Schubert's oeuvre, given that his style was already in a state of development before the period of illness, and that his final years represent a 'euphoric departure on a journey which was broken off in mid-flight'. He suggests instead of 'late' style that 'new' style may be more appropriate, an approach comparable to Walther Dürr's observation of 'new directions' in Schubert's compositional development in his instrumental music of the years 1826–28: these include 'an increased interest in contrapuntal techniques', '[further] attention to thematic, especially motivic and submotivic relationships', and 'a new kind of sonority'. See Ian Bostridge, *A Singer's Notebook* (London: Faber and Faber, 2011), 69; Benjamin K. Korstvedt, '"The Prerogative of Schubert's Late Style": Thoughts on the Expressive World of Schubert's Late Works', in *Schubert's Late Music*, 412–13; Hans-Joachim Hinrichsen, 'Is There a Late Style in Schubert's Oeuvre?', in *Rethinking Schubert*, 26; and Walther Dürr, 'Compositional Strategies in Schubert's Late Music', in *Rethinking Schubert*, 29–40. See also Lorraine Byrne Bodley, 'Introduction: Schubert's Late Style and Current Musical Scholarship', in *Schubert's Late Music*, 1–16; and Byrne Bodley, 'A Place at the Edge: Reflections on Schubert's Late Style', *Oxford German Studies* 44/1 (2015), 18–29.

Epilogue

and pleasure, or in Schiller's notion of the sensuous-infinite, accounts for the ways in which his music broadens the boundaries beyond the (untroubled) beauty with which it is readily associated.[2] Bound up with this is an approach that recontextualizes the perceived violence of Schubert's music, or 'volcanic outbursts',[3] well established in the literature, vis-à-vis the preoccupation with awe and terror at the time, as defined here through the writings of Burke, Kant, and Schiller. The grotesque similarly suggests connections between Schubert's music and wider artistic considerations. Sounds that push at the extremes, twisted and fused with their opposites, or disjuncture that shatters all frames of reference, find contextualization in themes of hybridity and metamorphosis central to the grotesque. These approaches highlight how death-related tropes open up pathways towards deeper understandings of Schubert's creative itinerary beyond the biographical realm.

The readings offered here carry wider implications for defining the gothic imagination at the intersection of sonic, textual, and visual elements. Here, too, is an emphasis on fluidity, as gothic tropes well established in literature and the visual arts play out, with multiple meanings, through the fusion of music and words. The chapters, besides expanding analytical approaches to Schubert, encourage a rethinking of how the gothic sounds, or looks, across literary studies and the visual arts. From this perspective, Schubert's approach, whether ghostly, sublime, or grotesque, offers a lens through which to reread literary excerpts quoted in the Introduction, or to reimagine the artwork discussed throughout. Such is the case with the depictions of the grave in chapter 1, from settings resonating with graveyard poetry of the eighteenth century, to those moving closer in spirit to ideas of the Romantic gothic explored in chapter 3 – wherein death alternates between something to fear and that which offers release beyond the realm of the living. The expansion of thought from the ghostly to the sublime and the grotesque not only highlights the ways in which gothic necropoetics evolved in the early nineteenth century, but also provides impetus for seeing or hearing interrelationships among aesthetic categories more widely.

The fluidity of gothic soundworlds, of tropes appearing both continuous and discontinuous, with traces of *memento mori*, coalesces in Schubert's Piano Sonata in B

---

[2]   For a critical reappraisal of Schubertian beauty – a topic that remains ripe for further hermeneutic exploration – see among others Scott Burnham, 'Schubert and the Sound of Memory', *Musical Quarterly* 84/4 (2000), 655–63; and Susan Wollenberg, *Schubert's Fingerprints: Studies in the Instrumental Works* (Farnham: Ashgate, 2011), 189: 'there are numerous instrumental movements in Schubert's oeuvre where beauty is allowed to flourish relatively untroubled: the slow movement of the B flat Piano Trio, D 898, is an example. Elsewhere, though, beauty is created alongside and in relation to those darker moods that colour it indelibly, thereby lending it an even greater profundity.'

[3]   Hugh Macdonald, 'Schubert's Volcanic Temper', *Musical Times* 119 (1978), 949–52. See further Wollenberg, *Schubert's Fingerprints*, 161–90; Susan McClary, 'The Impromptu that Trod on a Loaf: Or How Music Tells Stories', *Narrative* 5/1 (1997), 20–35; Elizabeth Norman McKay, *Schubert: The Piano and Dark Keys* (Tutzing: Schneider, 2009); and Michael Spitzer, 'Mapping the Human Heart: A Holistic Analysis of Fear in Schubert', *Music Analysis* 29/1–3 (2010), 149–213.

154   *The Gothic Imagination in the Music of Franz Schubert*

flat, D 960 (1828), a piece not readily associated with the gothic but whose vocabulary revolves around ideas explored throughout this study.[4] Pertinent here is the trill that enters *ex nihilo* in bar 8 of the first movement, which has been described as 'a ghostly, distant thunder',[5] a 'stranger',[6] and a 'cryptic gesture' (Example 5.1).[7] Its fusion of eeriness and disruption, stopping the main theme in its tracks, recalls tensions discussed in chapter 2 apropos the main themes of the *Grande Marche Funèbre* and the C minor Impromptu. The sounds of Schubert's graveyard settings, or the nocturnal settings explored in chapter 3, may appear worlds apart from the mood of the main theme in D 960, yet momentarily close as the trill rises up then dissolves into its surroundings. These allusions capture the power of individual sonorities to conjure the constellation of gothic ideas explored across the preceding chapters. Schubert's final Sonata can thus be heard as part of those earlier soundworlds while distinct in its treatment of trills (now muted rather than forceful) and evocation of death by association (rather than through explicit cues).

Intimations of the gothic resurface in the last four bars of the finale of D 960 (Example 5.2). The pattern of alternating chordal interjections followed by silence recalls the ending of 'Leichenfantasie' (Example 1.5), where the funereal music dissipates into three G minor chords, each punctuated by rests. It also brings to mind echoes of the closing bars in the Andante of the E flat Trio, where falling octaves in the violin and cello (marked *pianissimo*) recede into the silence between each statement.

Whereas those earlier instances share a triple *piano* dynamic marking, the forcefulness of the chords in the closing bars of D 960 suggests a rearing up of the eeriness latent in the trill in the opening bars of the first movement – a resistance to closure paralleling the endings of the slow movements of D 956 and D 959. The reduction to octave unisons in the penultimate bar (recalling the octave signal in the opening of the C minor Impromptu) distills the intricate entwining of presence and absence central to this Sonata and the wider corpus of songs and instrumental music examined here.

The rests in what is the final bar of the last piano sonata by Schubert speak poignantly, despite the lack of sound, to the central themes of this book. The gothic is at times tied to excess and distortion, or force of execution. At other times its traces are audible only through silence – in those confrontations with what lies beyond finite existence.

---

[4] On D 960, see Charles Fisk, 'What Schubert's Last Sonata Might Hold', in *Music and Meaning*, ed. Jenefer Robinson (Ithaca and London: Cornell University Press, 1997), 179–200; Nicholas Marston, 'Schubert's Homecoming', *Journal of the Royal Musical Association* 125/2 (2000), 248–70.

[5] Donald Francis Tovey, 'Franz Schubert (1797–1828)', in *The Mainstream of Music and Other Essays* (Oxford: Oxford University Press, 1949), 119.

[6] Peter Pesic, 'Schubert's Dream', *19th-Century Music* 23/2 (1999), 136–44, at 139.

[7] Joseph Kerman, 'A Romantic Detail in Schubert's *Schwanengesang*', in *Schubert: Critical and Analytical Studies*, ed. Walter Frisch (Lincoln, NE, and London: University of Nebraska Press, 1986), 48–64, at 59.

Example 5.1. Schubert, Piano Sonata in B flat major, D 960, I, bars 1–9. Franz Schubert. Sonata for Piano in B flat major D 960 (BA 10860), editor: Walburga Litschauer. © 2013 Bärenreiter-Verlag Karl Vötterle GmbH & Co KG, Kassel.

Example 5.2. Schubert, Piano Sonata in B flat major, D 960, IV, bars 537–40. Franz Schubert. Sonata for Piano in B flat major D 960 (BA 10860), editor: Walburga Litschauer. © 2013 Bärenreiter-Verlag Karl Vötterle GmbH & Co KG, Kassel.

Select Bibliography

The Gothic

Andriopoulos, Stefan, *Ghostly Apparitions: German Idealism, the Gothic Novel, and Optical Media* (Princeton, NJ: Zone Books, 2013).

Andriopoulos, Stefan, 'Occult Conspiracies: Spirits and Secret Societies in Schiller's "Ghost Seer"', in 'Dark Powers: Conspiracies and Conspiracy Theory in History and Literature', *New German Critique* 103 (2008), 65–81.

Baldick, Chris (ed.), *The Oxford Book of Gothic Tales* (Oxford: Oxford University Press, 2009).

Barack, Karlheinz et al. (eds), 'Grotesk', in *Ästhetische Grundbegriffe: Band 2, Dekadent bis Grotesk* (Stuttgart: J.B. Metzler Verlag, 2001), 880–98.

Berthin, Christine, *Gothic Hauntings: Melancholy Crypts and Textual Ghosts* (London: Palgrave Macmillan, 2010).

Botting, Fred, *Gothic* (New York: Routledge, 2014).

Botting, Fred and Catherine Spooner (eds), *Monstrous Media / Spectral Subjects: Imaging Gothic from the Nineteenth Century to the Present* (Manchester: Manchester University Press, 2015).

Bronfen, Elisabeth, *Over her Dead Body: Death, Femininity and the Aesthetic* (Manchester: Manchester University Press, 1992).

Bronfen, Elisabeth and Beate Neumeier (eds), *Gothic Renaissance: A Reassessment* (Manchester: Manchester University Press, 2014).

Burwick, Frederick, *The Haunted Eye: Perception and the Grotesque in English and German Romanticism* (Heidelberg: Carl Winter Universitätsverlag, 1987).

Carruthers, Gerard and Liam McIlvanney (eds), *The Cambridge Companion to Scottish Literature* (Cambridge: Cambridge University Press, 2013).

Castle, Terry, 'The Spectralization of the Other in *The Mysteries of Udolpho*', in *The Female Thermometer: Eighteenth-Century Culture and the Invention of the Uncanny*, ed. Castle (New York: Oxford University Press, 1995), 120–39.

Cavallaro, Dani, *The Gothic Vision: Three Centuries of Horror, Terror and Fear* (London & New York: Continuum, 2002).

Chao, Noelle, 'Musical Listening in *The Mysteries of Udolpho*', in *Words and Notes in the Long Nineteenth Century*, ed. Phyllis Weliver and Katharine Ellis (Woodbridge: Boydell & Brewer, 2013), 85–102.

Connelly, Frances S., *The Grotesque in Western Art and Culture: The Image at Play* (Cambridge: Cambridge University Press, 2012).

Crawford, Joseph, '"Every Night, The Same Routine": Recurring Nightmares and the Repetition Compulsion in Gothic Fiction', *Moveable Type* 6 (2010), 1–9.

Crimmins, Jonathan, 'Mediation's Sleight of Hand: The Two Vectors of the Gothic in Mary Shelley's "Frankenstein"', *Studies in Romanticism* 52/4 (2013), 561–83.

Cusack, Andrew and Barry Murnane (eds), *Popular Revenants: The German Gothic and its International Reception, 1800–2000* (Rochester, NY: Camden House, 2012).

Davison, Carol M., 'Death and Gothic Romanticism: Dilating in/upon the Graveyard, Meditating among the Tombs', in *The Routledge Companion to Death and Literature*, ed. W. Michelle Wang, Daniel Jernigan, and Neil Murphy (New York: Routledge, 2020), 276–87.

Davison, Carol M. (ed.), *The Gothic and Death* (Manchester: Manchester University Press, 2017).

Davison, Carol M., *Gothic Literature 1764–1824* (Cardiff: University of Wales Press, 2009).

Davison, Carol M., 'Trafficking in Death and (Un)dead Bodies: Necro-Politics and Poetics in the Works of Ann Radcliffe', *Irish Journal of Gothic and Horror Studies* 14 (2015), 37–47.

DeLamotte, Eugenia C., *Perils of the Night: A Feminist Study of Nineteenth-Century Gothic* (Oxford: Oxford University Press, 1990).

Dent, Jonathan, *Sinister Histories: Gothic Novels and Representations of the Past, from Horace Walpole to Mary Wollstonecraft* (Manchester: Manchester University Press, 2016).

Esse, Melina, 'Donizetti's Gothic Resurrections', *19th-Century Music* 33 (2009), 81–109.

Ferguson, Frances, *Solitude and the Sublime* (London: Routledge, 1992).

Fillerup, Jessie, 'Lucia's Ghosts: Sonic, Gothic and Postmodern', *Cambridge Opera Journal* 28/3 (2016), 313–45.

Gamer, Michael, *Romanticism and the Gothic: Genre, Reception, and Canon Formation* (Cambridge: Cambridge University Press, 2000).

Gibson, Matthew, *The Fantastic and European Gothic* (Cardiff: University of Wales Press, 2013).

Groom, Nick, *The Gothic: A Very Short Introduction* (Oxford: Oxford University Press, 2012).

Harpham, Geoffrey Galt, *On the Grotesque: Strategies of Contradiction in Art and Literature* (Princeton, NJ: Princeton University Press, 1982).

Head, Matthew, 'Mozart's Gothic: Feelings for History in the Rondo in A minor, K. 511', *Keyboard Perspectives* 4 (2012), 69–114.

High, Jeffrey L., 'Schiller, Coleridge, and the Reception of the "German (Gothic) Tale"', Themenheft, 'The German Gothic', *Colloquia Germanica* 42/1 (2009), 49–66.

Hoffmeister, Gerhart, *European Romanticism: Literary Cross-Currents, Modes, and Models* (Detroit: Wayne State University Press, 1989).

Select Bibliography 159

Hogle, Jerrold E. (ed.), *The Cambridge Companion to Gothic Fiction* (Cambridge: Cambridge University Press, 2002).

Howard, Jacqueline, *Reading Gothic Fiction: A Bakhtinian Approach* (Oxford: Oxford Academic Books, 1994).

Hughes, William et al. (eds), *The Encyclopedia of the Gothic*, 2 vols (New York: John Wiley & Sons, 2015).

Lake, Crystal B., 'Bloody Records: Manuscripts and Politics in *The Castle of Otranto*', *Modern Philology* 110/4 (2013), 489–512.

Leikin, Anatole, 'Chopin and the Gothic', in *Chopin and his World*, ed. Jonathan D. Bellman and Halina Goldberg (Princeton, NJ: Princeton University Press, 2017), 85–102.

Lüdeke, Roger, 'Gothic Truth and Mimetic Practice: On the Realism of Schiller's *Geisterseher*', *European Romantic Review* 28/1 (2017), 37–50.

Maier, Edward K., 'Gothic Horror, the Windowless Monad, and the Self: The Limits of Enlightenment in Schiller's "Der Geisterseher"', *Colloquia Germanica* 3/4 (2006), 243–55.

Matthews, Samantha, *Poetical Remains: Poets' Graves, Bodies, and Books in the Nineteenth Century* (Oxford: Oxford University Press, 2004).

Mishra, Vijay, *The Gothic Sublime* (New York: State University of New York Press, 1994).

Moffitt, John, 'A Pictorial Counterpart to "Gothick" Literature: Fuseli's *The Nightmare*', in 'Haunting II', special issue, *Mosaic: An Interdisciplinary Critical Journal* 25/1 (March 2002), 173–96.

Morris, David B., 'Gothic Sublimity', in 'The Sublime and the Beautiful: Reconsiderations', *New Literary History* 16/2 (1985), 299–319.

Mulvey-Roberts, Marie, *The Handbook of the Gothic* (New York: Palgrave Macmillan, 2009).

Myron, Martin, 'Henry Fuseli and Gothic Spectacle', *Huntington Library Quarterly* 70/2 (2007), 289–310.

Napier, Elizabeth R., *The Failure of Gothic: Problems of Disjunction in an Eighteenth-Century Literary Form* (New York: Oxford University Press, 1987).

Parisot, Eric, 'Gothic and Graveyard Poetry: Imagining the Dead (of Night)', in *The Edinburgh Companion to Gothic and the Arts*, ed. David Punter (Edinburgh: Edinburgh University Press, 2019), 245–58.

Protano-Biggs, Laura, 'Bellini's Gothic Voices: Bellini, "Un grido io sento" (Alaide), *La straniera*, Act I', *Cambridge Opera Journal* 28 (2016), 149–54.

Punter, David (ed.), *The Edinburgh Companion to Gothic and the Arts* (Edinburgh: Edinburgh University Press, 2019).

Punter, David, *The Literature of Terror: A History of Gothic Fictions from 1765 to the Present Day* (New York: Longman Group, 1980).

Punter, David (ed.), *A New Companion to the Gothic* (Cambridge: Cambridge University Press, 2000).

Shapira, Yael, *Inventing the Gothic Corpse: The Thrill of Human Remains in the Eighteenth-Century Novel* (Cham, Switzerland: Palgrave Macmillan, 2018).

Smith, Andrew, 'The Gothic and the Sublime', in *Gothic Radicalism: Literature, Philosophy, and Psychoanalysis in the Nineteenth Century* (London: Palgrave Macmillan, 2020), 11–37.

Smith, Andrew, *Gothic Death 1740–1914: A Literary History* (Manchester: Manchester University Press, 2016).

Spooner, Catherine and Emma McEvoy (eds), *The Routledge Companion to Gothic* (New York: Routledge, 2007).

Townshend, Dale and Angela Wright (eds), *Ann Radcliffe, Romanticism and the Gothic* (Cambridge: Cambridge University Press, 2014).

Townshend, Dale and Angela Wright (eds), *The Cambridge History of Gothic*, Vol. 2: *The Gothic in the Nineteenth Century* (Cambridge: Cambridge University Press, 2020).

Trowbridge, Serena, 'Past, Present, and Future in the Gothic Graveyard', in *The Gothic and Death*, ed. Carol M. Davison (Manchester: Manchester University Press, 2017), 21–33.

Van Elferen, Isabella, *Gothic Music: The Sounds of the Uncanny* (Cardiff: University of Wales Press, 2012).

Ward, Maryanne C., 'A Painting of the Unspeakable: Henry Fuseli's "The Nightmare" and the Creation of Mary Shelley's "Frankenstein"', *Journal of the Midwest Modern Language Association* 33/1 (2000), 20–31.

Webber, Andrew J., *The Doppelgänger: Double Visions in German Literature* (Oxford: Oxford University Press, 1996).

Wright, Angela and Dale Townshend (eds), *Romantic Gothic: An Edinburgh Companion* (Edinburgh: Edinburgh University Press, 2015).

Franz Schubert (Primary Source Material)

Deutsch, Otto Erich, *Schubert: Die Dokumente seines Lebens* (Kassel: Bärenreiter Verlag, 1964, repr. 1980 and 1996); *Schubert: A Documentary Biography*, trans. Eric Blom (London: J.M. Dent & Sons, 1947); and *The Schubert Reader: A Life of Franz Schubert in Letters and Documents*, trans. Blom (New York: W.W. Norton & Co., 1949).

Deutsch, Otto Erich, *Schubert: Die Erinnerungen seiner Freunde* (Wiesbaden: Breitkopf & Härtel, 1957, repr. 1983); *Schubert: Memoirs by his Friends*, trans. Rosamund Ley and John Nowell (London: Adam and Charles Black, 1958).

Dürr, Walther, Arnold Feil, Christa Landon et al. (eds), *Franz Schubert: Neue Ausgabe sämtlicher Werke* [NSA] (Kassel: Bärenreiter, 1964–).

Dürr, Walther, Arnold Feil, Christa Landon et al. (eds), *Franz Schubert: Thematisches Verzeichnis seiner Werke in chronologischer Folge von Otto Erich Deutsch*, NSA, VIII/4 (Kassel: Bärenreiter, 1978).

Dürr, Walther and Andreas Krause (eds), *Schubert Handbuch* (London: Panther Books, 1971; orig. pub. Cassell & Co., 1951).

Hilmar, Ernst, *Franz Schubert in seiner Zeit* (Vienna: Hermann Böhlaus Nachf., 1985), trans. Reinhard G. Pauly as *Franz Schubert in his Time* (Portland, OR: Amadeus Press, 1988).

Hilmar, Ernst and Werner Bodendorff, *Franz Schubert: Dokumente 1801–1830*, Vol. 1: *Texte, Programme, Rezensionen, Anzeigen, Nekrologe, Musikbeilagen und andere gedruckte Quellen, Addenda und Kommentar* (Tutzing: Veröffentlichungen des IFSI, 2003).

Hilmar, Ernst and Margaret Jestremski (eds), *Schubert Lexikon* (Graz: Akademische Druck- und Verlagsanstalt, 1997).

Litschauer, Walburga (ed.), *Neue Dokumente zum Schubert-Kreis: Aus Briefen und Tagebüchern seiner Freunde* (Vienna: Musikwissenschaftlicher Verlag, 1986).

Waidelich, Till Gerrit (ed.), *Franz Schubert: Dokumente, 1817–1830*, Vol. 1: *Texte, Programme, Rezensionen, Anzeigen, Nekrologe, Musikbeilagen und andere gedruckte Quellen* (Tutzing: Hans Schneider Verlag, 1993).

Franz Schubert (Aesthetics and Expressive Worlds)

Barry, Barbara, 'Schubert's *Quartettsatz*: A Case Study in Confrontation', *Musical Times* 155 (2014), 31–49.

Barry, Barbara, '"Sehnsucht" and Melancholy: Explorations of Time and Structure in Schubert's *Winterreise*', in *The Philosopher's Stone: Essays in the Transformation of Musical Structure* (Hillsdale, NY: Pendragon Press, 2000), 181–202.

Barry, Barbara, 'A Shouting Silence: Further Thoughts about Schubert's "Unfinished"', *Musical Times* 151 (2010), 39–52.

Binder, Benjamin, 'Disability, Self-Critique, and Failure in Schubert's "Der Doppelgänger"', in *Rethinking Schubert*, ed. Lorraine Byrne Bodley and Julian Horton (New York: Oxford University Press, 2016), 418–36.

Black, Brian, 'Lyricism and the Dramatic Unity of Schubert's Instrumental Music: The Impromptu in C Minor, D. 899/1', in *Drama in the Music of Franz Schubert*, ed. Joe Davies and James William Sobaskie (Woodbridge: Boydell & Brewer, 2019), 233–56.

Black, Brian, 'Remembering a Dream: The Tragedy of Romantic Memory in the Modulatory Processes of Schubert's Sonata Forms', *Intersections* 25/1–2 (2005), 202–28.

Black, Brian, 'The Sensuous as a Constructive Force in Schubert's Late Works', in *Rethinking Schubert*, ed. Lorraine Byrne Bodley and Julian Horton (New York: Oxford University Press, 2016), 77–108.

Bostridge, Ian, *Schubert's Winter Journey: Anatomy of an Obsession* (London: Faber & Faber, 2015).

Select Bibliography

Botstein, Leon, 'Realism Transformed: Franz Schubert and Vienna', in *The Cambridge Companion to Schubert*, ed. Christopher H. Gibbs (Cambridge: Cambridge University Press, 1997), 13–35.

Brendel, Alfred, 'Schubert's Piano Sonatas, 1822–1828', in *Musical Thoughts and Afterthoughts* (Princeton, NJ: Princeton University Press, 1976), 57–74.

Bretherton, David, 'In Search of Schubert's Doppelgänger', *Musical Times* 144 (2003), 45–50.

Brett, Philip, 'Piano Four-Hands: Schubert and the Performance of Gay Male Desire', *19th-Century Music* 21/2 (1997), 149–76.

Burnham, Scott, 'Beethoven, Schubert and the Movement of Phenomena', in *Schubert's Late Music: History, Theory, Style*, ed. Lorraine Byrne Bodley and Julian Horton (Cambridge: Cambridge University Press, 2016), 35–51.

Burnham, Scott, 'The "Heavenly Length" of Schubert's Music', *Ideas* 6/1 (1999).

Burnham, Scott, 'Landscape as Music, Landscape as Truth: Schubert and the Burden of Repetition', *19th-Century Music* 29 (2005), 31–41.

Burnham, Scott, 'Schubert and the Sound of Memory', *Musical Quarterly* 84/4 (2000), 655–63.

Burnham, Scott, 'Thresholds Between, Worlds Apart', in 'Schubert's String Quintet in C major, D. 956', ed. William Drabkin, special issue, *Music Analysis* 33/2 (2014), 156–67.

Byrne Bodley, Lorraine, *Franz Schubert: A Musical Wayfarer* (New Haven: Yale University Press, 2023).

Byrne Bodley, Lorraine, 'In Pursuit of a Single Flame? On Schubert's Settings of Goethe's Poems', *Nineteenth-Century Music Review* 13/2 (2016), 11–33.

Byrne Bodley, Lorraine, 'Introduction: Schubert's Late Style and Current Musical Scholarship', in *Schubert's Late Music: History, Theory, Style*, ed. Byrne Bodley and Julian Horton (Cambridge: Cambridge University Press, 2016), 1–16.

Byrne Bodley, Lorraine, 'Music of the Orphaned Self? Schubert and Concepts of Late Style', in *Schubert's Late Music: History, Theory, Style*, ed. Byrne Bodley and Julian Horton (Cambridge: Cambridge University Press, 2016), 331–56.

Byrne Bodley, Lorraine, 'A Place at the Edge: Reflections on Schubert's Late Style', *Oxford German Studies* 44/1 (2015), 18–29.

Byrne Bodley, Lorraine, *Schubert's Goethe Settings* (Farnham: Ashgate, 2003).

Byrne Bodley, Lorraine and Julian Horton (eds), *Rethinking Schubert* (New York: Oxford University Press, 2016).

Byrne Bodley, Lorraine and Julian Horton (eds), *Schubert's Late Music: History, Theory, Style* (Cambridge: Cambridge University Press, 2016).

Clark, Suzannah, *Analyzing Schubert* (Cambridge: Cambridge University Press, 2011).

Daverio, John, *Crossing Paths: Schubert, Schumann, and Brahms* (New York and Oxford: Oxford University Press, 2002).

Select Bibliography

Daverio, John, '"One More Beautiful Memory of Schubert": Schumann's Critique of the Impromptus, D. 935', *Musical Quarterly* 84/4 (2000), 604–18.

Davies, Joe, 'Franz Schubert, Death, and the Gothic', in *Schubert's Piano*, ed. Matthew Gardner and Christine Martin (Cambridge: Cambridge University Press, 2024).

Davies, Joe, 'Interpreting the Expressive Worlds of Schubert's Late Instrumental Works' (DPhil dissertation, University of Oxford, 2018).

Davies, Joe and James William Sobaskie (eds), *Drama in the Music of Franz Schubert* (Woodbridge: Boydell & Brewer, 2019).

Dunsby, Jonathan, 'Adorno's Image of Schubert's "Wanderer" Fantasy Multiplied by Ten', *19th-Century Music* 29/1 (2005), 209–36.

Dürr, Walther, 'Compositional Strategies in Schubert's Late Music', in *Rethinking Schubert*, ed. Lorraine Byrne Bodley and Julian Horton (New York: Oxford University Press, 2016), 29–40.

Dürr, Walther, 'Schuberts Ossian-Gesänge. Vom Lied zur Szene', in *Schubert: Interpretationen*, ed. Ivana Rentsch and Klaus Pietschmann (Stuttgart: Franz Steiner, 2014), 11–26.

Dürr, Walther, 'Über Schuberts Verhältnis zu Bach', in *Johann Sebastian Bach: Beiträge zur Wirkungsgeschichte* (Vienna: Kongressbericht Wien, 1992), 69–79.

Erickson, Raymond (ed.), *Schubert's Vienna* (New Haven, CT: Yale University Press, 1997).

Feurzeig, Lisa, *Schubert's Lieder and the Philosophy of Early German Romanticism* (Farnham: Ashgate, 2014).

Fisk, Charles, *Returning Cycles: Contexts for the Interpretation of Schubert's Impromptus and Last Sonatas* (Berkeley: University of California Press, 2001).

Fisk, Charles, 'Schubert Recollects Himself: The Piano Sonata in C Minor, D. 958', *Musical Quarterly* 84/4 (2000), 635–54.

Fisk, Charles, 'What Schubert's Last Sonata Might Hold', in *Music and Meaning*, ed. Jenefer Robinson (Ithaca and London: Cornell University Press, 1997), 179–200.

Frisch, Walter, '"You Must Remember This": Memory and Structure in Schubert's String Quartet in G Major, D. 887', *Musical Quarterly* 84/4 (2000), 582–603.

Gibbs, Christopher H. (ed.), *The Cambridge Companion to Schubert* (Cambridge: Cambridge University Press, 1997).

Gibbs, Christopher H., '"Komm geh mit mir": Schubert's Uncanny "Erlkönig"', *19th-Century Music* 19/2 (1995), 115–35.

Gibbs, Christopher H., *The Life of Schubert* (Cambridge: Cambridge University Press, 2000).

Gibbs, Christopher H., 'Schubert's *Tombeau de Beethoven*: Decrypting the Piano Trio in E-flat Major, Op. 100', in *Franz Schubert and his World*, ed. Gibbs and Morten Solvik (Princeton, NJ: Princeton University Press, 2014), 241–98.

Gibbs, Christopher H. and Morten Solvik (eds), *Franz Schubert and his World* (Princeton, NJ: Princeton University Press, 2014).

Gingerich, John, 'Remembrance and Consciousness in Schubert's C-Major String Quintet, D. 956', *Musical Quarterly* 84/4 (2000), 619–34.

Gingerich, John, *Schubert's Beethoven Project* (Cambridge: Cambridge University Press, 2014).

Gingerich, John, '"Those of Us Who Found our Life in Art": The Second-Generation Romanticism of the Schubert–Schober Circle, 1820–25', in *Franz Schubert and his World*, ed. Christopher H. Gibbs and Morten Solvik (Princeton, NJ: Princeton University Press 2014), 67–114.

Gingerich, John, 'Unfinished Considerations: Schubert's "Unfinished" Symphony in the Context of his Beethoven Project', *19th-Century Music* 31/2 (2007), 99–112.

Gramit, David, 'The Intellectual and Aesthetic Tenets of Franz Schubert's Circle' (PhD dissertation, Duke University, 1987).

Gramit, David, '"The Passion for Friendship": Music, Cultivation, and Identity in Schubert's Circle', in *The Cambridge Companion to Schubert*, ed. Christopher H. Gibbs (Cambridge: Cambridge University Press, 1997), 56–71.

Gülke, Peter, 'In What Respect a Quintet? On the Disposition of Instruments in the String Quintet D 956', in *Schubert Studies*, ed. Eva Badura-Skoda and Peter Branscombe (Cambridge: Cambridge University Press, 1982), 173–85.

Gülke, Peter, *Schubert und seine Zeit* (Laaber: Laaber-Verlag, 1991).

Gülke, Peter, 'Zum Bilde des späten Schubert: Vorwiegend analytische Betrachtungen zum Streichquintett, Op. 163', in *Musik-Konzepte. Franz Schubert*, ed. Heinz-Klaus Metzger and Rainer Riehn (Munich: Edition Text+Kritik, 1979), 107–66.

Hallmark, Rufus, 'The Literary and Musical Rhetoric of Apostrophe in *Winterreise*', *19th-Century Music* 35/1 (2011), 3–33.

Hascher, Xavier, '"In dunklen Träumen": Schubert's Heine-Lieder through the Psychoanalytical Prism', *Nineteenth-Century Music Review* 5/2 (2008), 43–70.

Hascher, Xavier, 'Narrative Dislocations in the First Movement of Schubert's "Unfinished" Symphony', in *Rethinking Schubert*, ed. Lorraine Byrne Bodley and Julian Horton (New York: Oxford University Press, 2016), 127–46.

Hascher, Xavier (ed.), *Le style instrumental de Schubert: sources, analyse, évolution* (Paris: Publications de la Sorbonne, 2007).

Hascher, Xavier, 'Eine "traumhafte" *barcarola funebre*: Fragmente zu einer Deutung des langsamen Satzes des Streichquintetts D 956', in *Schubert und das Biedermeier, Beiträge zur Musik des frühen 19. Jahrhunderts: Festschrift für Walther Dürr zum 70. Geburtstag*, ed. Michael Kube (Kassel: Bärenreiter, 2002), 127–38.

Hatten, Robert S., 'Schubert the Progressive: The Role of Resonance and Gesture in the Piano Sonata in A, D. 959', *Intégral* 7 (1993), 38–91.

Hatten, Robert S., 'Schubert's Alchemy: Transformative Surfaces, Transfiguring Depths', in *Schubert's Late Music: History, Theory, Style*, ed. Lorraine Byrne Bodley and Julian Horton (Cambridge: Cambridge University Press, 2016), 91–110.

Select Bibliography

Hatten, Robert S., *Interpreting Musical Gestures, Topics, and Tropes: Mozart, Beethoven, and Schubert* (Bloomington: Indiana University Press, 2004).

Hinrichsen, Hans-Joachim, *Franz Schubert* (Munich: C.H. Beck, 2011).

Hinrichsen, Hans-Joachim, 'Is There a Late Style in Schubert?', trans. Lorraine Byrne Bodley, in *Rethinking Schubert*, ed. Byrne Bodley and Julian Horton (New York: Oxford University Press, 2016), 17–28.

Hirsch, Marjorie W., *Romantic Lieder and the Search for Lost Paradise* (Cambridge: Cambridge University Press, 2007).

Hirsch, Marjorie W., *Schubert's Dramatic Lieder* (Cambridge: Cambridge University Press, 1993).

Hirsch, Marjorie, 'Schubert's Reconciliation of Gothic and Classical Influences', in *Schubert's Late Music: History, Theory, Style*, ed. Lorraine Byrne Bodley and Julian Horton (Cambridge: Cambridge University Press, 2016), 149–70.

Howe, Blake, 'The Allure of Dissolution: Bodies, Forces, and Cyclicity in Schubert's Final Mayrhofer Settings', *Journal of the American Musicological Society* 62/2 (2009), 271–322.

Howe, Blake, 'Bounded Finitude and Boundless Infinitude: Schubert's Contradictions at the "Final Barrier"', in *Schubert's Late Music: History, Theory, Style*, ed. Lorraine Byrne Bodley and Julian Horton (Cambridge: Cambridge University Press, 2016), 357–82.

Howe, Blake, 'Whose *Winterreise*?', *Nineteenth-Century Music Review* 13/1 (2016), 113–22.

Hyland, Anne M., 'In Search of Liberated Time, or Schubert's Quartet in G Major, D. 887: Once More between Sonata and Variation', *Music Theory Spectrum* 38/1 (2016), 85–108.

Hyland, Anne M., 'The "Tightened Bow": Analysing the Juxtaposition of Drama and Lyricism in Schubert's Paratactic Sonata-Form Movements', in *Irish Musical Analysis: Irish Musical Studies* 11, ed. Julian Horton and Gareth Cox (Dublin: Four Courts Press, 2014), 17–40.

Johnson, Graham, *Franz Schubert: The Complete Songs*, 3 vols (New Haven and London: Yale University Press, 2014).

Kinderman, William, 'Franz Schubert's "New Style" and the Legacy of Beethoven', in *Rethinking Schubert*, ed. Lorraine Byrne Bodley and Julian Horton (New York: Oxford University Press, 2016), 41–60.

Kinderman, William, 'Schubert's Piano Music: Probing the Human Condition', in *The Cambridge Companion to Schubert*, ed. Christopher H. Gibbs (Cambridge: Cambridge University Press, 1997), 155–73.

Kinderman, William, 'Schubert's Tragic Perspective', in *Schubert: Critical and Analytical Studies*, ed. Walter Frisch (Lincoln, NE, and London: University of Nebraska Press, 1986), 65–83.

Kinderman, William, 'Wandering Archetypes in Schubert's Instrumental Music', *19th-Century Music* 21/2 (1997), 208–22.

Select Bibliography

Korstvedt, Benjamin K., '"The Prerogative of Late Style": Thoughts on the Expressive World of Schubert's Late Works', in *Schubert's Late Music: History, Theory, Style*, ed. Lorraine Byrne Bodley and Julian Horton (Cambridge: Cambridge University Press, 2016), 404–25.

Kramer, Lawrence, *Franz Schubert: Sexuality, Subjectivity, Song* (Cambridge: Cambridge University Press, 1998).

Kramer, Richard, 'Against the Grain: The Sonata in G (D. 894) and a Hermeneutics of Late Style', in *Schubert's Late Music: History, Theory, Style*, ed. Lorraine Byrne Bodley and Julian Horton (Cambridge: Cambridge University Press, 2016), 111–33.

Kramer, Richard, *Distant Cycles: Schubert and the Conceiving of Song* (Chicago: University of Chicago Press, 1994).

Kramer, Richard, 'Schubert's Heine', *19th-Century Music* 8/3 (1985), 213–25.

Krause, Andreas, *Die Klaviersonaten Franz Schuberts: Form, Gattung, Ästhetik* (Kassel: Bärenreiter, 1992).

Kube, Michael, 'Zur Satztechnik in Schuberts Sonate für Klavier, Violine und violoncello, B-Dur D 28 (Triosatz)', in *Bach und Schubert: Beiträge zur Musikforschung* (Munich: Katzbichler, 1999), 15–22.

Kurth, Richard, 'Music and Poetry, A Wilderness of Doubles: Heine–Nietzsche–Schubert–Derrida', *19th-Century Music* 21/1 (1997), 3–37.

Lindmayr-Brandl, Andrea, 'Music and Culture in Schubert's Vienna', in *The Cambridge Companion to Schubert's 'Winterreise'*, ed. Marjorie W. Hirsch and Lisa Feurzeig (Cambridge: Cambridge University Press, 2021), 11–23.

Macdonald, Hugh, 'Schubert's Volcanic Temper', *Musical Times* 119 (1978), 949–52.

Mak, Su Yin, 'Et in Arcadia Ego: The Elegiac Structure of Schubert's *Quartettsatz* in C Minor (D. 703)', in *The Unknown Schubert*, ed. Barbara M. Reul and Lorraine Byrne Bodley (Farnham: Ashgate, 2008), 145–53.

Mak, Su Yin, 'Formal Ambiguity and Generic Reinterpretation in the Late Instrumental Music', in *Schubert's Late Music: History, Theory, Style*, ed. Lorraine Byrne Bodley and Julian Horton (Cambridge: Cambridge University Press, 2016), 282–306.

Mak, Su Yin, 'Schubert as Schiller's Sentimental Poet', *Eighteenth-Century Music* 4/2 (2007), 251–63.

Mak, Su Yin, *Schubert's Lyricism Reconsidered: Structure, Design and Rhetoric* (Saarbrücken: Lambert, 2010).

Mak, Su Yin, 'Schubert's Sonata Forms and the Poetics of the Lyric', *Journal of Musicology* 23/2 (2006), 263–306.

Marston, Nicholas, 'Schubert's Homecoming', *Journal of the Royal Musical Association* 125/2 (2000), 248–70.

McClary, Susan, 'Constructions of Subjectivity in Schubert's Music', in *Queering the Pitch: The New Gay and Lesbian Musicology*, ed. Philip Brett, Gary Thomas, and Elizabeth Wood (New York and London: Routledge, 1994), 205–33.

McClary, Susan, 'The Impromptu that Trod on a Loaf: Or How Music Tells Stories', *Narrative* 5/1 (1997), 20–35.

McClary, Susan, 'Pitches, Expression, Ideology: An Exercise in Mediation', *Enclitic* 7 (1983), 76–86, repr. in *Reading Music: Selected Essays* (Farnham: Ashgate, 2007), 3–14.

McClelland, Clive, 'Death and the Composer: The Context of Schubert's Supernatural Lieder' in *Schubert the Progressive: History, Performance Practice, Analysis*, ed. Brian Newbould (Aldershot: Ashgate, 2003), 21–35.

McKay, Elizabeth Norman, *Franz Schubert: A Biography* (Oxford: Oxford University Press, 1996).

McKay, Elizabeth Norman, *Schubert: The Piano and Dark Keys* (Tutzing: Schneider, 2009).

Messing, Scott, *Marching to the Canon: The Life of Schubert's 'Marche Militaire'* (Rochester, NY: University of Rochester Press, 2014).

Messing, Scott, *Schubert in the European Imagination*, 2 vols (Rochester, NY: University of Rochester Press, 2006).

Messing, Scott, *Self-Quotation in Schubert: 'Ave Maria', the Second Piano Trio, and Other Works* (Rochester, NY: University of Rochester Press, 2020).

Muxfeldt, Kristina, *Vanishing Sensibilities: Schubert, Beethoven, Schumann* (New York: Oxford University Press, 2011).

Perry, Jeffrey, 'The Wanderer's Many Returns: Schubert's Variations Reconsidered', *Journal of Musicology* 19/2 (2002), 374–416.

Pesic, Peter, 'Schubert's Dream', *19th-Century Music* 23/2 (1999), 136–44.

Plantinga, Leon, 'Schubert, Social Music and Melancholy', in *Rethinking Schubert*, ed. Lorraine Byrne Bodley and Julian Horton (New York: Oxford University Press, 2016), 237–50.

Reul, Barbara M. and Lorraine Byrne Bodley (eds), *The Unknown Schubert* (Farnham: Ashgate, 2008).

Rushton, Julian, 'Schubert, the Tarantella, and the *Quartettsatz*, D. 703', in *Variations on the Canon: Essays on Music from Bach to Boulez in Honor of Charles Rosen on his Eightieth Birthday*, ed. Robert Curry, David Gable, and Robert L. Marshall (Rochester, NY: University of Rochester Press, 2008), 163–71.

Samuels, Robert, 'The Double Articulation of Schubert: Reflections on *Der Doppelgänger*', *Musical Quarterly* 93/1 (2010), 192–233.

Samuels, Robert, 'Schubert's Instrumental Voice: Vocality in Melodic Construction in the Late Works', in *On Voice*, ed. Walter Bernhart and Lawrence Kramer (Amsterdam: Rodopi, 2014), 161–78.

Sobaskie, James William, 'A Balance Struck: Gesture, Form, and Drama in Schubert's E-flat Major Piano Trio', in *Le style instrumental de Schubert: sources, analyse, évolution*, ed. Xavier Hascher (Paris: Publications de la Sorbonne, 2007), 115–46.

Sobaskie, James William, 'The "Problem" of Schubert's String Quintet', *Nineteenth-Century Music Review* 2/1 (2005), 57–92.

Sobaskie, James William, 'Schubert's Self-Elegies', *Nineteenth-Century Music Review* 5/2 (2008), 71–105.

Sobaskie, James William, 'Tonal Implication and the Gestural Dialectic in Schubert's A Minor String Quartet', in *Schubert the Progressive: History, Performance, Practice, Analysis*, ed. Brian Newbould (Aldershot: Ashgate, 2003), 53–79.

Spitzer, Michael, 'Mapping the Human Heart: A Holistic Analysis of Fear in Schubert', *Music Analysis* 29/1–3 (2010), 149–213.

Stanley, Glenn, 'Schubert Hearing *Don Giovanni*: Mozartian Death Music in the "Unfinished" Symphony', in *Schubert's Late Music: History, Theory, Style*, ed. Lorraine Byrne Bodley and Julian Horton (Cambridge: Cambridge University Press, 2016), 193–218.

Stein, Deborah, 'The End of the Road in Schubert's *Winterreise*: The Contradiction of Coherence and Fragmentation', in *Rethinking Schubert*, ed. Lorraine Byrne Bodley and Julian Horton (New York: Oxford University Press, 2016), 355–82.

Suurpää, Lauri, *Death in Winterreise: Music-Poetic Associations in Schubert's Song Cycle* (Bloomington: Indiana University Press, 2014).

Suurpää, Lauri, 'Longing for the Unattainable: The Second Movement of the "Great" C major Symphony', in *Schubert's Late Music: History, Theory, Style*, ed. Lorraine Byrne Bodley and Julian Horton (Cambridge: Cambridge University Press, 2016), 219–40.

Taylor, Benedict, 'Schubert and the Construction of Memory: The String Quartet in A Minor, D. 804 ("Rosamunde")', *Journal of the Royal Musical Association* 139/1 (2014), 41–88.

Thym, Jürgen, 'Invocations of Memory in the Last Songs', in *Schubert's Late Music: History, Theory, Style*, ed. Lorraine Byrne Bodley and Julian Horton (Cambridge: Cambridge University Press, 2016), 383–404.

Tunbridge, Laura, 'Saving Schubert: The Evasions of Late Style', in *Late Style and its Discontents: Essays in Art, Literature, and Music*, ed. Gordon McMullan and Sam Smiles (New York: Oxford University Press, 2016), 120–30.

Wen, Eric, 'Schubert's *Wiegenlied*: The Andante sostenuto from the Piano Sonata in B♭, D. 960', in *Schubert's Late Style: History, Theory, Style*, ed. Lorraine Byrne Bodley and Julian Horton (Cambridge: Cambridge University Press, 2016), 134–48.

Wolff, Christoph, 'Schubert's "Der Tod und das Mädchen": Analytical and Explanatory Notes on the Song D 531 and the Quartet D 810', in *Schubert Studies: Problems of Style and Chronology*, ed. Eva Badura-Skoda and Peter Branscombe (Cambridge: Cambridge University Press, 1982), 143–71.

Wollenberg, Susan, 'The C major String Quintet D 956: Schubert's "Dissonance" Quintet?', *Schubert durch die Brille* 28 (2002), 45–55.

Wollenberg, Susan, '"Dort, wo du nicht bist, dort ist das Gluck": Reflections on Schubert's Second Themes', *Schubert durch die Brille* 30 (2003), 91–100.

Wollenberg, Susan, 'From Song to Instrumental Style: Some Schubert Fingerprints', in *Rethinking Schubert*, ed. Lorraine Byrne Bodley and Julian Horton (New York: Oxford University Press, 2016), 61–76.

Wollenberg, Susan, 'Schubert's Dramatic Lieder: Rehabilitating "Adelwold und Emma", D. 211', in *Drama in the Music of Franz Schubert*, ed. Joe Davies and James William Sobaskie (Woodbridge: Boydell & Brewer, 2019), 85–106.

Wollenberg, Susan, *Schubert's Fingerprints: Studies in the Instrumental Works* (Farnham: Ashgate, 2011).

Wollenberg, Susan, 'Schubert's Poetic Transitions', in *Le style instrumental de Schubert: sources, analyse, évolution*, ed. Xavier Hascher (Paris: Publications de la Sorbonne, 2007), 261–77.

Wollenberg, Susan, 'Schubert's Transitions', in *Schubert Studies*, ed. Brian Newbould (Farnham: Ashgate, 1998), 16–61.

Youens, Susan, '"Der Mensch ist zur Geselligkeit geboren": Salon Culture, Night Thoughts and a Schubert Song', in *Musical Salon Culture in the Long Nineteenth Century*, ed. Anja Bunzel and Natasha Loges (Woodbridge: Boydell & Brewer, 2019), 167–84.

Youens, Susan, 'Echoes of the Wounded Self: Schubert's "Ihr Bild"', in *Goethe and Schubert: Across the Divide*, ed. Lorraine Byrne and Dan Farrelly (Dublin: Carysfort Press, 2003), 1–18.

Youens, Susan, *Heinrich Heine and the Lied* (Cambridge: Cambridge University Press, 2007).

Youens, Susan, 'Of Dwarves, Perversion, and Patriotism: Schubert's "Der Zwerg", D. 771', *19th-Century Music* 21/2 (1997), 177–207.

Youens, Susan, 'The "Problem of Solitude" and Critique in Song: Schubert's Loneliness', in *Schubert's Late Music: History, Theory, Style*, ed. Lorraine Byrne Bodley and Julian Horton (Cambridge: Cambridge University Press, 2016), 309–30.

Youens, Susan, 'Reentering Mozart's Hell: Schubert's "Gruppe aus dem Tartarus", D. 538', in *Drama in the Music of Franz Schubert*, ed. Joe Davies and James William Sobaskie (Woodbridge: Boydell & Brewer, 2019), 171–204.

Youens, Susan, *Retracing a Winter's Journey: Schubert's 'Winterreise'* (Ithaca, NY: Cornell University Press, 1991).

Youens, Susan, *Schubert's Late Lieder: Beyond the Song-Cycles* (Cambridge: Cambridge University Press, 2002).

Youens, Susan, *Schubert's Poets and the Making of Lieder* (Cambridge: Cambridge University Press, 1996).

Index

Page numbers in *italic* refer to figures; page numbers in **bold** refer to music examples. References to the footnotes are indicated with a suffix 'n.'. Roman numerals refer to pages in the Foreword.

Alexander I 57

Bach, Johann Sebastian 19 n.70, 81
Baroque style, musical references to 19, 59, 79, 81, 104, 107
beautiful dead, the 36–43
Beckett, Samuel 1, 116
Beethoven, Ludwig van 56, 92, 93 n.13, 97 n.28
beginnings (of works) xiv, 59–66
Blair, Robert: 'The Grave' 23, 24, 27
Blechen, Carl: 'Gotische Kirchenruine' 9, *11*
Bostridge, Ian 152 n.1
boundaries, blurring of 4
 animate and inanimate objects 148
 beauty and terror 42–43, 73
 beginnings and endings 82–86, 147
 day and night 98
 dream and reality 33–34, 111
 gothic and Romantic elements 5–6, 9, 18–19, 101
 harmonies, in octave doubling 38
 life and death 33–34, 42, 47, 50, 72–74, 78, 91, 93 n.11, 130–31, 141–42
boundaries, prising open of, in the grotesque 123, 126, 130–31, 142
Brendel, Alfred 142
Brillenburg Wurth, Kiene 143
Brinkmann, Reinhold 82
Bronfen, Elisabeth 5
Bruchmann, Franz von:
 'Schwestergruss' 20 n.73, 24, 37–43, **39**, **40–41**, 90, 104, 107, 109, 142
Bruchmann, Justine von 37
Bruchmann, Sybilla von 37, 38, *39*
Burke, Edmund 8, 94–95
Burnham, Scott 88 n.57, 97–98 n.30, 127 n.18, 139 n.35, 141 n.39

Byrne Bodley, Lorraine 2–3, 21 n.80, 148

Callot, Jacques 125
Claudius, Matthias: 'Der Tod und das Mädchen' 68, 78 n.40, 103
Collin, Matthäus von
 'Der Zwerg' 16–17, 69, 111, **113**
 'Nacht und Träume' 1, 116, **117**, **118**
Connelly, Frances S. 126, 136
Craigher, J.N.: 'Totengräbers Heimweh' 24, 44–50, **48**, **49**, **51**, **52**, 64, 78, 98, 111

dactylic pattern, as emblem of death 38, 50, 53, 68, 78 n.40, 139
danse macabre genre 130–31
death
 in biography and art 1–3
 blurring of boundaries between life and 33–34, 42, 47, 50, 72–74, 78, 91, 93 n.11, 130–31, 141–42
 and the gothic 4–12, 13–14, 16–17
 and sleep 96–104, 109
 stylistic features signifying 38, 50, 53, 66, 68, 78 n.40, 91, 131, 139
 and the supernatural 6–8, 14–15, 26–27 n.13, 103
 see also graves and graveyards; night
defamiliarization, as element of the grotesque 127–29
distortions 66–77 *see also* grotesquerie
double vision 19, 87, 88
doubles and doubling 53–58
 beginnings xiv, 59–66
 Doppelgängers 18–19, 56–57, 87–88
 endings 82–86
 the returning past 27, 38–39, 53–56, 59, 77–81, 86–87, 98, 151

172   *Index*

doubles and doubling (*cont'd*)
  case studies   59–88
    Fantasy in F minor for four hands, D
      940   56, 77–81, **79, 80, 82**, 83–86,
      85, 87
    Grande Marche Funèbre, D 859   55–56,
      57, 59, **60, 61**, 74 n.36, 86
    Impromptu in C minor, D 899/1   xiv,
      56, 59–60, **62**, 64, 66–74, **67–68**,
      73, 75, 78, 82–83, **83**, 86–87, 88
dreams   10 n.48, 33 n.19, 33 n.21, 72, 111, 116,
  123, *124*, 136–39
Dürr, Walther   152 n.1

eeriness   19, 33, 39, 43, 64, 90, 154
endings (of works)   82–86

fantasia, stylistic characteristics   143 n.50
Fiorillo, Johann   123
Fisk, Charles   56, 72, 82 n.46, 142
French overture, musical references to   59,
  79, 81, 104, 136 n.31
Freud, Sigmund   86
Friedrich, Caspar David: 'Abbey in an Oak
  Forest'   9, *10*, 97–98
Fry, Paul   47
fugal writing   81
Fuseli, Henry: 'The Nightmare'   123, *124*

Gamer, Michael   4
ghosts and ghostliness   6–8, 12–13, 17–18, 39,
  42–43, 44
Gibbs, Christopher H.   56, 73
Gingerich, John   18, 147 n.55
Goethe, Johann Wolfgang von
  description of the gothic (Strasbourg
    cathedral)   8–9, 59, 79
  'An den Mond'   97 n.28
  'Erlkönig'   26 n.13, 69, 73, 90, 103
  'Nachtgesang'   102, 103–4
  'Wanderers Nachtlied II'   97
gothic, the
  defining   3–6, 58, 59, 153–54
  hearing, in Schubert's music   12–19,
    150–54
graves and graveyards   9, 12–13, 15–16, 23–24
  case studies   25–52
    'Grablied für die Mutter,' D 616   36–37,
      43, 109
    'Leichenfantasie,' D 7   24, 25–34,
      28–29, 30, 32, 35–36, 89, 154
    'Schwestergruss,' D 762   20 n.73, 24,
      37–43, **39, 40–41**, 90, 104, 107,
      109, 142

'Totengräbers Heimweh,' D 842   24,
  44–50, **48, 49, 51, 52**, 64, 78, 98, 111
Grillparzer, Franz Seraphicus
  'Bertas Lied in der Nacht'   101–7, **105, 106**
  Die Ahnfrau   103
grotesquerie   9–12, 119–27, 152–53
  hybridity   125, 130–35, 143
  metamorphosis   125–26, 142–47
  rupture   136–42
  case studies   127–49
    Klavierstück in E flat minor, D
      946/1   130–33, **131, 132**
    Piano Sonata in A major, D 959   18,
      142–49, **143, 144–46**
    String Quintet in C major, D 956   98
      n.30, 136–42, **137–38, 140–41**,
      147–48
    'Wanderer' Fantasy in C major, D
      760   119–23, **120–22**, 127–28,
      129, 142

Hades   16, 72, 133 n.28
Hardenberg, Georg Friedrich Philipp von
  (Novalis)   89, 90–92, 94
Harpham, Geoffrey Galt   125–26
Haydn, Joseph   78 n.39
Head, Matthew   143 n.50
Heine, Heinrich
  'Der Atlas'   44, 148–49
  'Der Doppelgänger'   18–19, 87–88
Hell   16, 72, 133 n.28
Hinrichsen, Hans-Joachim   152 n.1
Hirsch, Marjorie W.   18, 68, 143, 146, 147
  n.55
Hoffmann, E.T.A.   10–12, 93 n.13, 125
Hölty, Ludwig Christoph Heinrich   97
hybridity, as element of the grotesque   125,
  130–35, 143

instrumental genres, hearing the gothic
  in   18 *see also individual works under*
  Schubert, Franz

Jean Paul   53, 57, 124–25 n.9, 143 n.51
Johnson, Julian   136 n.30

Kant, Immanuel   95
Kenner, Josef: 'Grablied'   44, **46**
Kinderman, William   78 n.40, 142
Korstvedt, Benjamin K.   2, 152 n.1
Kosegarten, Ludwig: 'Nachtgesang'   102,
  103–4
Kotzebue, August von   17–18
Kramer, Richard   20 n.73, 37, 87

Index 173

Krummacher, Friedrich Adolf: 'Die Nacht' 91, 92

late style 20–21, 123 n.5, 151–52
Levy, Janet 59 n.22
Lübeck, Georg Schmidt von: 'Der Wanderer' 97, 98, 119

Macpherson, James (Ossian) 14–16, 89–90
Matthisson, Friedrich von: 'Der Geistertanz' 12–13, 23, 24, 104
Mayrhofer, Johann: 'Nachtstück' 96–101, **99, 100–1**
McKay, Elizabeth Norman 142
metamorphosis, as element of the grotesque 125–26, 142–47
Monroe, Jonathan 94
Mozart, Wolfgang Amadeus 27, **31**
Müller, Wilhelm: 'Der Leiermann' 98, 148

Napier, Elizabeth 4
night 14–16, 89–96, 133
    case studies 96–118
    'Bertas Lied in der Nacht,' D 653 101–7, **105, 106**
    'Nacht und Träume,' D 827 1, 116, **117, 118**
    'Nachtstück,' D 672 96–101, **99, 100–1**
    'Der Unglückliche,' D 713 107–11, **110–11, 112, 114, 115**
nightmares 123, 124
nocturnal imagery *see* night
Novalis (Georg Friedrich Philipp von Hardenberg) 89, 90–92, 94
November, Nancy 78 n.39

octave doubling, use of 24, 27, 36, 43, 47–50, 60, 64, 92, 104, 151
ombra style 16, 17, 18, 68
Ossian (James Macpherson) 14–16, 89–90

pain and pleasure combined 8, 94, 95, 107–15, 116
parricide 13–14
past, the returning 27, 38–39, 53–56, 59, 77–81, 86–87, 98, 151
Pfeffel, Gottlieb: 'Der Vatermörder' 13–14, 18
Pichler, Caroline: 'Der Unglückliche' 107–11, **110–11, 112, 114, 115**
political context 57–58
presence and absence xiv, 64, 83, 154
Punter, David 58

Radcliffe, Ann: *The Mysteries of Udolpho* 6–7

rhythmic features, significance
    dactylic pattern 38, 50, 53, 68, 78 n.40, 139
    double- and triple-dotted 79, 104
    repeated triplets 15, 38, 66
Richter, Jean Paul 53, 57, 124–25 n.9, 143 n.51
Romanticism 5–6, 9, 18–19, 47, 57, 87–88, 90–91, 101
rupture, as element of the grotesque 136–42

Schelling, Friedrich 86
Schiller, Friedrich
    and the sublime 93, 95, 98–101, 104, 108
    Der Geisterseher 7
    'Gruppe aus dem Tartarus' 16, 18, 42 n.30, 68, 72, 133 n.28
    'Leichenfantasie' 24, 25–34, **28–29, 30, 32, 35–36,** 89, 154
    'Thekla: Eine Geisterstimme' 42, **43**
Schlechta, Franz: 'Totengräberweise' 47
Schlegel, Friedrich 9, 124, 133
Schober, Franz von
    'Schatzgräbers Begehr' 23–24
    'Todesmusik' 91–92
Schubert, Franz
    biographical readings of his music 1–3, 56, 142 n.47
    diary entry on conflating opposites 126
    late style 20–21, 123 n.5, 151–52
    letter to Leopold Kupelwieser 1–2
    letter to Franz von Schober 107–8 n.45
    as living son of (dead) Mozart 27
    on pain and pleasure 107–8 n.45
    political context of his life 57–58
    works
        'An den Mond' (Goethe), D 259 97 n.28
        'An den Mond' (Hölty), D 193 97
        'Der Atlas,' D 957/8 44, 148–49
        'Bertas Lied in der Nacht,' D 653 101–7, **105, 106**
        'Death and the Maiden' String Quartet in D minor, D 810 38, 68, **69, 70,** 130
        Des Teufels Lustschloss, D 84 17–18
        'Der Doppelgänger,' D 957/13 18–19, 87–88
        'Du bist die Ruh,' D 776 98
        'Erlkönig,' D 328 26 n.13, 69, 73, 90, 103
        Fantasy in G minor for four hands, D 9 60, **63,** 74
        Fantasy in C minor for four hands, D 48 60, **63,** 74
        Fantasy in C major, 'Wanderer,' D 760 119–23, **120–22,** 127–28, **129,** 142

174   *Index*

Schubert, Franz: works (*cont'd*)
    Fantasy in F minor for four hands, D
        940   56, 77–81, **79, 80, 82,** 83–86,
        85, 87
    'Frühlingstraum,' D 911/11   136–39 n.33
    Fugue in E minor, D 952   81
    'Der Geistertanz,' D 15, D 15A, D
        116   12–13, 23, 24, 104
    'Grablied,' D 218   44, **46**
    'Grablied für die Mutter,' D 616   36–37,
        43, 109
    Grande Marche Funèbre, D 859   55–56,
        57, 59, **60, 61,** 74 n.36, 86
    'Gretchen am Spinnrade,' D 118   2 n.4
    'Gruppe aus dem Tartarus,' D 583   16,
        18, 42 n.30, 68, 72, 133 n.28
    'Hagars Klage,' D 5   98
    Impromptu in C minor, D 899/1   xiv,
        56, 59–60, **62,** 64, 66–74, **67–68,**
        73, 75, 78, 82–83, **83,** 86–87, 88
    Klavierstück in E flat major, D
        946/2   133, **134, 135**
    Klavierstück in E flat minor, D
        946/1   130–31, **131, 132**
    'Kolmas Klage,' D 217   14–16
    'Leichenfantasie,' D 7   24, 25–34,
        28–29, 30, 32, 35–36, 89, 154
    'Der Leiermann,' D 911/24   98, 148
    'Der Lindenbaum,' D 911/5   91 n.8
    'Nacht und Träume,' D 827   1, 116,
        117, 118
    'Die Nacht' (Uz), D 358   92, 92–93
        n.11, 109
    'Die Nacht' (Ossian), D 534   15–16,
        89–90
    'Die Nacht' (Krummacher), D
        983/4   91, 92
    'Nachtgesang' (Goethe), D 119   102,
        103–4
    'Nachtgesang' (Kosegarten), D
        314   102, 103–4
    'Nachthymne,' D 687   90–92
    'Nachtstück,' D 672   96–101, **99, 100–1**
    Notturno in E flat major for piano trio,
        D 897   139 n.34
    Octet in F major, D 803   18
    Piano Sonata in A minor, D 784   64,
        65, 92
    Piano Sonata in A minor, D 845   64, **66**
    Piano Sonata in G major, D 894   20
        n.73, 33 n.21
    Piano Sonata in A major, D 959   18,
        142–48, **143, 144–46**
    Piano Sonata in B flat major, D 960   2,
        153–54, **155**

Piano Trio in B flat major, D 898   153 n.2
Piano Trio in E flat major, D
    929   53–55, **54, 55,** 56, 60, 69–72,
    71–72, 74, **75, 76–77,** 78, 79, 83,
    84, 86–87, 88, 154
Quartettsatz, D 703   79 n.41
'Schatzgräbers Begehr,' D 761   23–24
Schwanengesang, D 957 (*see* 'Der Atlas';
    'Der Doppelgänger')
'Schwestergruss,' D 762   20 n.73, 24,
    37–43, **39, 40–41,** 90, 104, 107,
    109, 142
String Quartet in D minor, 'Death and
    the Maiden,' D 810   38, 68, **69,**
    70, 130
String Quartet in G major, D 887   33
    n.21, 79 n.41, 136 n.31
String Quintet in C major, D 956   98
    n.30, 136–42, **137–38, 140–41,**
    147–48
Symphony in B minor, 'Unfinished,' D
    759   66
Symphony in C major, 'Great,' D
    944   143 n.51
'Thekla: Eine Geisterstimme,' first
    setting, D 73   42 n.30
'Thekla: Eine Geisterstimme,' second
    setting, D 595   42, **43**
'Der Tod und das Mädchen,' D 531   68,
    78 n.40, 103
'Todesmusik,' D 758   91–92
'Totengräbers Heimweh,' D 842   24,
    44–50, **48, 49, 51, 52,** 64, 78, 98,
    111
'Totengräberweise,' D 869   47
'Der Unglückliche,' D 713   107–11,
    110–11, 112, 114, 115
'Der Vatermörder,' D 10   13–14, 18
'Der Wanderer,' D 489   97, 98, 119
'Wanderer' Fantasy in C major, D
    760   119–23, **120–22,** 127–28,
    129, 142
'Wanderers Nachtlied II,' D 768   97
Winterreise, D 911   56, 91 n.8, 98, 136–39
    n.33, 148
'Der Zwerg,' D 771   16–17, 69, 111, **113**
Schumann, Robert   143
Shelley, Mary: *Frankenstein*   10–12
silence, use of   33, 37, 74, 78, 154
sleep   96–104, 109, 123 *see also* dreams
Smith, Andrew   5, 6, 10
Sobaskie, James William   2, 21 n.80
spectrality *see* ghosts and ghostliness
Stanley, Glenn   66
Streinsberg, Josef Ludwig von   36

Streinsberg, Maria Anna   36
sublime, the   8–9, 93 n.13, 94–96, 98–101, 104, 107, 111, 152–53
supernatural, the   6–8, 14–15, 26–27 n.13, 89–90, 103

Taylor, Benedict   148 n.58
tremolo, use of   14, 15, 16, 17, 18, 24, 27, 31, 34, 56, 64, 68, 69, 91, 92, 111, 128, 131, 133, 147, 148–49

uncanniness   73, 86–88, 148 n.58
Uz, Johann Peter: 'Die Nacht'   92, 92–93 n.11, 109

van Elferen, Isabella   4, 86

Walpole, Horace   6
wanderer motif   96–97, 98
Ward, Maryanne   123
Webber, Andrew J.   57
Wen, Eric   2
Winter, Robert   142
Wollenberg, Susan   56, 139 n.36, 142, 153 n.2

Youens, Susan   16, 27, 33–34, 103, 128, 133 n.28, 139 n.33, 149
Young, Edward   45, 89, 108